JOHN VENN AND THE CLAPHAM SECT

JOHN VENN

From a portrait by John Downman, 1782, in the possession of Dr. J. A. Venn, President of Queens' College, Cambridge, and reproduced in *Annals of a Clerical Family*, p.121

JOHN VENN
AND THE
CLAPHAM SECT

by

MICHAEL HENNELL

LUTTERWORTH PRESS

LONDON

TO PEGGY,
MY WIFE

Printed in Great Britain by
Latimer, Trend & Co. Ltd., Plymouth

Contents

Abbreviations

THE following abbreviations have been given for the works most used for reference in the footnotes:

Sermons: Sermons by the Rev. John Venn, M.A., Rector of Clapham. In Three Volumes (Fourth edition 1822).

Annals: Annals of a Clerical Family: being some account of the family and descendants of William Venn, Vicar of Otterton, Devon 1600–1621, by John Venn, Fellow and President of Gonville and Caius College, Cambridge (1904).

Life of H. Venn: The Life and a selection from the Letters of the late Rev. Henry Venn, M.A., successively Vicar of Huddersfield, Yorkshire, and Rector of Yelling, Huntingdonshire, Author of "The Complete Duty of Man", etc. The Memoir of his Life drawn up by the late Rev. John Venn, M.A., Rector of Clapham, Surrey. Edited by the Rev. Henry Venn, B.D., Incumbent of Drypool, Yorkshire; late Fellow of Queens' College, Cambridge (Second edition 1835).

Life of Wilberforce: The Life of William Wilberforce by his sons, Robert Isaac Wilberforce, M.A., Vicar of East Farleigh, late Fellow of Oriel College; and Samuel Wilberforce, M.A., Rector of Brighstone. In Five Volumes (1838).

Correspondence of Wilberforce: The Correspondence of William Wilberforce, edited by his sons, Robert Isaac Wilberforce, M.A., Vicar of East Farleigh, late Fellow of Oriel College; and Samuel Wilberforce, M.A., Archdeacon of Surrey, Rector of Brighstone. In Two Volumes (1840).

Preface and Acknowledgments

THE VENNS have always been their own biographers. It seems something of an impertinence, therefore, for someone outside the Venn family to attempt a Venn biography. John Venn himself left an unfinished memoir of his father, which was completed by Henry Venn of C.M.S. and included by him in his edition of his grandfather's letters. Henry Venn also left in manuscript the first chapter of what he called "Sketch of Life of John Venn of Clapham" together with a document entitled "Sketch of the Character of the late John Venn of Clapham" and some brief notes he intended to use in editing his father's correspondence. John Venn himself had gathered together a large number of family papers covering a period of 200 years. From these he made notes for a private family history he entitled "Parentalia". His grandson, also John Venn, followed his example and, while President of Gonville and Caius College, Cambridge, wrote *Annals of a Clerical Family* which contains the only substantial account of John Venn of Clapham previously published. Like the other monographs included in his book, this essay is a model of domestic biography and extremely valuable to anyone attempting something bigger. The background material is taken from John Venn of Clapham's collection and the mass of personal papers he and Henry Venn of C.M.S. handed on to the next John Venn. His son, Dr. J. A. Venn, President of Queens' College, Cambridge, has given me free access to this rich collection of family papers. No author could have been treated more generously than I have been by Dr. and Mrs. Venn on all occasions. Dr. Venn kindly read the section on Cambridge and made many helpful suggestions. The details of the Venn family papers will be found in the bibliography at the end of the book.

My interest in the Clapham Sect goes back to 1941 when, as a student at Wycliffe Hall, Oxford, I read Sir Reginald Coupland's *Wilberforce* and re-read Elie Halévy's *History of the English People in 1815*. I followed up some of the references the latter contained and came to the conclusion that the social record of the Clapham Sect had possibly been misjudged by most religious and social historians of the period. Gradually this subject became the focus of my research. Though not the main subject of the present volume there is material in the third and fourth chapters which may reinforce the defence of this group made by Dr. E. M. Howse in *Saints in Politics* in 1952.

After I had done about two years' research Dr. Max Warren showed me the *Account of a Society for Missions to Africa and the East* and suggested my writing this book. For its shortcomings he is in no way responsible, but much of the inspiration that has kept me going has come from him. For more than twelve years I have enjoyed the stimulus of his friendship, conversation and trenchant criticism. His knowledge of the period, his informed interest in Charles Simeon, and his deep understanding of the history and purpose of the society he serves so well, have all been invaluable to me. He has read the final manuscript for me and the many drafts that preceded it. Canon Gordon Hewitt has also read the final draft and most of its predecessors. At every stage I have had the benefit of his wide experience of publishing and writing. Canon Charles Smyth and Professor Norman Sykes have given me gracious and unstinting help almost from the time I embarked on research.

I was invited by the Church Missionary Society to give the James Long Lectures for 1955. The material used in these four lectures is distributed through the book. I have to thank Canon Eric Abbott, who was then Dean of King's College, London, for his kind hospitality, the Reverend Douglas Webster for making the practical arrangements, and also my audience, most of whom were not deterred from attendance by the rail strike of that year.

The bibliography contains details of the manuscript sources

used in this book in addition to the Venn papers. Here I should like to acknowledge my debt to the Church Missionary Society, the Reverend C. Tremayne of the Elland Society, Mr. C. E. Wrangham, the Rector of Clapham (the Reverend A. C. Raby), the late Mr. F. S. Bull of Newport Pagnell, the Secretary of the Cowper Museum at Olney, the Principal of Ridley Hall, Cambridge, and Mr. E. M. Forster, who in his delightful biography, *Marianne Thornton*, draws attention to some Thornton papers in the Wigan Public Library.

I have spent long hours in many libraries, not least in the British Museum Reading Room where two kind vicars, the Reverend R. C. Taylor and the Reverend D. M. Lynch, allowed their assistant curate to work in parish time. Miss J. Ferrier and Miss D. M. Pratt (a great-granddaughter of Josiah), have been most kind at the C.M.S. Library as have, more recently, the staff of the Manchester Central Library. I spent five months at St. Deiniol's Library, Hawarden, whilst the Reverend Dr. A. R. Vidler was Warden. I am most grateful to him for his encouragement and also for permission to reproduce, at the end of the fifth chapter, material that has already appeared in *Theology*, May 1957.

This book has been so long in writing that many of those who have helped me have died before my task was complete. These include the Reverend W. A. Kelk (formerly Editor of *The Record*), Dr. M. G. Jones (biographer of Hannah More), Sir Reginald Coupland, Mr. J. Battley (formerly M.P. for Clapham), and Mr. S. J. Hicks (formerly Churchwarden at Clapham Parish Church). Mrs. Wendy Rodger, who did most of the typing for me, died last summer; the rest was done by her mother, Mrs. Rockliff, and Miss Joyce Tweedle: to all of whom I am most grateful.

I am indebted to many other friends, especially to the Principals of Ridley Hall and St. Aidan's College, Birkenhead, in whose colleges most of the book has been written; to Dr. G. D. Ramsay, Mr. John Walsh, Mr. R. E. Waterfield, Mr. E. P. Hennock, Miss K. Duff, Miss D. Stephen, Mr. T. Alford, Mr. A. Pollard, and not least to Mr. H. B. Wells and the Reverend A. R. Milroy who kindly read the proofs for me. Mr. Wells also made himself responsible for the index.

Finally I am indebted to my wife to whom this book is justly dedicated, for she has helped me at every turn and borne patiently with a husband writing a book.

St. Aidan's College MICHAEL HENNELL
Birkenhead
November 9, 1957

1

FATHER AND SON

To understand the Venns one must understand the Evangelical Revival, and to understand the Evangelical Revival we must look briefly at the eighteenth-century Church.

The older historians' picture of profligacy, pluralism, absenteeism, nepotism, ignorance and heresy is partially true, but somewhat overdrawn. The higher clergy were mostly rich, drawing their income from a string of benefices whose pastoral care was left to an ill-paid curate, and promotion was chiefly through influence: it is said that Bishop Sparke of Ely provided so well for his family that "one could find one's way across the Fens at night by all the little Sparkes in the best country livings". The lower clergy were exceedingly poor and underpaid, living in cut-throat competition for benefices: "passing rich on £40 a year" is applied by Goldsmith to Irish clergy, but there were clergy in England who received no more. In spite of poverty many of the country clergy took advantage of the newly formed alliance of squire and parson and endeavoured to live the lives of country gentlemen with a taste for sport and high society.

However, pluralism, absenteeism and clerical ignorance were not novelties in the eighteenth century, nor in the post-Reformation Church of England; rather they were remnants of medieval church life which the Reformation had not touched. There is abundant evidence in the sixteenth and seventeenth centuries of the same disorders, but the failure of the Church to do anything to meet the needs of the increasing and shifting population of England during the early years of Industrial Revolution showed how great was the need of reform; further, the efficient re-organization of the 1830s and the industriousness of the Victorian Church makes the earlier period look blacker than it really was. There is considerable evidence of genuine piety and pastoral care in diocese and parish alike; the bishops in particular were conscientious men, whose work was made particularly difficult to execute, as the Whig party to whom they owed their appointment insisted on their presence in the House of Lords while Parliament was in session: this revived the medieval situation of bishops spending more time in London than in their dioceses. The Hanoverian clergy may be censured for being subservient, but few of them can fairly be accused of wilful negligence. It is an interesting fact that though Evangelical clergy found that the bishops gave very qualified support to such enterprises as the Church Missionary Society, the same clergy found them worthy of real respect.

There was, however, a serious decline in church life. After 1660 administration of the Sacrament of Holy Communion became increasingly infrequent;[1] for instance, the Visitation of Archbishop Herring of York revealed that out of more than 800 parishes in his Province only 72 had a monthly celebration, and less than half had two services on Sunday.[2] In reaction against the fervour and intolerance of the seventeenth century, almost any doctrine could be held without offending clerical opinion, provided it was neither taught nor practised with fervour. In the desire for a quiet life emotion and feeling had been banished from their proper place in religion and a vigorous personal faith had been replaced by a prudential morality. In addition, the age of Newton and Boyle was an age of exciting scientific discovery; this caused a shift in theological interest from the blessings of redemption to those of creation, from the saving mercies of God to the wisdom and benevolence of the Creator, from the Bible to the book of Nature, from belief in the Holy Spirit to belief in the Divine Reason. The Evangelical Revival was a return to those doctrines which were at a discount, as Gladstone well says in his *Gleanings*: "It aimed at bringing back on a large scale, and by an aggressive movement, the Cross,

[1] Even before 1660 the Holy Communion was celebrated as a rule monthly in the towns and seldom more than six times a year in the country.

[2] N. Sykes, *Church and State in England in the XVIIIth Century* (1934), p. 251.

and all the Cross essentially implies, both into the teaching of the clergy, and into the lives as well of the clergy as of the laity."[1]

It was on this issue that John Venn himself criticized the majority of his fellow-clergy. In one of his *Letters to a Young Clergyman*, which appeared in the *Christian Observer* in 1807, he has left a picture of two types of conscientious country clergy; here is the first one:

> Your neighbour Mr. S. makes no scruple that his design in taking orders was to qualify himself to receive the income of some family preferment by which he might be enabled to live in a style of great comfort. His object he has attained: his house is commodious and in excellent repair, his garden is well-stocked, his wines of the best flavour, his table plentifully furnished, and he is surrounded by a number of cheerful friends with whom he lives on a footing of the most pleasant intercourse. At the same time S. has no conception that he neglects his duty; he resides generally at the parsonage, preaches regularly, takes the pains of writing out the best sermons he can find, and administers the Sacrament to any sick persons who desire it. He endeavours to do his duty, and he is thought by most to perform it very respectably. It is true he does not "travail in birth" with souls until Christ be formed in them, nor is he "instant in season and out of season" in his ministerial labours. It is no part of his plan to take extraordinary pains, nor does he see any necessity for it.[2]

Parson Woodforde could scarcely have given a more accurate picture of himself at Weston Longeville; here too is the country clergyman who has obtained the living he wanted, enjoys the pleasures of a gentleman and earns universal respect because he does his duty according to his own light and that of his parishioners. Mr. F., John Venn's second incumbent, demands considerably more of himself and his parishioners, whom he persuades to come regularly to church on time and with their prayer books; he has taken pains to improve the singing; he preaches his own sermons and instructs the young in the Catechism; furthermore, since he came to the parish the number of communicants has doubled. For all this John Venn commends him but censures him on one point; his lack of converting zeal.

[1] W. E. Gladstone, *Gleanings*, Vol. 7 (1880), p. 207.
[2] *Christian Observer* (1806), pp. 208–9.

It was this passion for souls that the eighteenth century church lacked, and it was this that the Evangelical Revival brought. But when it came it was condemned as "Enthusiasm" and "Enthusiasm" to the upper and middle classes then was what Communism is to many to-day: a bogey to be feared and a demon to be exorcised. When the Revolution broke out in France, Jacobins and Enthusiasts were considered the twin enemies of respectable people. Hannah More was once, after a visit to her friend Dr. Porteous, Bishop of London, going on to stay with John Venn at Clapham, but the coachman had strict instructions to set her down at the Plough Inn, as his lordship's carriage must not be seen outside the Rectory gate of a notorious Evangelical. John Venn was himself refused entry to Trinity College, Cambridge, solely on the grounds that he was the son of an Evangelical clergyman. The contrast between the approach of the Latitudinarian scholar and the Evangelical preacher is well brought out in one of John Venn's letters, in which he writes:

> Infidelity in the common people is a new enemy which we have to encounter. The most successful way of encountering it I am inclined to think would be rather to lay down the truth and to appeal to the conscience than to combat error. For the last century past our learned divines have been wholly employed in defending Christianity and that by argument ingenious, solid and true. They have confuted to the entire satisfaction of every admirable mind the objections of the infidels, and yet strange to tell infidelity has never been more prevalent than during that period and has even been gaining ground considerably. I don't however find that in those congregations where the endeavours of the preacher are chiefly directed to awaken the conscience to a sense of sin against God, Deism gains ground, but the reverse; and this seems to show the true method by which it is most effectually to be resisted; indeed where a sacred reverence for God and spiritual things is wrought in the heart, the change to infidelity is extremely difficult, but when there is already a carelessness about the soul, an indifference to the Gospel, and a dry barren morality which does not interest the heart, there the transition to infidelity is very easy and natural. For what use are the principles of religion which are not perceived to be attended with any power?[1]

[1] J. Venn to E. Edwards, Aug. 1, 1794 (MS.).

Suspicion as to their doctrines, their methods and their personal characters kept Evangelicals for a long period from high office in the Church, and, except where they were provided for by lay patronage, they were also excluded from important livings; no Evangelical was a member of a cathedral staff till Isaac Milner became Dean of Carlisle in 1792 and there was no Evangelical bishop on the bench till the appointment of Henry Ryder to be Bishop of Gloucester more than twenty years later. Evangelicals, on their part, declared that the doctrines they taught were those of the Bible and the Prayer Book, and that their contemporaries were true to neither; "if men", said William Romaine, "called the plain doctrines of scripture and the church 'enthusiam'," he hoped to live and die "a Church of England enthusiast".[1] Because they held certain doctrines in common, and because they were treated as a people by the rest of the Church, Evangelicals were drawn much closer together, becoming a party, over against the rest of the Church to some extent, with a common pattern of parochial life and teaching.

In other matters, which have been the subject of later criticism, Evangelical clergy resembled their brethren more closely than has often been supposed. To the evils of the many administrative abuses Evangelicals were by no means blind. John Newton for instance writes: "Pluralities are the great opprobrium of our church; and the earnestness with which they are sought and seized by those whose care is not for the flock but the fleece should make faithful ministers very cautious how they countenance such mercenaries by their example." Newton said this to discourage the practice of some of his friends who held more than one living with the hope of keeping the Gospel in the second living by employing a curate. John Venn did something very like this: while Rector of Clapham he was presented by Samuel Thornton with the sinecure Rectory of Great Tey in Essex, which brought him £300 a year but no duties, as the parish was already divided in two with a vicar in each part. Venn, although he expressed himself doubtful "of the propriety of holding two livings with cure of souls", allowed himself the extra source of income to provide for his large family, partly because there were two resident clergy with

[1] Romaine, *Works*, *IV*, p. cclxii.

whom the Rector could not interfere until they retired or died, and partly because it would enable him as Rector to appoint their successors, or successor. The year before he died he won a court case ratifying his right of presentation to the Vicarage of Great Tey. It is significant that a devout Evangelical should, as late as the first decade of the nineteenth century, allow himself to become a pluralist with so little moral justification.

Evangelicals, however, were seldom "sporting parsons".[1] John Venn enjoys relating to his friend Edward Edwards the contribution Richard Cecil had made at the Eclectic Society when the subject was: "Should a clergyman bear arms?" Cecil said: "If I was Archbishop I would advise the clergy to arm; I would say to them: 'You are now of no use in the world, but you are excellently qualified to be soldiers. You can scour the country over hedge and ditch as well as any persons. You are fine, stout, jolly fellows; who are so fit to be soldiers? Who know the country so well? Who are better marksmen? Who can use their muskets better? But as for the Methodists let them not enter your corps. They are only fit to pray and preach. Let them mind their own business.' "[2] This did not mean that Evangelicals necessarily deprived themselves of all outdoor enjoyment. If Henry Venn neither rode out hunting nor coursed with hounds, if he neither shot wild fowl nor fished for trout in a Yorkshire stream, he was frequently away from his parish on long horse-rides, partly on preaching tours, but mainly for health and pleasure. John inherited both his father's riding cloak and his love of horse-riding. Furthermore, on one occasion at least a friend remembers accompanying him as he ranged over Clapham Common with a gun.

One further thing must be said of the character and history of the Revival itself. The Revival within the Church of England was no offshoot of Methodism (Griffith Jones of Llanddowror was preaching in Wales "the Evangelical doctrines of the Re-

[1] G. W. E. Russell says that among the mid-Victorian Evangelical clergy whom he knew as a boy, hunting was thought wicked by some though no one condemned shooting. "My father was an inveterate fox-hunter, and our vicar, who was a fine horseman, said, with marked expression, 'I too should like to hunt, if I could hunt with a field of saints'." G. W. E. Russell, *The Household of Faith* (1906, 3rd edition), p. 234.

[2] J. Venn to E. Edwards, May 4, 1798 (MS.).

formation" while John Wesley was still a boy); rather, there were in England between 1730 and 1750 a number of Evangelical conversions of which those of Whitefield and the Wesleys appear to be the earliest, but none of the others were the result of their work or preaching. William Romaine, although Wesley's contemporary at Oxford, never associated with the Holy Club and owed his faith to his Huguenot upbringing; Grimshaw of Haworth, Adam of Winteringham and Henry Venn himself were converted through an independent study of the Bible, Walker of Truro through a conversation with his old schoolmaster, and John Newton whilst crying to God for mercy during a storm at sea. These men revived their own parishes and sometimes the surrounding district, but they did not regard the world as their parish as Wesley did, though they corresponded with him, attended on occasion his conferences and invited him to preach in their churches. Some, like Henry Venn, were prepared to itinerate, although others like Walker and Adam rebuked Wesley for ecclesiastical irregularity. The truth is that Wesley's highly centralized machinery of annual conferences, class meetings, lay-preachers and stewards, did not fit easily into the framework of Anglicanism and, in fact, after Wesley's death, worked with great success outside it.

There were other clergy who refused to countenance any move that would endanger their being forced outside the Church of England, and chief among these were Samuel Walker of Truro, the leader of the Cornish Evangelicals, Henry Venn the leader of the Yorkshire Evangelicals, and John Newton, leader of the London Evangelicals. Walker died in 1761, the year after Venn arrived in Huddersfield, and Newton came to London in 1779, eight years after Venn had left Yorkshire for Yelling where he became father rather than leader to another group—the Cambridge Evangelicals, whose real leader (Charles Simeon) he guided and trained. His own son, John Venn, had imbibed the same principles and ideas as Simeon from the same source. The debt which John Venn owed to his father was so great that we shall not understand the son unless we have considerable knowledge of the life and character of the father.

From Queen Elizabeth I's reign till the present century at

least one member of the Venn family has been in Holy Orders. Henry Venn's father, Richard Venn, for many years Rector of St. Antholin's, Watling Street, was a strict High Churchman with Jacobite leanings. He was the first London clergyman to refuse his pulpit to George Whitefield. He also showed a High Churchman's aversion to Dissenters, which was shared by his son who constantly assaulted the son of a Dissenting minister who lived in the same street. From 1742–47 Henry Venn was at Jesus College, Cambridge, where he was a Rustat scholar. He was a keen cricketer and reckoned one of the best in the University. In the week before he was ordained he was playing for Surrey against all England; after the game he threw his bat down, saying, "Whoever wants a bat which has done me good service, may take that: as I have no further occasion for it." When asked the reason he replied, "Because I am to be ordained on Sunday; and I will never have it said of me 'Well struck, parson'."[1] He was ordained by Bishop Gibson of London, but he served a curacy at Barton near Cambridge, which he held together with a Fellowship at Queens'. In 1750 he became curate to the Rev. Adam Langley, who held the livings of St. Matthew's, Friday Street, and West Horsley, near Guildford. He was in London for the summer and in West Horsley for the winter. In 1754 he became curate of Clapham.

During his first curacies he read a number of "pious books", including Law's *Serious Call*. The challenge of this book affected him the same way as it affected John Wesley. Though neither found Law's theology ultimately satisfactory and later criticized it severely, his writings did awaken in both men a sense of sin and a thirst for God, which made them seek in the Bible the Christ who justifies by faith alone.

Henry Venn made this discovery shortly before his appointment to Clapham. He seems to have been left in sole charge in the parish, for the parish records contain no reference to the Rector, Sir James Stonhouse,[2] who appears to have resided on his family estate at Radley. Here Venn met John Thornton, the merchant prince, who soon after his arrival was converted

[1] H. Venn, *Life of H. Venn* (1835), pp. 13, 14.

[2] He is not to be confused with his Evangelical cousin, also James Stonhouse, lecturer of All Saints, Bristol, who succeeded him in the baronetcy in 1792.

through the influence of Martin Madan and who was to become, in Charles Smyth's apt words, "the Nuffield of the Evangelical Revival". The friendship between Henry Venn and John Thornton was deep and lasting and the families were closely associated for more than a century.

Henry Venn's connection with the leaders of the Methodist Revival dates from this period. In March 1754 Venn wrote to Wesley for a personal charge, and in 1756 he attended Wesley's conference at Oxford. In the following year he itinerated with Madan and Whitefield and stayed with the Countess of Huntingdon at Clifton. In the same year Whitefield preached twice in Clapham Church and henceforward frequently in John Thornton's house. Henry Venn himself was the first parochial clergyman in the neighbourhood of London to preach extempore.

It was also about the time of his move to Clapham that Henry Venn met his first wife, Eling Bishop. She was a daughter of the Reverend Thomas Bishop, D.D., who lived at Ipswich and held no less than four Suffolk livings. In spite of this accumulation of benefices Dr. Bishop, who was extravagant as well as learned, left his family in comparative poverty.[1] For the benefit of his own family Henry Venn wrote *A Sketch of the Life of Eling Venn* which is exceedingly informative. He was very fond of nicknames and though he wrote to her as "Syphe" he called her "Mira" in this brief memoir, and it is as Mira that she seems to have been generally known.

Mira was only thirteen when her father died; she already showed promise of becoming a woman of uncommon loveliness, "but very soon", writes her future husband, "must this charming flower lose its most lovely appearance for the Lord was pleased to visit her with the smallpox of so malignant a sort as to change in some degree the features of her face, and to leave her, compared with her former figure, much altered for the worse".[2] Mira determined to make herself an eligible wife and competent mother by proficiency in all those skills required in the running of a home; her husband says that apart from her shoes she made all her clothes herself. Such training proved

[1] J. Venn, *Annals*, p. 221.
[2] Sketch of Life of Eling Venn by her husband, H.V. (MS.), p. 34.

invaluable to the future mistress of Huddersfield Vicarage; it also provided her with a trade when her mother died in 1749, for she joined her sister Martha as a dressmaker at Teddington and it was here that Henry Venn met her.

They seem to have been drawn together by a common concern for Christian truth. Henry was still groping his way towards some understanding of the implications of his new-found faith, while Mira's conventional beliefs had been severely shaken by a reading of the Bible, and by obeying an injunction of her mother's diligently to prepare herself for receiving the Holy Communion on her twenty-first birthday. Henry Venn introduced his fiancée to several of his Christian friends, including Romaine and the Wesleys. From the latter she seems to have imbibed, and to have imperfectly understood, ideas of Christian Perfection against which she reacted with such violence that she drove her husband far into the Calvinistic camp and caused a sad rupture between him and John Wesley at Huddersfield.

However this may be, Mira seems to have been a vivacious intelligent girl with a strong, attractive personality, and John Venn's short description of his mother accords well with the longer account his father and John Riland have left.[1] "In this lady", writes John Venn in his Memoir, "Mr. Venn found a mind congenial with his own—the most sincere and exalted piety, directed by a sound judgement, and enriched by a sweetness of disposition and animation, which rendered her particularly interesting as a companion and friend."[2]

By the end of 1756 Henry had returned to duty at Clapham and on May 10, 1757, he and Mira were married in Clapham Church. Henry Venn writes: "As soon as we were married, we lived at Clapham in Surrey, a favourite village where many London merchants, having acquired fortunes, chose their country seats, desiring in general, only to enjoy themselves. To such the doctrine of the Gospel preached with zeal and boldness was very offensive."[3] As an example of this he relates that when

[1] J. Riland, who was H. Venn's curate at the time, wrote in November, 1767 *A Sketch of the Character of Eling Venn* which he called *Eusebia*. Two copies in manuscript are extant among the Venn Family Papers.

[2] *Life of H. Venn*, pp. 25–26.

[3] Sketch of Life of Eling Venn by H.V. (MS.).

Eling, their first child, was nearly a year old and "Jack was soon expected to make his appearance" a woman tried to persuade Mira "to repress the disgusting earnestness of her husband" saying that it was alienating possible friends who might otherwise have been of considerable financial assistance to the curate's impecunious and growing family. To which Mira replied: "The Master Mr. Venn serves is too great and too good ever to see him or his real losers for faithfulness in his service." Little wonder her husband's narrative continues: "In the following year, grieved at the obstinate rejection of the Gospel during five years by almost all the rich (and there were but few poor in the place), I accepted a living unexpectedly offered to me by my very affectionate friend, the Earl of Dartmouth."[1] In fact the patron was not Lord Dartmouth, but his friend, Sir John Ramsden, whose family had almost owned Huddersfield for centuries. Sir John appointed Venn on Lord Dartmouth's recommendation.

The offer was made two or three months before John's birth; Henry Venn postponed his journey north till John was three months old. He then took horse for Yorkshire. One night he found himself staying at the same inn on the Great North Road as John Wesley.[2] He received a great welcome at Huddersfield; at one service, he told his wife, there seemed to be over three thousand people. The prospect of an enthusiastic congregation seemed infinitely preferable to the rich and self-satisfied church people of Clapham, but he did not make up his mind quickly. The living was worth less than £100 per annum and Venn feared leaving his family destitute if either he died young or were to run into serious debt. "By this change of situation," he says, "our income was reduced by more than one half. However, believing . . . several things to be true which were misrepresented, and supposing the small income in so cheap a country would be sufficient to live upon, I determined to move to Huddersfield."[3]

In 1760 Huddersfield was an overgrown industrial village with a population of about five thousand. It was an important

[1] Sketch of Life of Eling Venn by H.V. (MS.), pp. 13, 14.
[2] G. G. Cragg, *Grimshaw of Haworth* (1947), p. 88.
[3] Sketch of Life of Eling Venn (MS.).

centre of wool manufacture.[1] The importance of Venn's appointment can hardly be over-estimated in the history of the Revival, for Huddersfield was the first of the growing industrial communities to receive an Evangelical incumbent. Venn's like-minded contemporaries were mostly situated in remote villages, Grimshaw at Haworth, Fletcher at Madeley, Hervey at Weston Favell. The only man whose responsibility corresponded in size to Venn's was Samuel Walker of Truro. As Bishop Ryle says, Venn was the only early Evangelical who could number his lawful parishioners by thousands.[2]

From the outset Henry Venn drew crowds to the parish church. His preaching was vigorous and direct, full of lucid exposition of the Scriptures and enhanced by racy anecdotes. These addresses were so challenging to those who heard them that many sought his help in private interviews. The children in the vicarage soon grew accustomed to seeing these inquirers waiting to see their father: Eling, the eldest tells us what she remembered:

> I used to hear Ruth (the maid) come running across the long passage; the door would open and she would say, "A man wants to speak to you about his soul." "Tell him to come in," my father would say. I remember the look of many of them to this day, with channels upon their black cheeks, where the tears were running. "Oh, Sir!" they would begin at once to say with eagerness, "I have never slept since last Thursday night. Oh Sir, your sermon." ... This would happen three or four times in the morning. "There was quite a troop of t' young beginners," as Ruth used to say.[3]

It appears to have been Venn's deliberate policy not so much to visit people in their homes as to encourage them to seek him out in this way. In the outlying parts of the parish he preached in the open air and held meetings for young people, and once a fortnight he instructed the children in the Catechism. It was from his father that John learnt the practical value of the Catechism. He also learnt a somewhat surprising method of enforcing "Sunday Observance". On Sunday the vicar's most ardent

[1] As yet there were no factories. Weaving was done in cottages in the town and surrounding villages, many of which lay within the parish boundary.

[2] Ryle, J. C., *Christian Leaders* (1889), p. 269.

[3] J. Venn, *Annals*, p. 82.

supporters, known as the "Venn people", patrolled the streets to see that all was quiet and urge those they met to go to church. Henry Venn was also successful in persuading shopkeepers and travellers to desist from Sunday sales.

Venn's real success, however, lay in the changed lives of many who came to hear him. These included a successful woollen manufacturer named Thomas Atkinson, William Hey, the distinguished Leeds surgeon, and a large number of boys including Joseph Cockin and Samuel Bottomley, both of whom have written their memoirs.[1] They were two of the twenty-two men who offered for the ministry during Venn's decade at Huddersfield. All, however, had to look outside the Church of England for their training, as the established Church had no funds available for the training of poor boys. Such a fund came into existence in 1777 as part of the work of the Elland Society, which has supported Evangelical candidates ever since. This society had been founded by Henry Venn in 1767; some account of it is given in the next chapter.

The child John must have met many of the leading Evangelicals when they visited his father; one parishioner commented "there was a new one every week". Wesley, Whitefield, Romaine, Newton, Grimshaw, Adam, Fletcher, Madan, all visited Huddersfield. The Countess of Huntingdon stayed at least once in the vicarage and Lord Dartmouth attended the church when he was in the district. Wesley was not always welcome at the parish church, for Venn disagreed with the Methodists on two points; firstly, he could not accept Wesley's doctrine of Christian Perfection, and secondly he could not persuade Wesley to remove his preachers from Huddersfield, though he protested there was now "a Gospel Minister" at the parish church. Venn's discrimination against Wesley was possibly occasioned and certainly encouraged by Mira, whose views, Stillingfleet once told the younger Henry Venn, were thought by most of the Vicar of Huddersfield's friends "far too Calvinistic".[2] After his wife's death Venn's Calvinism gradually moderated and he no longer cared whether a minister of the Gospel called himself Arminian or Calvinist; moreover he taught his son to mistrust

[1] Memoirs of J. Cockin (1841).

[2] H. Venn, Diary of a Visit to Yorkshire (MS.).

such labels. The effect of being brought up in the atmosphere of warring religious parties had a salutary effect on John, who came to have no use for what he calls "the sub-divisions of the religious world".[1]

Of the clergy nearer home, two became particular personal friends of the Venn family. One was James Stillingfleet, a descendant of Bishop Stillingfleet of Worcester, who was for some years in charge of a proprietary chapel at Bierley near Bradford and later became Rector of Hotham. "Stilo", as Henry Venn called him, became the closest of his clerical friends and John came to regard him almost as a second father. The other was John Riland, one of Henry Venn's curates.

Both men have left some record of their impressions of the relationship between Henry Venn and Mira, and Riland in his *Eusebia*, which is a manuscript life of Mira, gives some description of their habits. Stillingfleet told the younger Henry Venn, "She [Mira] had too much influence over her husband. She led him entirely, though he was not aware of it. Yet I often thought that he had fallen into the conduct he so severely condemns in his chapter in *The Duty of Man* respecting conjugal duties, of giving up his authority like an officer in the army to his soldiers. She was a very clever woman and he was the most uxorious man I ever knew—devotedly fond of her."[2] John Riland, who had lived in Huddersfield Vicarage since his arrival in 1765, would confirm what Stillingfleet says of Henry Venn's "uxoriousness", but he would agree to little else. He maintains in *Eusebia* that Mira submitted to her husband even in the most trifling matters and that Henry Venn was master of his own household. Nevertheless, bearing in mind that Riland was particularly devoted to Mira, we are inclined to accept Stillingfleet's picture of Henry Venn as a "hen-pecked husband" and are therefore bound to ask what would have been the influence of such a mother on a sensitive child like John Venn, had she lived as long as his father. Nevertheless it was to his mother that John owed his sensitive, nervous temperament and inclination to moods of deep depression.[3]

[1] See p. 262.
[2] H. Venn, Diary of a Visit to Yorkshire (MS.).
[3] J. Cunningham, *The Velvet Cushion* (1814), pp. 162–3.

Even if the managing of her husband must be placed on the debit side of Mira's account, the managing of her household and young family must assuredly be placed on the credit side. The living of Huddersfield was worth only £100 a year, and the Venns soon had five children instead of two; John's younger sisters, Jane, Frances and Catherine were all born in Huddersfield. It was undoubtedly Mira's self-taught domesticity and practical economy that helped them to win through. Economy, however, did not lead to meanness in either of John's parents; rather the reverse was true, for both were exceedingly generous. John Riland says that Mira used to buy more meat than the family required so that she could send something to those she knew to be destitute; she also gave away clothes. Riland found she wanted to give something to everyone he mentioned who was in need, so he stopped mentioning them. Mira, in her turn, made her husband empty out his pockets before he went visiting to ensure he did not give away what was so badly needed at home. When he handed his successor a register of the parish the word "poor" was marked against many names, and "very poor" against others. Asked for an explanation Venn said that from the "poor" he took nothing and to the "very poor" he always gave something.

In spite of financial stringency the Venns employed two maids, and some of the time, at least, Henry Venn employed a manservant. Mira was never strong and seldom well; after Catherine's birth she decided if she were to recover her strength and were free from further child-bearing, she would economize on food and employ only one maid; but she never really recovered. In 1767 she was sufficiently better for her husband to take a continental "tour" on horseback. Two successive nights Venn dreamt that his wife was ill—this made him hurry home: she died within four days of his arrival. John was at boarding-school at Leeds; he too had a dream, a sort of vision of his mother on the morning of her death, before the news was brought to him. He often spoke about this in later life, and it seems to have left a deep impression on his young and sensitive mind.

After Mrs. Venn's death the two maids stayed to look after the children—one of these was Ruth Clark. She came from Hull where she had been the play-fellow of two poor boys, Joseph and Isaac Milner. She was a devoted Christian and a devoted servant of the Venn family, who were extremely fond of her.[1] However, Ruth Clark's influence was soon overshadowed by the coming to the vicarage of another woman of charm and character, Priscilla Riland, the wife John Riland married in August 1768. Priscilla Hudson[2] was one of Henry Venn's earliest converts and had been a great friend of both Mira and himself. Within a year of Mira's death Henry Venn proposed to Priscilla Hudson but she refused him. This is evident from a letter he wrote her at the time of his engagement to Mrs. Katherine Smith in which he quotes a friend of Mrs. Smith as saying: "If you and your children are not happy with Mrs. S. I will publicly declare the fault is wholly your own—had I an own brother to settle to-morrow I know not a woman I would so soon see him united to," to which Henry Venn adds, "there is but one I could have preferred, I answered to myself". Henry Venn and his family were all extremely happy with "Mrs. S.", but she was not only his second wife but his second choice of wife. However, Henry Venn did not grieve seriously over his rejection but recommended John Riland to try where he had failed.[3] When the Rilands came to live in the vicarage, Mrs. Riland did her best to take Mira's place as the children's mother. The two families fed and lived together even after the Rilands had a daughter of their own. John, as well as his sisters, seems to have retained his affection for the Rilands throughout his life and their children frequently stayed at Clapham Rectory.

Henry Venn's marriage to Katherine Smith took place in

[1] When John Venn was Rector of Clapham he found Ruth Clark a house for her retirement and his son Henry Venn wrote a tract about her entitled *The Single Talent Well-Employed.*

[2] In the marriage register of Huddersfield Parish Church she appears as Ann Hudson. "Priscilla" was probably Henry Venn's own name for her.

[3] In reply to a request from John Riland via his wife for a curate, Venn writes: "I know not anyone to recommend, for curates are like wives: a great comfort or a great cross. And though I did venture to recommend him one of the latter, and succeeded marvellously, I must not expect to find a curate as able to please and fulfil the duties of his place, as a Priscilla" (*Life of H. Venn*, p. 224). Letters incidentally are always addressed to Mrs. Riland and they begin M.B.P., which stands for "My Beloved Priscy".

July 1771. She was a clergyman's daughter and a widow. In spite of Henry Venn's confession of another preference, the second marriage proved as happy as the first and all the children seem to have found in "Marie Venn", as her husband called her, a real mother, and were as happy with her as her friend prophesied they should be.

1771 was also the year that Henry Venn, now suffering severely from consumption, left Huddersfield for Yelling in Huntingdonshire.[1] "I go to Yelling a dying man", he wrote to Mrs. Riland, but in fact he recovered his health and lived another twenty-seven years.

John was eight when his mother died and had already shown himself a promising child, intelligent, easily disciplined, and resolved since the age of five to be a preacher like his father, "determining to compel the disobedient to come in *vi et armis*, if milder methods would not succeed; for you were determined to make use, you said, of a good oaken trowel, to bring them to their sense of sin, if your discourses and entreaties should fail. In a few years more, I saw you gaining fast the meaning of Latin and Greek words, and by the help of an excellent teacher, promising to be a scholar."[2] The "excellent teacher" was probably Mr. Shute of Leeds,[3] to whose boarding-school John was sent at the age of seven. Here he met Henry Jowett, who was two or three years his senior. During term John used to spend his Sundays with Henry Jowett's family in Leeds, where his father had a prosperous business. In the Jowett home he also met Henry's three brothers John, Benjamin and Joseph: the family moved to London in 1771 but Joseph and Henry were both at Cambridge when John went up six years later.[4] In 1769

[1] It was a Chancellor's living and was offered him by Chief Baron Smythe, one of the Evangelical laity.

[2] *Life of H. Venn*, p. 271.

[3] It may have been Sutcliffe and not Shute, as it was of Sutcliffe that Venn had such a high opinion as a scholar and teacher, but the context implies that Mrs. Venn was still alive at the time.

[4] The Jowetts originally came from Bradford. Henry Jowett (1719–1801) was converted under Whitefield's preaching, while apprenticed to a hat manufacturer in Camberwell. In 1751 he set up as a skinner and furrier in Leeds; here his friendship began with Henry Venn and William Hey, the surgeon. In 1771 the Jowetts moved back to London, having purchased a warehouse in Bermondsey; at this time John, the eldest son, took over his father's business. In 1790 John Jowett bought Newington Butts, which became a centre of Evangelical piety and

both John Venn and Henry Jowett were transferred to Hipperholme Grammar School, which was nearer Halifax than Leeds. The Master was the Reverend Richard Sutcliffe, vicar of Lightcliffe, who was an able classical scholar and who so secured the confidence of Henry Venn that when after a year the family moved south to Yelling, John stayed on at Hipperholme.

John spent his holidays with the Jowetts and other of his father's Yorkshire friends. It seems that he saw neither his new home at Yelling nor his stepmother till the summer of 1772, a year after her marriage to his father. At Yelling he also met Martin Madan, who was impressed by John's intelligence and suggested that he should be sent to Westminster, his own old school. Henry Venn, however, had heard disquieting rumours about the morals of the boys at Westminster; these decided him to send John back to Hipperholme.

In spite of distance, Henry Venn tried to supervise his son's progress and conduct to some extent. "If John should call on you," he writes to Mrs. Riland, "as perhaps he will, tell him I wrote to him the 24th of December at Mr. Elmsall's, and ordering him to write me word back before he went to school what book he was reading, and he has never taken the least notice of my letter—I shall not therefore write to him again until he does."[1] And to Mr. Whitaker, a Huddersfield clothier, with whom he spent the Easter holidays one year: "Jack I understand has been at your house, I hope he behaved well and seemed sensible of your kindness to him."[2]

In 1775 John had to leave Hipperholme, as he was now fourteen, which was the usual leaving age. "It would have been extremely in his favour had Mr. Sutcliffe been able to have taught him one year longer. He would have been fit for the university and superior to most in learning when they enter

musical culture—all the Jowetts being keen musicians. John Jowett was a member of the original C.M.S. Committee (John Venn was probably responsible for his election), but he died in 1800 a year after the Society was formed and a year before his father. One of John Jowett's sons was William Jowett, the first graduate to go overseas as a C.M.S. missionary. Benjamin Jowett, the famous Master of Balliol, was a grandson.

[1] H. Venn to Mrs. Riland, Jan. 29, 1772 (MS.).

[2] H. Venn to T. Whitaker, May 3, 1773 (MS.).

there."[1] It may surprise us that Henry Venn should consider sending a boy of fifteen to the university, but he would have been no exception; for the young William Pitt, who was born the same year as John, was only fourteen when he entered Pembroke College, Cambridge. "I was at a loss", Henry Venn tells Stillingfleet, "where to find a master but have determined, at length, to put him under Mr. Milner, at Hull, for a year. If you go there I hope you will call upon him. He seems, indeed, to be all I could wish, and still continues fixed in his choice of being a preacher of Christ."[2]

Isaac Milner, then a Cambridge undergraduate, called for John on his way to Hull and took him to his brother's school. John stayed as a boarder in the Milners' house.[3]

> Upon his return to Yelling at midsummer, 1774, great was his father's eagerness to ascertain his progress and within a few minutes of his arrival at the house the Greek and Latin books were spread on the table. His father's countenance fell as he proceeded in his examination and it was soon discovered that the son had lost ground during the year he had spent in Hull—for Mr. Milner at this time was so deeply engaged in the preparation of his Church History that his scholars were sadly neglected. Mr. Venn determined that his son should not return to Hull and began with great energy to instruct him himself till he should fix upon another tutor.[4]

Mr. Sutcliffe, fortunately, was prepared to take him as a private pupil; meanwhile there was little vacation for John. His father writes: "I send Jacky again to his old master—none as I can find, are equal to him. Since he has been at home I have read much Horace and some of Herodotus."

On his return to Hipperholme, John not only made up lost ground with his studies, but also revealed progress in his spiritual life. The coach in which he was travelling to Yorkshire was involved, or nearly involved, in a dangerous accident; Henry Venn considered this escape particularly significant: "It was a memorable era in your life, to me and yourself, when

[1] H. Venn to Mrs. Riland, Aug. 28, 1773 (MS.).

[2] *Life of H. Venn*, p. 204.

[3] John tells his sister Eling when he visits Hull in 1795: "Old Mr. Milner died last week under whose care I was as a boarder for about 12 months."

[4] H. Venn, Sketch of Life of John Venn of Clapham (MS.).

a sense of your wonderful preservation, in the article of danger in the stage-coach, going to Hipperholme, made a deep impression upon you. All the children of God can record such interpositions; and by them have very many been brought to themselves."[1]

It seems to have been during his last year at school that John's mind was moving in the direction his father had always desired, and towards the conclusion for which he had so often prayed. "Finished Janeway's *Life*—a most excellent book indeed. O may I imitate his example! What communion had he with God! What love of souls!"[2] He also mentions reading Beveridge's *Private Thoughts* at this time, Whitefield's *Life*, etc. Other extracts exhibit great tenderness of conscience and contrition for sin and he notices the day on which he first discovered some signs of religious feelings in one of his school-fellows.[3]

At length he wrote to his father, who eagerly replied. So careful was he that Mr. Sutcliffe should neither read nor censor the letter, he sent it to his former curate, George Burnett, at Elland, asking him to deliver it personally to the boy. He evidently had no objection to Burnett reading it, for the covering notice is written on the same sheet as the first page of the letter to John. John's own letter has unfortunately not been preserved. His father's reply begins:

Dear Jacky,

I desire to be very thankful to the Lord for his great goodness in bringing you to feel with an afflicted mind, that you are a very wicked and sinful creature. And I am very much pleased with you for letting me know the state of your soul—and your declaration that you would wish to be most unreserved as a friend with me. It is in that relation, I hope we shall pass the few years which, it is probable, I may be continued to you. Instead therefore of being shy to ask my advice, and to open to me your own heart as

[1] Letter written to John Venn on his twentieth birthday, March 9, 1779, printed in *Life of H. Venn*, pp. 271–2. Belief in special providences is a characteristic of the early Evangelicals; John Newton's *Authentic Narrative*, for instance, abounds in them.

[2] *Life of John Janeway*, by James Janeway, 1672. The first edition had an introduction by Richard Baxter. In 1884 John Venn of Hereford came across his father's copy. He was so impressed by it that he republished it in a cheap edition, with a brief preface. He makes no reference to its influence over his father.

[3] H. Venn, Sketch of Life of John Venn of Clapham (MS.).

pride would have you do (lest I should not have a good opinion of you), apply to me, as one who has age and experience, and great pleasure in making all I have useful to you and your sisters.

Henry Venn then proceeds to tell his son at great length that the conviction of sin which he is experiencing comes from God who has also provided a remedy for the disease, "as a sick patient deplorably wounded, prizes the medicine, and the giver of it, which are working his cure, so every man must be sick of sin, and sorely wounded by it, in order to prize the admirable Physician, who is given for the healing of the nations." He sympathizes with his son in his want of "spiritual company" at school, but comforts him by saying "a single stranger in a strange country is much on his guard—but when we are with those from whom we expect much help, we are apt to grow careless ourselves, and foolishly conclude we may relax our guard without danger." The letter ends: "And now I commend you to God—Watch and pray—Read God's Holy Word, begging Him to teach you the meaning of it—to make it plain to your soul and you shall prosper—and grow in grace and in the love and knowledge of our Lord and Saviour Jesus Christ, to whom be glory for evermore."[1]

The letter not only tells us something of John's religious experience, it also tells us something of his character. The picture is of a shy retiring boy who, after a struggle, has opened his heart to his father. This trait of shyness, which is frequently mentioned even by John himself, never left him, though in some measure he conquered it when he became Rector of Clapham. John, as his father frequently told him, much resembled his mother. Although there is no trace in his make-up of Mira Venn's quarrelsomeness and desire for mastery, her nervous temperament reappeared both in the moods of depression which, like her, he endured, and in an awkward reserve, which was perhaps his counterpart of her meddlesomeness. J. W. Cunningham, who was for a time John Venn's curate, says that the vigour and *joie de vivre* which Henry Venn perpetually radiated "only gleamed occasionally" in his son, when stirred by the company of close friends, or by the sight of majestic scenery or by "the grand themes of religion".[2] It is also possible that

[1] *Ibid.*

[2] J. W. Cunningham, *The Velvet Cushion*, pp. 166–7.

Henry Venn's very exuberance may well have pushed John back into himself and, as frequently happens, a dominating though humble father crippled the development of his son's personality; consequently maturity came late. It is highly significant that although John sometimes found it easier to confide in his elder sister, Eling, than in their father, he never resented the part Henry Venn played in his life.

In the relationship between John and Henry Venn there is a superficial parallel with that which existed between Edmund Gosse and his father nearly a century later. Both were sons of pious Evangelical parents who intended their only sons for some sort of Christian ministry; both lost their mothers at the age of seven; both their fathers after an interval of a few years married again; in both cases there was a marked difference in temperament; but there the parallel ends. Edmund Gosse was an only child, and for many years his father's only companion. Henry Venn had a large family and many friends. Though solemnity had its place at Yelling Rectory it never predominated as it did in Gosse's Devonshire villa. At Yelling, joy and wit were always bursting through: there was nothing stuffy or superficial about the home atmosphere, and an Evangelical Anglican home in the 1770s was very different from a Plymouth Brethren home in the 1860s. Henry Venn was prepared to read and learn from books by Roman Catholics; Philip Gosse could scarcely contemplate the possibility of Roman Catholics being saved. In the case of the Gosses there was a clash of temperaments and eventually rebellion; in the case of the Venns the difference was recognized, but there was no attempt on the father's side to coerce the son into his own mould. When John Venn was a schoolboy, and even more when he was an undergraduate, Henry Venn wrote him pages of advice and instruction, but his letters never bore the inquisitorial character of Philip Gosse's. Henry Venn may have been an anxious and at times an interfering parent, but he was never a bully.

As a result he was to his son "that dear and admirable man to whom indeed under God I owe almost every blessing I enjoy in life",[1] and Cunningham says that in his preaching and teach-

[1] J. Venn, Introductory Memoir to "Parentalia" (MS.).

ing, John Venn, "of all the men I ever saw . . . most delighted to represent God under the image of a father. It was to him the most honourable and most interesting of all titles, and he transferred it to the being he loved best."[1] "No curse of time," John says in a sermon on the Parental Character of God, "will ever obliterate the memory of that unvarying kindness, that incessant solicitude, that perpetual watchfulness, that affectionate sympathy in my trouble, that abounding joy in my happiness, which for so many years I daily witnessed."[2] And again, in a sermon John Venn preached on "True Regard to God the Great Preservative from Sin", he says: "The true fear of God . . . is a filial fear; the fear which a son feels of a father whom he at once reveres and loves."

Such a son will be eager to please and reluctant to displease or disobey such a father. "He will not obey him from any mere motive of interest, nor yet from mere dread of his displeasure: he will not obey in these things only which coincide with his own inclination, while he refuses what would cost him any effort of self-denial; he will not show reverence in external acts, or in his father's presence only; but there will be in him a steady prevailing principle of regard, which will make his heart and his life in union with each other, which will incline him to his duty with an irresistible force."[3] Here is the underlying idea of the relationship that existed between John and his father, an ideal which was to be more positively realized as John outgrew his shyness and rejoiced in his father's companionship and in doing those things that pleased him.

Two other things stand out with regard to John's character at this time, to which there is some reference in the letters; one is his sweet disposition, the other his continuing determination to become "a pastor in the Church of Christ". "He assures me

[1] J. W. Cunningham, *The Velvet Cushion*, pp. 167–8. cf. "I have long been accustomed to attach to the word Father every idea that is consoling, tender, affectionate; I have witnessed repeatedly the tender anxiety of my personal earthly parent on my account, and have been accustomed to transfer it to my heavenly Father who gave to my earthly one all that was kind and excellent in him, and to consider the same love and tenderness as eminently residing in him with the difference of an infinite superiority in everything good." J. Venn to Miss H. More, June 3, 1813 (MS.).

[2] *Sermons*, Vol. II, pp. 292–3.

[3] *Sermons*, Vol. III, pp. 20–1.

he had rather be a minister of Christ than a prince. He speaks well."[1]

Little wonder that when Henry Venn finally took John away from Hipperholme at the end of 1775, he should be apprehensive not only of his own ability as a teacher, but of his example as a minister of Christ. "At Christmas my son, who is as tall as I am, and promises to be as tall as Mr. Riland, comes home, and I shall have great need more than common of your prayers that whilst he lives with me he may see nothing that will hurt his precious soul and take off the force of those instructions I shall be daily giving him, nothing but what will win his affection, even without the word, to Christ; and make him feel that the Knowledge of Him is the way of peace and joy."[2]

With his intellectual progress at Hipperholme Henry Venn was well pleased. "He has been taken good care of in his learning at Hipperholme, and reads every day two hundred lines in Homer without a translation—and passes with exactness."[3] On his return to Yelling he continued to apply himself diligently to his work. "My son has been my pupil since the 16th of December. And my heart perhaps too much intent on his qualifying himself with all learning for the ministry, makes me spend much time with him. At present, my son is everything that I could wish—a sweet temper indeed, and very serious,[4] joining with devotion in our meetings in the evening, and intent to please me by studying closely."[5] With his father, John studied Greek, Latin and the New Testament but, "as I could not teach him to *write* good Latin, and I feared I might be most defective there, I accepted dear Mr. Robinson's proposal, and he is now at Leicester with him for two months, in order to receive a blessing from that lively, zealous, prudent, and able young minister, as well as to be perfected in the Latin tongue. I have no fear of my son's abilities, they are excellent. . . . Nothing can be better. I do not intend he should go to

[1] H. Venn to Stillingfleet, Jan. 20, 1775; *Life of H. Venn*, p. 222.

[2] H. Venn to Mrs. Riland, Sept. 30, 1775; partly reproduced, *ibid.*, p. 228.

[3] H. Venn to Mrs. Riland, July 4, 1775 (MS.).

[4] "Serious" here does not mean "solemn" but sincerely Evangelical; "serious views" were Evangelical views.

[5] H. Venn to Mrs. Riland, Feb. 7, 1776; *Life of H. Venn*, pp. 228–9.

college till he is nineteen; and I intend he shall study physic enough to be useful and learn to bleed."[1]

Thomas Robinson[2] had formerly been a Fellow of Trinity, whom Venn had come to know and admire. At Leicester he was at this time curate of St. Martin's, lecturer at All Saints', and Chaplain of Leicester Infirmary. In spite of the work these three offices involved he contrived to take private pupils in classes to prepare them for the university. Most of these were local boys, but John lived with him in his house. John stayed in Leicester three successive summers before going up to Cambridge. The arrangement worked well and John looked to Robinson for counsel and advice throughout his life.

Although a former wrangler, Robinson sent John for mathematics to William Ludlam, a retired Cambridge don living in Leicester. Ludlam's chief interest was mechanics and it was probably from him that John gained an interest in science and engineering which never left him. While at Cambridge he corresponded with Ludlam on lectures in this subject and asked for a longer book-list. One of the few early entries in his own *Annals* reads: "Mr. Daw gave me an electrical machine." That was eighteen months before he went up to the university. It is possible that William Ludlam's son, Thomas Ludlam, was suggested as Governor of Sierra Leone by John Venn. Another former Cambridge don who took a lively interest in John's intellectual and spiritual progress was the eccentric John Berridge of Everton. "He is as affectionate as a father to my son," writes Henry Venn, "and gives him many valuable books."[3] This interest and affection grew during John's time at the university.

John Venn spent the summer of 1777 at Leicester. His father

[1] H. Venn to J. Stillingfleet, quoted in H. Venn, Sketch of Life of John Venn of Clapham (MS.).

[2] Thomas Robinson (1749–1813). While Fellow of Trinity he served the curacies of Witcham and Wichford in the Isle of Ely and drew large congregations. At Leicester his hearers were said to number three thousand. In 1778 he was appointed to the living of St. Mary's, Leicester, through the influence of Thomas Babington. He died in 1813. He considered Henry Venn his prototype. Shortly after his death E. T. Vaughan published *Some Account of the Reverend Thomas Robinson, M.A., late Vicar of St. Mary's, Leicester* (1815).

[3] *Life of H. Venn*, p. 233. For an amusing account of Berridge and his influence see C. H. Smyth, *Simeon and Church Order* (1941), chapters IV and VI.

tells a cousin, John Brasier, that both Robinson and Ludlam gave an excellent account of his behaviour (what they said about his studies this time is not mentioned). After a break of three weeks at home John Venn went up to Sidney Sussex College, Cambridge, on October 23, 1777.

2

CAMBRIDGE AND LITTLE DUNHAM

In the eighteenth century the University like the Church had fallen on evil days; nevertheless quick and vigorous resurrection in the nineteenth century suggests that, as in the case of the Church, critics have been too sweeping in their condemnation.

In the University, as in Church and State, sinecures abounded. Oxford and Cambridge were infested by dons who neither lectured nor took pupils. A college fellowship in most cases involved both the taking of Holy Orders and temporary celibacy —a Fellowship in fact was not so much a stepping-stone to a university chair but to a college living sufficiently well-endowed to enable the incumbent to marry. D. A. Winstanley has pointed out that unless a don held college or university office he had no specified duties to perform and little incentive to advance his own scholarship or that of others. Those who failed to secure clerical preferment remained in the university leading a life of aimless ease.[1] Moreover it was perfectly possible for an undergraduate to be in residence for three years at a university without attending a single lecture. However, towards the end of the century the bishops required all ordination candidates at Cambridge to produce a certificate showing that they had attended a certain number of the lectures of the Norrisian Professor of Divinity.

Before 1820 it was difficult for a student wishing to read theology to find either books to read or a tutor to supervise his studies. Much of the teaching was done by private tutors, a system which lent itself, as we shall have occasion to see, to the prevailing corruption of the day. Most of the examinations

[1] D. A. Winstanley, *Unreformed Cambridge* (1935), p. 261.

were oral. In the case of Cambridge mathematics predominated. As this subject was not taught in many schools, a large number of students began their university careers with an almost complete ignorance of the subjects they were chiefly to be examined in. The northern schools were on the whole more progressive; in this John Venn was fortunate in having been at Hipperholme.

In the eighteenth century, as well as the familiar academic division into scholars and commoners, undergraduates were divided socially into four classes; noblemen, fellow-commoners, pensioners and sizars. Noblemen and fellow-commoners were drawn from noble, county and wealthy families; they were exempt both from lectures and examinations if they so wished. Sons of noblemen received the M.A. automatically instead of B.A. and that without tests, whereas many fellow-commoners were often content to leave the university without a degree. The main difference between them was that noblemen paid higher fees than fellow-commoners. The majority of the undergraduates were pensioners, mostly sons of clergy and professional men, often receiving financial aid in the form of an exhibition from school. Below them were the sizars, sons of the poorer clergy and small farmers. Their fees were low and service was originally required in return; though this was becoming obsolete by the end of the eighteenth century and though they were now no longer "gyps" given the privilege of working for degrees, they were never allowed to forget that they were charity boys: as late as 1770 Isaac Milner, as a sizar of Queens', was required to ring the chapel bell and serve the first dish to the Fellows at dinner.[1]

These distinctions account for an outburst in a letter from Henry Venn to a cousin:

> On Monday last your nephew was admitted to Sidney College, where both his grandfathers were before him. But oh, what a wound to my pride: he is admitted in the same rank as his father and Dr. Conyers were, a sizar. Will not this offend you too? Why should not we be a little higher in the world and make some figure? Who can be comfortable or even contented to remain

[1] See Winstanley, *op. cit.*, pp. 197–203, and M. Milner, *Life of I. Milner* (1838), p. 6.

towards the fag end of the gentry, if we are allowed even to rank amongst them? O money! money! money! in abundance that our hearts cry out for. Yet what is this universal idol able to do? To create a right spirit? No. To make us excellent and happy? No. To arm us again to the evils and crosses of life? No. Only to dress out, and feed, and lodge, in a larger house, or to carry about in a shining chariot, a poor vile carcase and a sinful soul.[1]

However, in April 1777, six months before he went into residence, John Venn won a scholarship which enabled him to advance from sizar to pensioner; he also received a grant from the Fishmongers' Company.

The fact that John should go to Cambridge was not accepted by his father as a matter of course; in 1775 he tells Stillingfleet that he has asked Christopher Stephenson[2] to meet him in Oxford. "I want to know the state of religion amongst the students there, and incline to send Jacky there than my neighbouring university. We are so bad that some clergymen who are not over-serious almost scruple to send their sons, on account of the dissipation and extravagance there."[3] That there was cause for alarm is confirmed by Gunning, who describes the years when in fact John was in residence as "the very worst part of our history".[4] Henry Venn met Stephenson and five other like-minded students, but his inquiries about the state of the university did not convince him of the superiority of Oxford to Cambridge morality and in October 1776 he took John with him to enter him at a college for the following year. He first applied to Trinity, but the Master and Tutor were nervous of admitting the son of a notorious "Methodist". They then moved on to Sidney Sussex, where John was examined at some length by two of the Fellows. "He acquitted himself extremely well", Henry Venn tells Brasier, "and had great honour paid him, with appearances of all encouragement if he behaved well. This,

[1] H. Venn to Miss Martha Bishop, Oct. 9, 1776, in H. Venn, Sketch of Life of John Venn of Clapham (MS.).

[2] Christopher Stephenson of Worcester College, later presented to the living of Olney by Lord Dartmouth. See J. S. Reynolds, *The Evangelicals at Oxford* (1953), pp. 48–9.

[3] H. Venn to J. Stillingfleet, Feb. 17, 1775 (MS.).

[4] H. Gunning, *Reminiscences of the University, Town and County of Cambridge* (1855), preface, p. XII.

considering the name he bears, I thought very extraordinary. But I met with so much civility in Cambridge as made me astonished at the goodness of my God. What is infinitely better, there are some excellent students, who will be my son's companions, and are in earnest seeking the salvation of their souls."[1]

On October 23, 1777, John Venn took up residence in college. Numbers were small; possibly not more than six hundred in the whole university. At this time only two colleges had more than fifty resident members *in statu pupillari* and only seven more than forty. Sidney Sussex was the third smallest college with between fifteen and twenty men excluding the Fellows.[2] Cambridge itself was then a country town of some eight thousand inhabitants.[3] "Last week", his father told a correspondent, "my son left me to reside in College after near two years stay in my house. I am not able to express my thankfulness for his good behaviour and application to his studies. He is put under an admirable tutor, Mr. Hey. . . . He is very candid and very kind to my son."[4] Dr. J. Venn in the *Annals* says that Dr. Hey was probably by far the best college tutor in Cambridge at the time.[5] Although brother of Henry Venn's friend, William Hey, Dr. Hey was no "enthusiast".[6]

The first problem for John Venn was the furnishing of his rooms. His father writes from Yelling:

> On Friday between eleven and twelve you may, without the help of Dollond's telescope,[7] discover a phenomenon which no one ever saw before, a cartload of books belonging to J. V. Sid. Coll. Camb. . . . Pray take care and put your letters under lock

[1] Quoted by H. Venn in Sketch of Life of John Venn of Clapham (MS.).

[2] J. A. Venn, *Alumni Cantabrigienses*.

[3] H. C. G. Moule, *Charles Simeon* (1892), p. 6.

[4] *Annals*, pp. 115–16.

[5] He was also probably the most successful lecturer, drawing large audiences to his lectures on Morality and as Norrisian Professor of Divinity gaining a great reputation in that subject.

[6] In fact his lectures on the Trinity were so conciliatory to the Unitarians that they caused considerable embarrassment to Isaac Milner and Joseph Jowett when they were passed for publication by the University Press in the nineties. See Smyth, *op. cit.*, pp. 107–8.

[7] This family heirloom is still in the possession of Dr. J. A. Venn, John Venn's great-grandson.

and key. . . . Pray take care that your bed be thoroughly dry, and lay for the first night or two in your waistcoat, breeches and stockings. Before John[1] comes, will you buy some brass hooks to hang pictures on—a dozen—John will pay for them—I send you a guinea for the surplice.[2]

The next day John received another letter from his father which is a medley of advice on spiritual discipline and further hints on health and personal habits. John is to ride early as he did at Leicester in order to give him ample time for study and devotions.

> Be attentive to your health. Be sure, stand much. You cannot study hard and sit without smarting for it, especially if you incline your body. Every other morning attend to your mouth and clean it well with snuff, which I find of great service to my teeth, and so does your Mama.[3]

In a later letter he adds:

> I am glad you keep your room neat and clean—it is for your credit and comfort too. How do your books suit the shelves? have you room for them? I hope you mind your teeth and your posture in reading, making good use of your desk and standing full half your time.[4]

In the *Annals* there is a description of John Venn's appearance. "In stature he was rather below medium height, about five feet seven inches or thereabouts, and slender during his youth, though in after life he became somewhat corpulent."[5] A portrait was taken by John Downman of him just before he left college. "It is a small one, representing him after Downman's fashion, in profile, as a rather handsome, fine-featured young man. He is dressed in the somewhat elaborate style which custom then required at College hall, with his hair carefully powdered."[6]

[1] Henry Venn's manservant.

[2] To John Venn, Oct. 29, 1777 (MS.).

[3] H. Venn to J. Venn, Oct. 30, 1777 (MS.), not included in copy of letter in *Life of H. Venn*, pp. 241–3.

[4] H. Venn to J. Venn, Nov. 11, 1777 (MS.). Quoted in part in *Life of H. Venn*, p. 248.

[5] *Annals*, p. 121. The author says he owes this description of his grandfather to the latter's younger son, also called John Venn.

[6] *Ibid.* The portrait is reproduced as frontispiece.

John Venn's son Henry says that he questioned some of his father's contemporaries about his academic work. He was told that his father did not work particularly hard at his set subjects, namely classics and mathematics, but was inclined to read far more discursively in subjects that interested him; apart from history these subjects were chiefly scientific. If he had lived in the twentieth century John Venn would have probably taken a degree in physics or engineering, for his notebooks are full of notes on optics, astronomy, hydrostatics and mechanics, all illustrated by neat diagrams. John Venn's own diaries contain references to "machines" he was given, which he assembled for his father to the latter's great delight. His grandson says that among the family possessions he inherited were the Dollond telescope, a sextant, chronometer watch, dividing compasses.[1] He kept up his scientific studies while at Little Dunham, and all his life he was prepared to experiment with the latest inventions, whether they were grates or Rumford cooking-stoves or lighting appliances. In 1795 a fire in the nursery of Clapham Rectory was brought under control by "a watering engine" John Venn had purchased against such an emergency. In 1809 he himself installed a water-closet in Clapham Rectory. He was one of the earliest members of the public to make use of Jenner's discovery of vaccination, which he introduced not only to his family but to his parish.[1]

Other interests included shorthand, astronomy, heraldry and all branches of antiquarian knowledge. He also took care to cultivate a good style of reading and speaking. Sidney Sussex as a college was in advance of most other colleges in offering prizes for classics and mathematics. John Venn competed for both and was examined for six hours on nine successive days. He obtained neither prize, but Hey told Henry Venn that "taking classics and mathematics together" he was the best.[2]

John Venn's favourite pastimes were boating and riding. At Cambridge he was known as "Admiral of the Cam". He bought at least two boats, one of which he shared with two friends; this boat was twenty feet long and was kept at St. Ives. He also occasionally appeared on the Cam in a canoe. In his second long

[1] *Annals*, p. 122. Also see p. 143.
[2] *Annals*, p. 117.

vacation, with his friend Francis Wollaston, he took a large sailing-boat up the Thames to Mortlake "and had a most narrow escape under Chelsea Bridge".[1] On the occasion of this holiday his family completely lost trace of him; two days before the incident on the Thames Edward Venn of Bow Lane received this request from his uncle at Yelling: "I write now to beg you will find out, or advertise a young volunteer enlisted under the host of heaven, who has already exceeded his furlough five days and it is not known by the company to which he belongs, where he now is. Pray find him out as soon as possible"[2]—otherwise he will miss Stillingfleet on a short visit from Hotham. Henry Venn wrote to another relation in similar terms but with no avail. John reached home two days after "Stilo" had departed.

John Venn's modesty and ability at Cambridge seem to have impressed many people, including the senior members of his own college. In a letter, Berridge tells John Thornton:

> Jacky is the top branch of the tree, highest and humblest. His abilities seem equal to anything he undertakes, and his modesty is pleasing to all that behold him. He has daily hours for retirement for waiting secretly on his God . . . and he is so recollected in his talk, that I seldom hear him speak a trifling thing. His behaviour in College has turned the hearts of the Master and the Fellows entirely to him, who were very averse, and even injurious for a season, on account of his being the son of a Methodist clergyman.[3]

His father also found him a pleasant companion and was greatly impressed by his spiritual growth during his time as a student. He tells Mrs. Riland, "I assure you I can learn from him; he hath a deeper insight into the Scripture than was ever given to me," and he adds, "He rather too much fixes upon the dark side of things, and sees more of the fall of man, the infinite

[1] *Ibid.*, p. 120.

[2] H. Venn to E. Venn, undated (MS.).

[3] Berridge's *Works*, edited by R. Whittingham (1838), pp. 414–15. This was the only suggestion there is that John Venn was regarded with contempt by the members of the Senior Common Room, because his father was known to be a "Methodist". All that Henry Venn himself has written emphasizes the surprising courtesy his son was shown. There may, however, have been a period when he was made to feel that his views were not acceptable to authority, which he was able to convert to respect and affection, through the quality of his character.

evil of sin and the purity of God, than of grace, mercy, peace; and is rather inclined to be cast down than cheerful."[1] In another letter he tells Mrs. Riland: "He is more and more earnest, but much more Dr. Venn's son than mine."[2] The Dr. Venn he refers to is his own eldest brother, Edward Venn of Ipswich; however, if J. W. Cunningham is right,[3] John's tendency to earnestness and morbidity did not come from his father's side of the family at all, but from his mother's; it was from her that he inherited moods of melancholia to which his father was a complete stranger.

John Venn was certainly quieter and more solemn than his father; he also found hard work much less congenial than his father did. At Cambridge, as accomplishment in many fields came with ease he was not inclined to over-exert himself in any, nor did he always complete what he had begun. During his final year he was invited by the Master to assist him with the new college library; Henry Venn thought it necessary to tell John that he must not come home at the end of term unless the Master said he was satisfied that his work in the library was completed; "in this matter," he advises, "you must do violence to your natural indolence and persevere. How glad should I be that there was need of a curb, instead of a spur, respecting your application to study, and that you could persevere as well as begin with some spirit."[4] John's own son, Henry, wrote that his father was "of a retiring and somewhat indolent constitutional temperament".[5] There were physical reasons for this tendency to laziness; during his last year at Cambridge he became subject to violent feverish and liverish attacks which assailed him at intervals for the rest of his life. Added to this was a reserve which, as we have already noted,[6] he did not really overcome till he reached Clapham.

Later this solemnity and listlessness were set off by an impish wit, not unlike his father's but more polished. There can be

[1] H. Venn to Mrs. Riland, Sept. 20, 1781 (MS.).
[2] H. Venn to Mrs. Riland, Jan. 21, 1782 (MS.).
[3] See p. 31.
[4] H. Venn to John Venn, Nov. 1, 1781 (MS.).
[5] H. Venn, Sketch of the Character of the late Revd. John Venn of Clapham (MS.).
[6] See p. 31.

little doubt his Cambridge friends were already seeing something of this side of his character; but he seems to have kept it from his father, who was disturbed by John's reserve and timidity, particularly in relation to himself. Nelly, John's eldest sister, thought he should realize this and wrote him a long letter on the subject, asking John to be more open with his father about his spiritual convictions and opinions; if he finds he cannot speak about them to his father in conversation he should try to put them into a letter. "We know not . . . what are the feelings of a father's heart to an only son, towards a son too, whose whole conduct has been so pleasing to him, this little instance excepted. . . . Be an example to your sisters in this as you have been, and are, in every other respect."[1]

John was only too aware of his own shortcomings. Soon after taking his Tripos he received a letter from John Thornton questioning him seriously on his call to the ministry. In a lengthy reply John adds to a paragraph on his own insufficiency and sinfulness, that might have been written by any Evangelical ordinand of the day, this illuminating sentence: "Extremely timid by constitution, unwilling to converse and afraid of giving offence, I confess I startle at my own weakness, and that want of faith which is alone able to support me."[2]

A young man, naturally reserved in character, with a tendency to indolence and brooding, is unlikely to prove himself a leader amongst his contemporaries. Nevertheless John Venn quickly became the leader of those "excellent students" about whom Henry Venn had written to Brasier, who were "in earnest seeking the salvation of their souls". Henry Jowett, though two years John Venn's senior, was one of them. In later years he told the younger Henry Venn that through his father's influence were first formed "those little societies of religious young men, which proved, I believe, a help and comfort to many".[3] It was owing to his father's initiative that John began these groups, but their growth and success were the fruit of his own powers of spiritual leadership enhanced by frequent and wise counsel from Yelling. From the first, Henry Venn thought

[1] Eling Venn to John Venn, April 28, 1781 (MS.).
[2] To John Thornton, March 14, 1781 (MS.).
[3] Preface to *Sermons*, p. lx.

caution and discretion essential. There is a note of warning in a letter he sent John during his first term at college:

> I am very glad that you, with the three friends you mention, intend to meet on Sundays—I suppose, by turns, in each other's rooms. But I would not have you increase your number on several accounts. Your knowledge of each other and confidence of friendship will enable you to speak without fear and freely: but more would be a bar to such freedom, and prove a snare by tempting you to speak for commendation. More would draw upon you the eyes of each college, and expose you to needless ridicule, and prove an offence, which few young people are able to bear. It would have the appearance of making a party and lead to several disagreeable consequences. There is no occasion that you should mention your meeting to any one and if there should be other serious young men desirous of such improvement on the Sunday they should make another party; and so on—three or four making up a company. When you are together your great temptation will be to levity of mind—a sort of merriment very unseasonable—when you should be conversing, with all your attention, upon subjects of infinite moment. But if you are honest, meekly to reprove the first appearance of that spirit, you will succeed, and the Lord Jesus will, according to His promise, be in the midst of you.[1]

How these groups were divided up, whether they met by colleges, we do not know, but we do know that during his first Christmas vacation John told his father he had eight "serious" companions; a year later there were eleven. However, there must have been some larger meetings in which the students indulged in "unseasonable merriment" and displayed "levity of mind", for after one visit Henry Venn complained "I shall not call at Cambridge; my last visit there did not suit my spirit. There were too many, and the conversation about nothing."[2]

The warning in the original letter may seem to us unnecessarily solemn. Doubtless Henry Venn had in mind the treatment of the six students who had been sent down nine years earlier from St. Edmund Hall, Oxford, for attending prayer meetings in a widow's drawing-room, which the University

[1] *Life of H. Venn*, pp. 242–3.
[2] H. Venn to J. Venn, Nov. 1, 1781 (MS.).

authorities maintained to be an illicit conventicle.[1] He would also be aware of the situation which arose at Cambridge when Rowland Hill, an undergraduate at St. John's, gathered a group of about a dozen men round him "to read the Greek Testament and other evangelical publications"[2] and to pray together. For counsel and support this group turned to John Berridge and Robert Robinson, a Particular Baptist minister. With Berridge's encouragement some of them assisted Robinson in preaching tours round the villages near Cambridge, and Hill did some preaching on his own account, which may well have been the reason for the Master of St. John's refusing to give him a college testimonial. As a result of these irregularities Hill and his friends had considerable difficulty in finding a bishop who would ordain them. Hill was never allowed to proceed further than the diaconate,[3] and the Surrey Chapel which his supporters built for him, though Anglican in worship, never received episcopal sanction.[4] Although Henry Venn had a great affection for Rowland Hill and was a frequent visiting preacher at Surrey Chapel, he had no desire for his son to be likewise shut out from the full Anglican ministry by gaining notoriety for being a dangerous "enthusiast", whilst still an undergraduate.

All Rowland Hill's group had gone down by the end of 1771, the year that Henry Venn came to Yelling, but he was soon searching for others with similar views. In August 1772 Venn spent a few days in Cambridge. He tells Mrs. Riland "I hope it may please God I may be of some service to the students: I go for no other purpose."[5] The visit evidently bore fruit, for in October he was able to tell Powley, "There are some excellent young men at college, who come to me from the university, as I was in hopes they would",[6] and two years later he mentioned "an extraordinary young man from St. John's College, Cam-

[1] J. S. Reynolds, *The Evangelicals at Oxford*, 1735–1871 (1953), pp. 34–41, and S. L. Ollard, *The Six Students of St. Edmund Hall expelled from the University of Oxford in 1768* (1911).

[2] C. H. Smyth, *Simeon and Church Order*, p. 178.

[3] See Smyth, *op. cit.*, 178–9 for an account of the group and their activities.

[4] L. E. Elliott-Binns, *The Early Evangelicals* (1953), pp. 232–3.

[5] *Life of H. Venn*, pp. 232–3.

[6] *Ibid.*, p. 198.

bridge, one Collins, I like him much".[1] It was from careful observation of how these men and their successors behaved, and how they came to be regarded by the university authorities and their fellow-students, that Henry Venn wrote as he did to his son. A letter, dated November 11, 1777, reveals in full Henry Venn's fear for him:

> My first advice is, that you should beware of the device Satan too successfully practises against novices in religion. When he perceives they are no longer kept asleep in profaneness or formality—no longer to be deluded with the pleasures of gross sin, or the love of fame or wealth—when he sees they are determined to come out of the world and be separate—he alters his method to destroy them. "Be more separate," he suggests, "distinguish yourself; *immediately* assume the preacher's office: neglect the peculiar duties of your age and station, and intrude into what does by no means yet belong to you: force your sentiments upon others; and consider yourself, even in your youth (without experience, without knowledge, observe!) to be a reformer, authorised to despise your elders, to be impatient of submission, to be heady, high-minded: and then, to complete the whole, abuse learning, and be confident you have an impulse from heaven and a divine call to justify all you do!"—Thus I have seen religious young men perverted and become unsufferably disagreeable, by their false ideas of religion, and a stumbling-block in the way of others; they themselves seldom recovering from their forward, proud spirit. Under the influence of this proud spirit, they are always for overdoing, and for needless, nay, absurd singularities. They will even court persecution, and then swell with the idea that they are treated for Christ's sake as the prophets and martyrs were of old. Take knowledge, therefore, of the important boundary between separation from the world and this offensive self-sufficient excess in things which our God does not require.[2]

Henry Venn knew only too well how easily human pride is mistaken for God's grace and selfish desire for God's guidance in the life of a young Evangelical, and how insufferable priggishness results. The type of Christian Henry Venn warns his son against being is by no means extinct. In contrast to this

[1] H. Venn to J. Stillingfleet, Aug. 11, 1774 (MS.).
[2] *Life of H. Venn*, pp. 243–8.

type he urges his son to cultivate a quiet but cheerful modesty, nurtured by prayer and Bible study.

> Whilst thus you lay the stress upon matters of utmost moment, you will receive the blessing of the Lord, you will win and attract both esteem and affection from many, you will put to silence the ignorance of foolish men by well-doing. Their idea of your religion is that it puffs you up—makes you think yourself better than all beside, actuating you by a spirit of singularity, and love to be admired; that you are a compound of ignorance, enthusiasm and spiritual pride. Nothing can convince them of their gross mistake or conquer their prejudices but humility, meekness, wisdom, and soundness of mind, which those who are really in Christ possess and manifest.[1]

During his time in Cambridge John Venn certainly avoided the dangers against which his father here warns him and manifested in some degree the virtues that are here commended. Moreover he was eminently successful in doing what Rowland Hill and the students at Oxford did, without bringing on himself or his friends the same penalties that they incurred. The weakness of his father's counsel was that it discouraged him from committing sins he was unlikely to indulge in and to develop virtues which he obviously already possessed. John, naturally a reserved person, was not likely to cheapen his faith by over-advertising it, and though he formed these small groups of religious friends, they were not well known in the university; it was not till three years after his conversion in King's Chapel that Charles Simeon discovered them.[2]

This did not mean that John was not prepared to stand firm and suffer abuse for his beliefs. "My son is now in the midst of his trials", Henry Venn tells Brasier:[3]

> Obliged to be in the company of the sons of Belial, with whom he is engaged in keeping exercise in the public schools; because he would not get drunk with them, nor exceed the bounds of strict temperance, they abused him for a Methodist, saying none but Methodists believed there was a judgement to come or that there was any harm in whoring or drinking; could the Method-

[1] *Life of H. Venn*, p. 246.

[2] See p. 54.

[3] H. Venn to J. Brasier, Feb. 25, 1780 (MS.).

> ists be extirpated there would be no qualms of conscience in the land: and when he would leave them, they came drunk and broke in pieces the door of his room, but he was not in it: they were not suffered to break his furniture in pieces. These are the young gentlemen who in two or three years' time, will be reading lectures on morality from their pulpits.

Here is to be seen the strength of John's character. He might be shy and unobtrusive, but he was no coward.

To his friends, much that was positive in his later development was already visible. Henry Jowett says of John: "Mr. Venn, I consider to have been the oldest friend I had among my equals. . . . After a separation of some years, he came into residence at college, a few months before I took my degree. But as I continued to reside in Cambridge, our intimacy was renewed and increased; and he then discovered that warmth of affection, and that soundness of judgement and principle, which gained him the esteem and love of all who knew him."[1] This accounts for the many lifelong friendships he made at Cambridge.

Henry Jowett was one of John Venn's closest friends. He became Fellow of Magdalene in 1779 and remained such till he succeeded John as Rector of Little Dunham in 1792. Their friendship survived an emotional upset three years earlier when both men were courting the same girl. Henry Jowett's elder brother, Joseph, was Fellow and Tutor of Trinity Hall[2] when John Venn reached the university and possibly gave him some coaching in classics. He was more senior and for that reason naturally more distant from John Venn than his brother was. The same could be said of Isaac Milner, who probably took little notice of the shy undergraduate whom he had once accompanied as a schoolboy to Hull. At Clapham they were to meet frequently as friends of William Wilberforce; at Cambridge they were not on the same level, for Milner was already enjoying the reputation of being the most formidable of the Moderators in the Senate House Examination, he was on the

[1] Preface to *Sermons*, p. IX.

[2] Joseph Jowett became Regius Professor of Civil Law in 1782 and retired to a college living in 1823. He was a tiny man with two great passions in life, the promotion of Evangelical religion and classical music. He organized concerts in the Hall. He and Isaac Milner tried to spend two evenings a week together in term.

verge of becoming Jacksonian Professor of Physics and was soon to be elected President of Queens'.[1] When Milner resigned his professorship in 1793 the rival candidates for the Chair were William Farish and Francis Wollaston: Wollaston was elected. These men were the greatest of John Venn's Cambridge friends. Farish was his own age, Wollaston three years younger.

William Farish had been elected to a Fellowship at Magdalene the same year as Henry Jowett. He became in turn Tutor of his college, Professor of Chemistry and finally Jacksonian Professor on Wollaston's retirement. He was for nearly forty years Vicar of St. Giles', Cambridge. He died in 1837. Venn had the greatest regard for Farish both as a scientist and as a man. He sent his eldest son, Henry, to study for a year with him before entering Queens'. "He has indeed," he tells his son, "the greatest intuition on every subject of science which I ever saw in any man; and I never knew him err in any opinion he advanced. With such a tutor you may learn much."[2] In the next letter he asks Henry whether he helps Farish to erect and dismantle the models with which he illustrated his popular lectures on "industrial chemistry".[3] "Dear W. Farish" is often mentioned in John Venn's letters and diaries. Although there is little evidence of mutual correspondence, Farish was a frequent visitor at Dunham and Clapham. When John Venn lost his first wife Farish hastened to Clapham to be with him, when Farish himself was dangerously ill Venn hurried to Cambridge. While there he wrote to his children: "I had always depended

[1] Milner was elected Jacksonian Professor in 1783 (the year after Venn went down), and President of Queens' in 1788. In 1792 he became Dean of Carlisle, resigning his Chair but not his College. A brilliant pupil like Wollaston might write of Milner as Moderator "Milner, a most good-humoured man", but Gunning says "He was in the habit of calling dull and stupid men *sooty fellows*; and when he had a class of that description to examine, he would call out to the Moderators, who were at the other end of the Senate House, 'In rebus fuliginosis versatus sum'." Gunning, *Reminiscences*, Vol. I, p. 83.

[2] J. Venn to H. Venn, March 18, 1813 (MS.).

[3] As other lectures on chemistry were available, Farish devoted himself to explaining the application of chemistry to industry. During vacations he visited the new factories in the north and midlands and then made models of the various machines and instruments employed in them. These visual aids not only made his lectures popular, they also provided entertainment for the children of guests who visited him. See C. H. Smyth, "William Farish", *Magdalene College Magazine*, Dec. 1937, pp. 282–3.

on his kind advice and care towards you, had I been taken away I should have been glad for you to have looked up to him as your faithful friend and your most judicious adviser."[1] Farish recovered and after John Venn's own death more than amply fulfilled his duties as guardian to his friend's sons.

The influence of this shy, eccentric don[2] over undergraduates was immense, second only to that of Simeon, whom he outlived by a year. It was to Magdalene and not to King's that Evangelical parents sent their sons and the Elland Society their candidates, although Milner's appointment as President of Queens' created a diversion and an alternative.[3] Gunning says that he had heard the Master of Magdalene declare that "he thought there must be something in the air of Magdalene that made men Methodists".[4] Possibly it was not so much the air as the influence of William Farish.

Francis Wollaston came up to Sidney when John Venn was in his third year. They seem to have become friends almost at once, for the entry in John's diary for October 12, 1779 reads: "My acquaintance with F. J. H. Wollaston began."[5] They shared two great enthusiasms, science and boating. Wollaston was John's companion in the sailing adventure on the Thames and years later they were corresponding about telescopes, John illustrating his arguments with neat diagrams. As late as 1810 John Venn breakfasted with Professor Wollaston at Cambridge. One letter, written from Little Dunham and too long to be quoted, is of special significance. In it John tries to comfort his friend at a time of deep personal loss. He warns him against escapism and urges him to listen to what God is saying to him through his sorrow. He goes on to suggest that it is possible that Wollaston has become so immersed in scientific research and teaching that he may well have forgotten his "duty as a minister of Christ". "Alas! How little honour is it to be the best chemist in Europe in comparison with being a useful minister of Christ. What comparison can there be between saving a soul and analysing a salt!" Nevertheless, "Science and amusement and

[1] J. Venn to his children, June 1810 (MS.).
[2] See *Annals*, p. 189.
[3] See C. H. Smyth, *Simeon and Church Order*, p. 215 n.
[4] Gunning, *op. cit.*, Vol. I, p. 239.
[5] John Venn's Diary (MS.).

company are useful in their proper places; you will know me too well to think that I would declaim against them in general. It is the abuse of them that prevails at Cambridge—an abuse which renders us careless and insensible upon the verge of eternity."[1] The letter ends with an apology for writing his friend a sermon and a warm invitation to come and stay at Dunham. This letter did more to convince Wollaston of the truth of John Venn's Evangelical convictions than earlier attempts at Cambridge, for he replies: "I cannot but be highly thankful for the advice and seriously attentive to the purport of it."[2] He admits John's gentle rebukes were not without foundation and he has heeded them. The offer to visit Dunham is accepted.

John Venn's other friends at Sidney included John and Robert Heslop, both of whom became Fellows, Robert Pointer and James Gambier. All these were probably members of John's religious society. One vacation John called on Pointer unexpectedly and found him "absorbed with horses and hounds". James Gambier was John's cousin; he stayed at Yelling for a year's tuition before going up in 1779. In term time Henry Venn was his tutor but during the long vacation John took over. Jemmy Gambier's predilection for port seriously alarmed his uncle, not so much because he disapproved, but because it was difficult to obtain sufficient supplies for a young man who drank four glasses a day. John was therefore instructed to order six dozen bottles in Cambridge before he came home. Gambier was elected a "rural dean" of the Eclectic Society in 1792, no doubt at John Venn's instigation.[3]

Another probable member of the "holy group" was Henry Coulthurst, who was elected from St. John's to a Fellowship at Sidney in John's final year. He became Vicar of Holy Sepulchre as well, the following year about the same time that Simeon was inducted Vicar of Holy Trinity. It is quite possible that Simeon and Venn influenced this diminutive academic incumbent in an Evangelical direction, for Simeon reports to

[1] J. Venn to F. J. H. Wollaston, June 15, 1789 (MS.).

[2] F. J. H. Wollaston to J. Venn, June 25, 1789 (MS.).

[3] James Edward Gambier was son of W. J. Gambier of Camberwell and Mary Venn, Henry Venn's sister. He was for a time Rector of Langley in Kent. In 1792 he was elected a "rural dean" of the Eclectic Society.

Venn: "Mr. Coulthurst grows, I cannot tell you, how big a Christian",[1] and Henry Venn says of him, "He improves every time I see him."

Another friend was Christopher Atkinson, tutor of Trinity Hall and curate of St. Edward's Church, Cambridge. Smyth says of him, "He seems . . . to have been rather a colourless personality, and cuts a very minor figure in the records of the Evangelical Revival in Cambridge",[2] nevertheless it was through Atkinson that John Venn and Charles Simeon met.

The story of their first meeting on June 1, 1782 has often been told.[3] Simeon, after his conversion in 1779, endeavoured "to find out some minister who preached those truths which I loved and delighted in; and I attended at St. Mary's for a long time but to little purpose".[4] He must have been conspicuous either for his grotesque bearing or his unwonted display of piety, for both Atkinson and Venn had noticed him. Henry Venn "had often heard his son speak of this singular gownsman of King's College, and had advised him to get acquainted with him",[5] but John was too shy to make the first approach. About the time he gained his Fellowship, Simeon heard of Atkinson and transferred himself to St. Edward's. He had been attending there for some time before he had the opportunity of speaking *tête-à-tête* with Atkinson, who "manifested a union of heart with me, and introduced me the very next day to an excellent man, my dear friend, Mr. John Venn. . . . Here I found a man after my own heart, a man for whom I have retained the most unfeigned love to his last moments, and of whom I ever shall retain the most affectionate remembrance."[6]

The occasion was a tea-party in Christopher Atkinson's

[1] C. Simeon to J. Venn, Sept. 29, 1784 (MS.). "He was remarkably small with an extremely low but distinct voice," Gunning, *op. cit.*, Vol. II, p. 45. In 1790 he became Vicar of Halifax where he exercised a remarkable and effective ministry. He married one of the Whitakers, Huddersfield friends of the Venns.

[2] C. H. Smyth, *Simeon and Church Order*, p. 140.

[3] Smyth, *op. cit.*, pp. 139–143; W. Carus, *Memoirs of the Life of the Rev. Charles Simeon* (1847), pp. 21–24; H. C. G. Moule, *Charles Simeon*, pp. 25–27; *Annals*, p. 118.

[4] Carus, *op. cit.*, p. 21.

[5] *Ibid.*, p. 23.

[6] *Ibid.*, p. 23. Carus' *Memoirs* include a fragment of autobiography of Simeon's written in 1813, the year of John Venn's death.

rooms; Henry Jowett, though not mentioned by Simeon, was also present. John Venn has left two separate notes of the meeting in two separate diaries.[1] The first reads: "June 1: Commenced an acquaintance with Simeon of King's", the second: "1782, June 1: Drank tea at Atkinson's with Simeon, an undergraduate Fellow[2] of King's, a religious man, and Jowett." This was the beginning of John Venn's last week in Cambridge, but during that week he saw Simeon almost every day, for the diary continues: "June 2nd (Sunday): Drank tea with Jowett, Simeon (who preached his first sermon to-day at St. Edward's)[3] and Atkinson. 3rd: Called on Simeon, and walked with him to Trumpington. Supped with Simeon and Atkinson. 4th: Simeon and Atkinson drank tea with me. 6th: Called on Simeon and walked to Granchester."[4]

On the following day John Venn left Cambridge for good. A week later Simeon called on him at Yelling and stayed two days. John was on his own, the family being in London. The diary records: "13th: Simeon of King's walked over from Cambridge[5] to see me; walked on the terrace with him and in church. Family prayers extempore. 14th: Rode over with Simeon to Everton to introduce him to Mr. Berridge. 15th: Walked with Simeon in the church; he returned after dinner."[6] The visit to Everton was the first of many that Simeon made, but it was not as important to him as his second visit to Yelling a month later to meet Henry Venn, in preparation for which he writes characteristically on July 14 to John:

> My dear friend, I propose with the blessing of God, riding over to Yelling on Tuesday morning next before eight o'clock, or at the furthest a quarter after; to converse with your father has long

[1] The first quotation is taken from a manuscript notebook which has brief and scattered jottings covering Venn's early years. The fuller diary quoted by Carus seems to be no longer extant.

[2] Members on the foundation of King's College became Fellows by routine and seniority. Simeon's turn came whilst still an undergraduate; he took his B.A. in January, 1783.

[3] He was ordained on May 26, 1782, while he was four months under the canonical age, and as yet without a degree.

[4] Carus, *op. cit.*, p. 24 n.

[5] A distance of fourteen miles.

[6] *Ibid.*, p. 24 n.

been my desire, and that I shall be both pleased and edified by it I have not the least doubt.

Your most affectionate friend in Christ,

C. SIMEON[1]

Simeon made the most of his day, for John notes: "Mr. Simeon came at eight, and stayed till half-past eight at night. After dinner I walked with him."[2] The last sentence suggests that Simeon was closeted with the Rector till dinner. Simeon returned to Cambridge so "pleased and edified" that he paid Henry Venn no less than six further visits in the next three months.

In Henry Venn Simeon found a father and the greatest human influence on his life and ministry;[3] in Simeon Henry Venn found a son in whom his soul delighted almost as exuberantly as it did in his own John; in fact, it can be argued that Henry Venn and Simeon had more in common than the father and the son. "With dear Simeon", Henry Venn writes to John in October, "I wish you to be much united; may you be as David and Jonathan. I greatly admire him and always am the better for being in his company."[4]

John Venn's university career ended neither successfully nor happily. In the examination for his degree he was placed Sixth Junior Optime.[5] He was bitterly disappointed. Nevertheless it is true that those who read what interests them rather than concentrating on what the examiners require, seldom do brilliantly; further, the strain told on him more than it would have done had he been stronger physically. However, there is no doubt, as Farish assured the younger Henry Venn, he was placed far below his real merit. The chief reason for this was that the method of classing candidates after they had been examined left much to be desired. The examination itself was conducted in the Senate House by Moderators, who published a provisional list of "brackets" or classes—they then proceeded

[1] *Annals*, p. 118, and Carus, *op. cit.*, p. 24 n.

[2] MS.

[3] See Smyth, *Simeon and Church Order*, chapter VI.

[4] H. Venn to J. Venn, Oct. 2, 1782 (MS.).

[5] The classification was First Class, Wranglers; Second Class, Senior Optimes; Third Class, Junior Optimes. The same terminology is used in the Mathematical Tripos to-day.

to a nearby tavern where tutors of private pupils pushed their candidates' claims, and the final list, therefore, became considerably rearranged.[1] 1781 was a particularly bad year: the same month as the examination had taken place, the Senate passed a grace excluding from honours all those who had read with private tutors within two years of sitting the Senior House Examination.[2] "Last Friday", Henry Venn tells Stillingfleet, "my son was admitted to the degree of B.A. He got some honour and the ablest examiners assure my friends he deserved a higher, and but for infamous partiality would have gained it. But his extreme diffidence even to agitate his mind violently, rendered him very unfit to answer questions in the deepest part of mathematics."[3] Henry Venn does not cite the tavern meeting as the sole cause of the poor result.

The examination itself was at this time mainly *viva voce*, though there was now some written work; each candidate was examined with his group or class. John Venn's diary gives a full account of examination week.

January, 1781.

Monday 15th: Went into the Senate House at 8 to be examined for my degree. At 9 breakfasted with Heslop. 9.30. Examined with my class (4th), by Milner and Prettiman; in Algebra and a little Newton. At 1. Dined with Fisher, King and Young. 2. Examined by Coulthurst, problems of Algebra with my class. 11. Called on Farish.

Tuesday: Breakfasted with Heslop at 9. 11. Examined by Cautley and Vince with my class in Natural Philosophy and Newton. Dined with King. 2. Examined by Sisson till 3.30 and at 4 did problems in geometry for Cautley with the class. At night with Jowett and Atkinson.

Wednesday: The day for Locke etc. Breakfasted with Heslop. Examined in our class by all the Moderators; little in Butler. King, Young dined with me. 2. Examined by Sisson and Parke of Peterhouse with Walmesley, Eyre and Illingworth. Fagged out with problems etc. and Algebra. Evening with Farish.

Thursday: Examined before breakfast with the three before mentioned, in Newton, very ill with headache and tired out. Did

[1] *Annals*, p. 120 n., and D. A. Winstanley, *Unreformed Cambridge*, Chapter II.

[2] Winstanley, *op. cit.*, pp. 332–3.

[3] Henry Venn to J. Stillingfleet in a draft. Henry Venn of C.M.S. wrote as an editorial note to be used in his proposed life of his father (MS.).

nothing all the rest of the day. Dined with Young, King and Fisher. Drank tea with Heslop, W.n,[1] and Gambier, just come from London, who all supped with me, after supper at 12 o'clock Baines came and told me I was 6th Junior Optime, it being just settled in the tavern—Ainslie, Pembroke, Senior Wrangler. Should have been higher had I been well but given in for Senior Optime by Moderators before they left the Senate House.

Friday: Wollaston breakfasted with me. I took my degree of Bachelor of Arts with the usual forms. My father and Mr. Mayor[2] came over with whom I dined at the Moseley, Coulthurst with us. Bachelors dined together.

Further disappointment awaited John Venn. The Master of Sidney, in spite of the poor showing in the examination, encouraged him in his hope of a Fellowship; with this in view John Venn stayed another year in college. He was treated by the Fellows as one of themselves, made a member of the Combination Room and given a key to the Fellows' garden. "But an unfortunate quarrel which took place on the first day of the examination between the Tutor, Mr. Hunter, and a Fellow, who was a friend of Mr. Venn (Coulthurst), suddenly reversed all these fair expectations. Mr. Hunter had made some remark to Mr. Venn respecting Mr. Coulthurst, which Mr. Venn thoughtlessly repeated to Coulthurst. The quarrel was so violent that the examination was put off for a few days. The Master conceived a prejudice against Mr. Venn as if he had combatted with Mr. Coulthurst. Subsequently the examination was deferred *sine die.*"[3]

Yet this double failure had its compensations, as his father fully realized. "By this appointment of God", he writes to Stillingfleet, "the young man is exercised and taught to know more the heart of those who are in trouble, and to speak to them, not by hearsay, awkwardly, as I did for some years."[4]

Added to all this and because of it, John Venn was taken seriously ill with a fever in the early spring. His father fetched him home, thinking "college as bad a place as a jail to be sick

[1] Obviously Venn's abbreviation for Wollaston.

[2] The Reverend John Mayor, Vicar of Shawbury, Shropshire, 1779–1806. The living was in the gift of Sir Richard Hill.

[3] H. Venn, Notes for Life of John Venn of Clapham (MS.).

[4] H. Venn to J. Stillingfleet, Oct. 9, 1782 (MS.).

in".[1] While on a visit at the end of July he was suddenly taken ill again and was sent home in a post-chaise. By September he was well enough to get up and eventually went to Clapham to convalesce, but was ill again there. In December he finally moved out of his rooms in college; he had scarcely occupied them since the week he met Simeon.

In John Venn's letter to Wollaston, from which we have already quoted, he includes a savage indictment of university life of his day,

> The very air of Cambridge seems infected by the breath of anti-Christ: everything serious dies in it. The constant company of young men in the bloom of youth and vigour of spirits, whose only aim is to enjoy pleasure and mirth, and whose conversation tends to divert and dissipate all religious thought; the studies also which are so intensely pursued there, and which are always at hand to fill up each vacancy left in conversation by news or wit, and which only brace the mind that it may relax again to mirth with greater enjoyment, have a dreadful effect upon the soul, and keep it, as it were in a state of intoxication. They cherish levity, thoughtlessness and negligence about spiritual things in the extreme, they leave no time for the mind to learn any thing right and indispose it for doing so.[2]

On the one hand this paragraph is as hostile as anything his father wrote about Cambridge and may betray something of the bitterness of John Venn's disappointment; on the other, though the picture of round after round of riotous enjoyment is familiar enough, the intense pursuit of study, albeit by short bursts, is a feature of eighteenth-century academic life for which it seldom receives credit.

Simeon, Farish, Coulthurst and both the Jowetts all held college Fellowships at the time that John Venn finally went down, and Wollaston was elected Fellow of Sidney the following year. John Venn spent ten of the next eleven years in a remote Norfolk village; here he continued some of those studies he would have liked to maintain had he remained in Cambridge, adding, to the long list of subjects that he dabbled in, the Hebrew language in order to enable him to read the Old

[1] H. Venn to J. Brasier, quoted in *Life of H. Venn*, p. 330.
[2] J. Venn to F. J. H. Wollaston, June 15, 1789 (MS.).

Testament in the original. Although his work as a country rector was not arduous he learnt considerably more about people and pastoral methods than he would have done as a university don whom eventually marriage might have pitchforked into a busy living. Little Dunham was probably a better preparation for the important work he was to do at Clapham than ten more years of academic life. Furthermore, a move which took him considerably further away from Yelling than Cambridge was no bad thing, for while in Cambridge he was always likely to be both directed and overshadowed by his father; in Norfolk he was close enough to pay frequent visits home, but far enough to develop an independence of character.

On his journeys between Dunham and Yelling, John Venn usually called on one or other of his Cambridge friends and nearly all of them stayed for shorter or longer visits at Little Dunham Rectory. Furthermore, three of them were prepared to ride on occasion to Thetford in order to build each other up in Christian fellowship. William Jowett tells how, when he was travelling with his uncle, Henry Jowett, they stopped at an inn for the night and at supper his uncle said, "This is the room where Farish, Simeon and myself (coming from Cambridge), used to meet Venn (coming from his living in Norfolk), and here we united in consultation and prayer."[1] In a sense these meetings may well have been a continuation of those small societies which John Venn himself had started in the university. Possibly the chief value of Venn's time at Cambridge was his development of quiet leadership in a group of friends who shared his religious views, who came to rely on his balanced judgment and valued the real affection he gave without stint to those who had penetrated his reserve. It is possible that leadership here prepared him for leadership later in the Eclectic Society, and, even more important, in the Eclectic's offspring —the Church Missionary Society.

On September 22, 1782, John Venn was ordained deacon by Dr. Thurlow, Bishop of Lincoln, at his residence at Buckden, on the title of his father's curacy. The final decision to be ordained was not made without a severe mental and emotional struggle. John seemed to have no doubts about his vocation till he was

[1] *Jubilee Volume of C.M.S.* (1848), p. 24.

midway through his university course; he then wrote to his father saying that for some months he had been questioning his fitness for the ministry and now can keep these doubts to himself no longer: because of his many faults and weakness of character he "cannot undertake this holy employment".[1] His father, however, regarded this sense of incapacity as a favourable sign. "I scarcely know one who has been remarkably successful in winning souls, and in a holy life, but he has not felt what Paul did—weakness, and fear and much trembling."[2] Elsewhere in the letter he tries to jolt his son out of "his present gloomy and unreasonable resolution", reminding him of the way his early life had been ordered to this end and adding, quite pertinently, that he was trained for nothing else. Although this letter was followed up by long conversations, John's fears were not easily allayed; six months later we find him writing to John Thornton "I fear to hurt the work I wish to promote."[3]

The Sunday following his ordination John Venn preached for the first time in Yelling Church. However, he was still far from well, so his father sent him to John Thornton's house at Clapham to see what a change of air could do. Meanwhile Henry Venn had time to think about the difficulties in which he was now involved by John's failure to obtain a Fellowship. He had found four years at a university expensive. He had hoped to have an unpaid part-time curate, employed and paid by a Cambridge college; instead he was responsible for his son's entire stipend and there were two full-time clergy to work in a parish of less than two thousand souls.

Providentially the stay in London not only saw a marked improvement in John's health, it also provided the solution to the problem of his future employment. The occasion was a sermon he preached at John Thornton's request at St. Giles', Camberwell, a church of which Thornton himself was patron and which was attended by the several relations of the Venns who lived in Camberwell. Edward Venn reported to Eling that

[1] *Life of H. Venn*, p. 338.

[2] *Ibid.*, p. 346. The letter is quoted in full in *Life of H. Venn*, pp. 340–8. It is not without significance that John Venn chose as his text for the opening of his ministry at Clapham, I Corinthians 2: 3: "I was with you in weakness, and in fear, and in much trembling." See p. 114.

[3] J. Venn to J. Thornton, March 14, 1781 (MS.).

her brother had preached to a full church and in the congregation were John Thornton and his sons, Henry and Robert and "all the Gambiers, Brasiers, Montagues etc.".[1] What he does not say is that John Brasier had a guest in his pew, by name Edward Parry.

Brasier and Parry had recently returned from India as comparatively young men. Parry, although only in his early thirties, was already a Director of the East India Company; he was also squire of Little Dunham in Norfolk. John had already met him on one occasion, for he and his wife, "as much in earnest as himself", had visited Yelling while John was home on vacation. The following year Henry Venn, his wife and Eling had dined at Little Dunham. In January John Venn received a letter from Edward Parry which begins:

> The presentation of the living of Little Dunham being vacant and in my gift I hope by the blessing of God to introduce the Gospel of our Lord Jesus Christ into this dark corner of the kingdom, and, as I trust, it has pleased the Lord to give you such views of that Gospel and the importance of preaching it to poor sinners, permit me, sir, to make you an offer of this presentation and to assure you we shall be happy not only to have you as a minister, but as a friend and neighbour at this place.[2]

He added that the net income was between £130 and £140.

It seems that Parry's offer may well have resulted as much from Brasier's intercession on the young preacher's behalf as on the favourable impression John had made in the pulpit. Obviously Brasier realized the difficult financial position at Yelling and pointed out to Parry how he could help himself and the Venns at the same time. After John had been instituted he wrote to his cousin saying that Brasier's kindness and interest demanded "a constant remembrance".[3] Certainly many of the letters that John Venn wrote from Little Dunham were addressed to John Brasier Esq. of Camberwell. These are mainly in the nature of progress reports.

The offer of the living was made in January. In February John Venn went to see the parish, on March 14th he was

[1] E. Venn to Miss E. Venn, Oct. 12, 1782 (MS.).
[2] E. Parry to J. Venn, Jan. 14, 1783 (MS.).
[3] J. Venn to J. Brasier, March 1783 (MS.).

ordained priest by Dr. Halifax, Bishop of Gloucester,[1] at the King's Chapel, St. James's, and two days later he was instituted Rector of Little Dunham. During the three months between his return from London and his removal to Dunham he had his first experience of parochial work, a locum at St. Neots. The vicar was absentee, the curate had been "forced to fly for his evil deeds", and the churchwarden, hearing he might obtain help for which he would not have to pay, applied to Henry Venn. In fact John did nearly all the work; he became so well-liked that the inhabitants signed a petition asking that he might be their new curate.

Little Dunham is a small Norfolk village, eight miles north-east of Swaffham and twenty miles east of King's Lynn. John Venn with characteristic precision has recorded in the Register that at the time of his induction the population consisted of "53 men, 47 women and 72 children; 172 in all". The church is mainly fifteenth century, and is imposing but small; the Rectory is next to it; both lie some way out of the village and must have increased the young Rector's sense of isolation. "The little thatched house at Dunham Parva", as his sister Nelly called it, seemed ideal for the needs of a very self-sufficient bachelor.

> I am, at length [he tells Brasier] completely settled in my little house, the parsonage of Little Dunham, and have entered into all the cares and troubles of housekeeping. You will inquire what is my household. I have six acres of land, in the middle of which stands my house; a parlour, a kitchen, a brewhouse, and a spare bed for a friend; a maid, a boy; a horse, a cow and two kittens. My cow furnishes me with milk and butter. I bake and brew for myself, and live in as comfortable a manner as I can desire.[2]

In spite of this he set about enlarging the house after he had been there barely four months, adding a parlour, study and two bedrooms over, of the same size, and a cellar under.[3] Some-one told John Thornton that "Jack had built him a house fit

[1] The ordination was to have been taken by the Bishop of Norwich, on March 11; presumably he was unable to come to London and the Bishop of Gloucester, who was holding an ordination service three days later, agreed to ordain him.

[2] J. Venn to J. Brasier, Aug. 8, 1783 (MS.).

[3] *Annals*, p. 126.

for a squire";[1] it was certainly bigger than he required for his own purposes, though he hoped to compensate for his isolation by having large parties of visitors. The repairs cost him £250. He made £25 by selling timber and mortgaged the house itself for £250. He also managed to increase the value of the stipend by £40 or £50 by raising the tithe in one-half of the parish to equal that in the other and by enclosing his glebe. As a country parson he was extremely well off, as he discovered when he exchanged pulpits with Ivory of Hindolveston. "The living", he writes to his sisters, "is but £30 a year, and the Parsonage house in which Mr. Ivory lives, a cottage. . . . He reserves only two rooms for his own use and the rest of his house is let to poor people who cook his victuals and wait upon him."[2] Venn thinks he would himself find such conditions too depressing, but cannot see why he should expect better treatment than his friend.

John Venn professed to like living alone and for a long time successfully resisted all pleas from his sisters to keep house for him. When he first arrived he was naturally concerned about his relations with the squire and his wife. He need not have worried, for the Parrys were true to their promise of making him both "friend and neighbour". "I am ashamed at their kindness to me which seems to increase every day. I am ashamed at having two such experienced Christians sit at the feet of such a novice as I daily find myself to be."[3] But he made no other friends and when the Parrys were away from Dunham "I am left without a single acquaintance, clergyman or layman, within the space of twenty-four miles. Yet", he adds significantly, "I thank God I am in very good spirits, and do not find a single hour heavy upon my hands."[4] He goes on to say that he spends his time on theology, mastering Hebrew so that he can read the Old Testament in the original, and watching the work of grace in his own soul and in that of his people. This mood of happy independence was not constant; there were other times when his attention was not held by Hebrew grammar, and he found

[1] H. Venn to J. Brasier, Sept. 22, 1786 (MS.).
[2] J. Venn to his sisters, May 28, 1784 (MS.).
[3] To Brasier, Oct. 28, 1783 (MS.).
[4] J. Venn to Miss E. Venn, Dec. 26, 1783 (MS.).

himself sighing for his friends and "forming a thousand plans for the enjoyment of their company".[1]

In fact he had many visitors including most of his Cambridge friends. One New Year's Day Simeon, Farish, and Coulthurst sat down with him to a turkey dinner. They all came separately at other times as did the Jowetts, Wollaston and John's future brother-in-law, George King. On one occasion after Coulthurst had been taking holiday duty for him, Venn found that most of his tea and sugar had been used. He was about to complain of his friend's over-indulgence when the maid confessed to stealing. He saw his Cambridge friends again on his way to Yelling and back. In 1786, John Thornton, doubtless in search of patrons willing to be bought out of their livings, was touring Norfolk with the Reverend Henry Foster as his chaplain. They stayed with John at Dunham Rectory and then took him with them for a week. Three weeks after their visit John Venn entertained for three nights a party of eight, who arrived in two post-chaises and a whisky, and consisted of the complete family from Yelling, Priscilla Riland,[2] John's uncle, Richard Venn and Eling's husband, Charles Elliott.

On December 20, 1785, Eling Venn had been married to Charles Elliott at Yelling; her father officiated and her brother gave her away. Charles Elliott was a middle-aged widower with several children; by profession he was a silk merchant and lived in Bond Street. John Venn became very attached to the man who had married his favourite sister; for their part when he became Rector of Clapham the Elliotts moved there to become his parishioners. Nelly and John were always great friends: during his first year at Dunham John received a number of urgent letters from his sister, either pressing him to allow her to keep house for him, or upbraiding him for being such a poor correspondent. Here is a belated reply from John to one of his sister's letters:

> What will my dear sister say that I have delayed writing so long? I hope a *great deal*. I hope she has been so severe upon me that now when I come with pitiful looks after the fury of the storm

[1] J. Venn to Miss E. Venn, July 1783 (MS.).
[2] Eldest daughter of the Rev. John and Mrs. Riland.

is over, she may relent a little, and perhaps bear to hear me make some excuse for myself, for you know it does not look decent, nor suit the dignity of human nature, to stand like a criminal caught in the fact, and have nothing to say in defence of oneself. My excuse then for the first week after I received your letter is extremely good. I was out all the week making the tour of Norfolk with the three Jowetts, who came to see me on Sunday and dined with me upon a roast goose. Then for *last* week, let me see—Oh, I was very poorly at the beginning of the week, having had a slight return of my old disorder, and you know if I had written then, I was so low-spirited, I should have talked of nothing, but my dismal solitude, my crazy house, my empty purse, and the necessity of a speedy marriage to set all to rights. So, I think I did very wisely not to terrify you with all my gloomy prospects.[1]

At last John agreed that she should come for a year. "I count the weeks till my sister comes, and have already engaged Mr. Jackson's chaise to fetch her in."[2] Nelly arrived at the end of July. The arrangement worked well: Henry Venn writes to Jane: "We read a letter from Joannes who is vastly pleased with his housekeeper and his housekeeper with her situation."[3] In July 1785 the year was up and John took Nelly back to Yelling, where she was needed because their stepmother was ill; by becoming engaged in September she made it impossible for Jane to become her successor at Dunham, which was the original arrangement, and John was left on his own till he himself married.

As to his work in the parish, he was able to do as he pleased and build up his own tradition, for there had been no resident clergyman at Little Dunham for seventy-five years. "Since I began this letter", he tells Brasier, "I have opened my commission by preaching to my flock upon the completeness of Christ's salvation. I have given notice there will be for the future, service, morning and afternoon, and a sacrament monthly. There were about fifty people; I have conversed with some and found a heart dreadfully self-righteous and a proud

[1] J. Venn to Miss E. Venn, summer 1783 (MS.).
[2] J. Venn to his sisters, May 28, 1789 (MS.).
[3] H. Venn to Miss J. Venn, Sept. 3, 1784 (MS.).

unhumbled spirit, which must be brought very low indeed before they can throw themselves in mercy at the foot of the Cross."[1] This was a very full rota of services for a village church in the eighteenth century.[2] The first two years must have been very discouraging; few of the fifty who came that first Sunday returned, sometimes his congregation can hardly have reached double figures and he was disappointed to find that most of those who made some response came from other villages. Nevertheless Parry told Henry Venn after John had been in the parish a year that he had had "great success at Dunham, for he believes five or six are really joined to the Lord".[3] Six months later Henry Venn was able to write not only of what John endured at the beginning, but how events had now taken a more favourable turn.

> He had a fever two years ago last February, which was frequently returning upon him. Last November, Mr. and Mrs. Parry, his friends, left him alone, not a Christian friend within twenty miles, his health gone; his servant maid, an Anabaptist, proud and arrogant to the last degree, and at the same time ignorant of her business, and dirty and disobedient, his people so set against the Gospel that one only would come to church all the winter, and but eleven more out of his parish; the season so very trying to an invalid, and he not of the alert and lively cast. You cannot conceive how much I felt for him, and how much we all prayed for him, for I feared greatly he would sink into a nervous lowness of spirits. On the contrary adored be the God who giveth songs in the night. He wrote us word he never was so happy in his life. And when he came over in March to visit us, instead of being advanced a *little*, he was grown exceedingly insomuch that I shall ever remember his prayers in the family, and his preaching was remarkably deep, and savoury, and experimental. Mr. Berridge was greatly affected with it.
>
> Now his circumstances are more pleasing to man. My eldest daughter keeps his house this year, Pome[4] is to go the next. His church is full and he has a society of seventeen who meet in his house every Lord's day evening. He will hear of no lady, "for

[1] J. Venn to J. Brasier, April 12, 1783 (MS.).
[2] See next chapter.
[3] H. Venn to Miss J. Venn, May 11, 1784 (MS.).
[4] H. Venn's nickname for Jane.

what will my sisters do", says he, "if my father is taken? If they were settled I should have no objection".[1]

The "society" that met in the Rectory each Sunday evening was reminiscent of Henry Venn's own "kitchen" meetings at Yelling, and was no doubt modelled on them. Such meetings were really an extension of family prayers from the parsonage to the parish; it was a usual custom of Evangelical clergy to open their family worship to their parishioners in this way.[2] At the time Henry Venn wrote they were a very recent innovation, but one which seemed to bring quick results; within two months numbers had risen to twenty-five and they were meeting twice a week,[3] and in May 1785 Simeon came to conduct a one-night mission.

> We have been happy in the company of that faithful and zealous minister of Christ, Mr. Simeon. He preached last night in my parlour one of the most lively and solid discourses I ever heard. The room and passage were full. Several stood at the door; all seemed much impressed, even the little children were not, I trust, without some share of the blessing. I was much pleased with the sight of almost all my old people who have been for some time separated from the Baptists.[4] We forgot, I trust, all party distinctions and met together as we shall one day, glorying, not in a sect, but in the cross of Christ. In this spirit I could not but rejoice when I beheld this desert become like a garden. When I looked two years back and compared this with three or four people whose eyes were beginning to be opened, and the principle of life scarce working in them, to the present assembly of seventy people, all hearing with attention, and many with apparent emotion and an understanding heart. God has not sent me in vain to this place, the Lord has, I doubt not a people here already, and the number will soon, I hope, increase. Several have within the course of this spring been brought under convictions, and there has begun to be within these last few weeks, a great revival of that spirit of

[1] H. Venn to James Ireland of Bristol, Sept. 24, 1784 (MS.).

[2] C. H. Smyth, *Simeon and Church Order*, pp. 25–26.

[3] "I have my people twice a week to prayers in my own house. We have sometimes five and twenty." To J. Brasier, Dec. 20, 1784 (MS.).

[4] In the letter quoted above, John Venn tells Brasier: "The Baptists disturb my people considerably, and I am very much afraid lest they should make divisions amongst them, and excite a spirit of rational religion consisting of doctrinal knowledge only without the heart being engaged." Possibly John Venn's maid, whom Henry Venn calls an Anabaptist, was a member of this body.

persecution which generally precedes a revival. Pray for us that no reproach may be brought by the misconduct of any who join with us in profession.[1]

Seventy people from a village of less than two hundred inhabitants is a very high proportion, though it is certain several of those who attended were from outside Dunham. It is interesting to speculate on whether these numbers were due to the careful preparation of John Venn, whose own meetings were growing steadily in size, or whether Simeon's reputation as a preacher and an unusual personality had penetrated this remote part of Norfolk. Whatever was the reason it did seem that, for the moment, Dunham was to experience, on its small scale, the same sort of transformation that Huddersfield had experienced during the ministry of Henry Venn, that Haworth had experienced under Grimshaw, and that was becoming increasingly known in countless other small towns and villages where the Holy Spirit was working through devoted Evangelical clergy; but somehow promise at Dunham never reached fulfilment. There was some response, it is true, in the neighbouring village of Sporle, where Henry Venn reports, "My son tells me he has preached to large congregations"; but adds significantly, "but he is much cast down, because none have come to him inquiring what they must do to be saved".[2]

One innovation he transplanted from Huddersfield which can have hardly made him popular in a country parish was his custom of visiting all the alehouses every Sunday evening, in order to prevent drunkenness or sports and to stop all "indecent jollity".[3] Whereas his father, through his laity, might succeed in keeping the Sabbath quiet, while retaining the affection and respect of his parishioners, it was a different matter for the young Rector of Dunham, looking little more than a boy, to achieve the same results, especially as he had to act as his own officer in the matter.

Nevertheless when Henry Jowett succeeded John Venn he

[1] J. Venn to J. Brasier, May 27, 1785 (MS.).

[2] *Life of H. Venn*, p. 435.

[3] He tells of this practice in a letter to the Rev. J. Brock of Bidborough, when he (Venn) was appointed patron of Brock's living. He urges Brock to do the same. J. Venn to J. Brock, Aug. 1, 1791 (MS.).

found evidence of several changed lives, including a Mr. Girling of Sporle and a well-known profligate of Swaffham, "but", Henry Jowett told the younger Henry Venn, "I never could find much success had attended him in his own parish."[1] This is significant because it suggests that when Rector of Little Dunham John Venn did not confine himself as strictly to his parish boundaries as he came to believe a "regular" minister of the Church of England should; it also shows he was least successful where he was best known. Henry Venn himself says that his father always spoke disparagingly of his work at Dunham and that he confessed he had never exerted himself as he should have done, that he found the people ignorant and "unimpressable", and that for the most part he preached extempore sermons that were not properly prepared. He also suggests that John Venn gave time that should have been given to his parish to scientific and literary pursuits and that, on one occasion at least, Henry Venn senior suggested that John should leave Dunham for a more arduous living. Even after John had been at Dunham for a year, his father wrote warning him against idleness. In his reply John says that he recognizes that lack of diligence is his besetting sin; he believes his poor health encourages him to be lazy, but thinks that if he were more energetic he might be fitter. However, he has been taking himself in hand—both Sunday sermons are now written out in full and he is working hard at his Hebrew.[2] The resolution about his sermons, we have seen, was not kept and we have no means of knowing whether he persevered with his Hebrew, but we do know that during the two years before his marriage he was ill on and off, and it may be then that he was in danger of degenerating into a younger edition of his neighbour, Parson Woodforde of Weston Longeville—albeit with an Evangelical accent.[3]

[1] H. Venn, Sketch of Life of John Venn of Clapham (MS.).

[2] J. Venn to H. Venn, Aug. 19, 1784 (MS.).

[3] The Rev. James Woodforde was Rector of Weston Longeville, which is 10 miles from Norwich and 15 miles from Little Dunham, from December 1774 till his death in 1803. (*Diary of a Country Parson*, ed. J. Beresford, 1924–1931.) Woodforde was a conscientious pastor but no one would accuse him of over-exertion.

Nevertheless John Venn was well aware of the danger. In August, 1788, he writes to Dr. Poynting: "In my retirement I find as much need of watchfulness, of self-examination, of secret prayer, of powerful and immediate help of God as you can want in the public life in which you now are." (MS.)

diocese; in 1783 before the bishop in the cathedral, the following year to deliver the annual sermon in behalf of the Charity Schools[1] at St. Andrew's, Norwich, and in 1786 he was the preacher at the Archdeacon's Visitation at Litcham. His subject on this last occasion was Justification by Faith; for him, "the capital doctrine of the Gospel".[2] It seems so to have roused the ire of his fellow clergy that he was not chosen by the bishop on any subsequent occasion as his select preacher; nevertheless Henry Venn was exceedingly pleased and insisted on his son's sermon being published.

Evangelicalism has always been, as Canon Smyth has reminded us, "the religion of the home".[3] However, the first problem of the young Evangelical, be he clerical or lay, was to find a possible partner of similar views with whom he could fall in love, marry and start a home. We have already seen, in the first chapter,[4] the suspicion and isolation which Evangelicals had to endure, and the confinement of their ministries to scattered and usually remote places. This meant that the search for a partner was often restricted to certain geographical areas and that competition was sometimes keen. In May 1789 John Venn wrote to his stepmother *en route* for Hull:

> You will ask what business I can have at Hull. I reply almost the most business of any, no less than what materially interests the future happiness of my life, the looking out for a wife. I have heard of several ladies at Hull who appear to be very suitable, Miss King in particular, who has been spoken of to me in the highest terms by several of my acquaintance. . . . She is represented to be very sensible, sweet-tempered, serious and accomplished; and when I have mentioned those four grand accomplishments few others can be wanting. Her fortune is £2,000 down, and £1,000 more at the death of her mother. Her brother, Mr.

[1] The Charity Schools were a practical outcome of the theology of divine benevolence; they were begun towards the end of the seventeenth century and were intended to provide an elementary instruction for the children of the poor from the pockets of the middle classes, who were exhorted to Christian generosity in sermons like the one John Venn preached. The attraction was not only the preacher but the parade of the children themselves. See M. G. Jones, *The Charity School Movement* (1938), especially pp. 58–59.

[2] J. Venn to C. Elliott, Nov. 17, 1789 (MS.).

[3] C. H. Smyth, *Simeon and Church Order*, p. 20.

[4] See pp. 14-15.

> King of Trinity you have seen. I must beg the cause of my journey not to be mentioned, as these matters are very ready to spread themselves, and were the news to reach Hull it would in a great measure defeat the end of my journey.[1]

He says he has drawn comfort in his intention from the Bible which says it is not good for man to live alone, and looking round he sees many instances "to encourage marriage and few to discourage it". This all sounds very mercenary, as if he were looking for a horse or a house rather than a wife. It is only fair to add that after he had met Kitty King his whole attitude changed, and the prospect of marrying money deterred him rather than spurred him on. His was not the only instance of close competition for a Hull bride with suitable theological opinions. On a subsequent visit six years later Venn received a letter from his friend, Henry Thornton, asking him to call on the Sykes family because of Thornton's interest in Marianne Sykes; however, he was not to mention the purpose of his visit. This must have been a difficult request with which to comply, for John Venn was in the company not only of his wife but of Edward Edwards and Edward Parry, now a widower; both of them were seeking wives in Hull. In Parry's case the object of his affection was Marianne Sykes. She, however, refused him and this made Thornton more bold to press his claims. They were married the following spring.

Prior to his excursion to Hull John Venn had little experience of courting, and, apart from his sisters, little of female company. While home for his first long vacation he had fallen in love with his cousin, Charlotte Gambier, who was staying at the Rectory and to whom he wrote a love-poem,[2] but Edward

[1] J. Venn to Mrs. H. Venn, May 4, 1789 (MS.).

[2] "Adieu to fair Sabena's gentle mien
Once loved and yet so little seen,
And you still fairer Charlotte, adieu
Amidst the throng I long have bowed to you.
In secret sighed to gain so rich a prize
But durst not meet the lustre of your eyes.
Adieu. In distant places I go to roam,
And leave my Charlotte here and leave my home;
Yet sometimes, oh recall me to your view
And think of him who often thinks of you."

The "distant places" were located in Leicester where he had gone to study with

Venn (another cousin and eight years older than John) was also a guest at Yelling, and it was he who proposed to her; they were married the following year.

Katherine King was the only daughter of William King, a successful Hull merchant. She was nine months younger than John Venn. Her two elder brothers were in Riga in their father's business, and the third, George, was a Fellow of Trinity, and for a time tutor to the Duke of Rutland. George King was on the edge of John Venn's circle of friends at Cambridge, and more than once had come with Wollaston to Dunham to stay with him. The King family had come under the influence of Joseph Milner's ministry and Milner was a frequent guest at their home. Katherine was known to be intelligent, vivacious, sensitive, and, in the religious sense, "serious"; she was much sought after—in fact she had broken off an engagement within twelve months of her meeting John Venn.

John arrived at Hull on May 6th. On the 7th he called on Joseph Milner and then went on to the Terrys at Newland where he stayed as a guest for eight days. How this was all arranged is not disclosed but it looks like a plot devised by John Venn and his old friend James Stillingfleet of Hotham, for the other guests included Stillingfleet and his wife, and Kitty King. John Venn and Kitty King saw much of each other during this week, usually in the company of a Miss Harvey; he told them stories and anecdotes, including ghost stories, and he also recounted the tale of Simeon's conversion. Kitty was delighted by her new companion:

> I returned the other day from Newland [she writes to her brother] after spending a very agreeable week with a schoolfellow of yours,[1] Mr. John Venn. My expectations were much raised from the high character I have heard you give of him; I must say I was not disappointed for I have seldom met with a man so agreeable and entertaining—he seems truly pious also. He often wished, and I too, that you had come down with him, but he had

Robinson, leaving Charlotte at Yelling. Sabena was Elizabeth Bishop, another cousin, who was presumably also a guest at the Rectory. Henry Venn includes this poem in his Manuscript Memoir as an example of his father's "youthful composition"; that it might have any other interest for his readers seems to have escaped him.

[1] They would have been at Joseph Milner's school for a year together.

not time to inform you, as his journey at this time was rather unexpected, otherwise you would have had no objection to have taken a voyage with him, I dare say. He talks of returning by sea, after spending a little time at Hotham. I hope to see him before he returns as he expects to see you at Cambridge.[1]

John, who must have carefully concocted the story of his intention to ask George King to come with him, was as desperately in love as he had hoped to be. On May 13th he left Newland with the Stillingflects for a week at Hotham. While there his hopes of marrying Kitty King were shattered by a letter from Henry Jowett laying a prior claim to her, as he had become attached to her during the previous summer.

This was a grievous blow. John felt he must sacrifice his new-found love to his old friendship, although he was very bitter about it, and wrote himself out to Farish saying that he was prepared to give her up for the sake of twenty-two years' friendship. To Jowett he wrote civilly. He wanted to leave for home as soon as possible, but as he was still determined to go by sea he had to wait for a week for a boat to Lynn. Meanwhile Stillingfleet, who was also a confidant of Kitty's, encouraged him and John heard from both Farish and Jowett, the latter partially withdrawing what he had said in his first letter. John called on Kitty on his way through Hull as he had promised, and alarmed her by his despondency: "Mr. Venn was so obliging as to call before he left Hull, and I was very sorry to see him so low and indifferent. He seems very nervous, and nervous people I do indeed pity."[2] He went almost straight from Dunham to Cambridge and saw both Jowett and Farish. Jowett apologized for his hastiness and confessed that he wondered whether he was opposing Providence as well as John by his action. Meanwhile Stillingfleet wrote to say that he had talked with Kitty, who gave the lie to Jowett's claim.

With the situation turning in his favour and having consulted his father, John now proposed to Kitty by letter. Kitty asked to be spared an immediate decision and given time to get to know him better. This was the end of June, but to visit Hull again soon was not easy; a locum at Dunham had to be pro-

[1] Miss K. King to G. King, May 12, 1789 (MS.).
[2] Miss K. King to G. King in H. Venn's MS. Life.

vided and a pupil whom he had taken could not be neglected. Eventually it was arranged that John Venn should exchange with Mr. Garwood, minister of one of the Hull churches, and that Mustard, his pupil, should go to Hull with him. This was arranged for the beginning of August. Meanwhile Stillingfleet came to stay first at Yelling and then at Little Dunham. At Yelling he gave Henry Venn an excellent account of Kitty and an amusing account of a lovesick John; at Dunham he encouraged the young lover, and on his way between the two places he called on Henry Jowett.

During August John saw Kitty both at Hull and Bridlington, but she did not make up her mind easily. She consulted her uncle, Robert Jarratt (also a cousin of John's) who urged her to put John out of his torture, but the same day she saw Joseph Milner who maintained the single state was better, though "the other" not wrong.[1] The entry in her notebook for August 17th reads: "Mr. Venn called after breakfast with some flowers from Newland. Caught me without my bonnet. I supped at my Uncle Jarratt's who repeated that all depended on me. Wished it did not."[1]

Within the next fortnight she made up her mind to marry John, though not before Mrs. King had applied to John Thornton concerning the character of her prospective son-in-law. Thornton was only too willing to do this and also to write enthusiastically about Kitty to Henry Venn. "She is indeed a treasure; and will be an example to every one."[2] John and Kitty became officially engaged on September 1st and on October 22nd they were married at Holy Trinity Church, Hull, by Robert Jarratt.

After the wedding they spent a further week at Hull and nearly three weeks at Yelling, with a visit to see and preach for the ageing Berridge thrown in. Two days visiting Cambridge friends followed. The modern idea of the honeymoon as the time when the couple remove themselves as far as possible from everyone they know was not yet conceived. "We got home on Saturday last at noon", John tells the Elliotts. "My father accompanied us to Cambridge. On Wednesday we dined with

[1] Both quoted by H. Venn in MS. Life from Kitty's notebook.
[2] *Life of H. Venn*, p. 475.

Mr. G. King at Trinity, drank tea at J. Farish's,[1] supped at Simeon's, breakfasted at Coulthurst's, dined at W. Farish's, drank tea at H. Jowett's, and breakfasted the next morning at Wollaston's. During the whole time my father was in such spirits that every one of us old men stood astonished at the vivacity of youth. We dined at Newmarket on Friday, where Mr. King accompanied us, and slept at Brandon, and the next morning came to Little Dunham by noon."[2]

Henry Venn was indeed delighted with his daughter-in-law. Her vivacity, her Christian sincerity, her readiness to sacrifice a wide circle of friends at Hull for the loneliness of Little Dunham, greatly appealed to him. Further, he realized that there was no trace of her husband's laziness in her character. "I hope", he confides to Stillingfleet,[3] "she will stir up her husband and urge him to spend himself in labours." He was not to be disappointed. Kitty eventually pointed out to John "You may find sufficient work even in this retired place, if you will only put yourself forward." Henry Venn was also quick to notice the change, and to Kitty herself he writes: "I will write only a line to congratulate you on the good progress we all perceive in your husband. We think him as much in spirits as he was when he first saw a certain lady at Newland. He now turns his eyes from the miseries of man to the blessings of the ransomed of the Lord."[4] No wife could have wished for more gratitude than that.

John Venn tried to overcome the problems of their isolation by increasing the number of visitors, by teaching Kitty to ride horseback alone and by purchasing a chaise to enable them to make the journey to Yelling together. Henry Venn disapproved of this latter move on grounds both of expense and appearance; he always strongly disapproved of clergy parading as high society.[5] Nevertheless John Venn was now considerably better

[1] J. Farish, brother of W. Farish, was a doctor in Cambridge and was the Venn family doctor.

[2] J. Venn to the Elliotts, Nov. 27, 1789 (MS.).

[3] H. Venn to J. Stillingfleet, Dec. 23, 1789 (MS.).

[4] H. Venn to Mrs. J. Venn, Jan. 28, 1792 (MS.).

[5] "Mr. Haweis has done much harm here—he and his lady dress extravagantly and live in all the pride of life which is so contrary to the spirit of the Christian minister." H. Venn writing from Bath to John at Leicester, July 15, 1777 (MS.).

off than his father; not only was his wife wealthy but she was a very efficient keeper of the family budget, and John, feeling that their chief need was "More society with people of our own rank and religious sentiments",[1] felt the expense justified. In 1792 his stepmother died and in the summer his father was so ill that he was persuaded to leave the parish in the hands of a curate, whose salary was £40 per annum; Charles Elliott paid half and John Venn paid half.

After being married a year Kitty gave birth to her first child, a son, called Henry after his grandfather. Kitty was exceedingly ill during her confinement, and the child lived only for a month. On December 2, 1791, Catherine Eling was born. Great care was taken to see she survived and John prevailed on Kitty to allow her to be "inoculated" for smallpox at only three months.[2] "Our dear Catherine Eling grows and thrives apace," he tells his father; "you would smile to see how much I nurse her."[3]

The year following his marriage was eventful for John Venn in many ways. In January he was appointed Chaplain to the Dowager Duchess of Hereford, one of the devout patrician ladies of the Countess of Huntingdon's circle. John Thornton had suggested John Venn and in honour of the occasion presented him with a scarf. Nothing is heard of John Venn fulfilling any duties in connection with this office; either it was a purely honorary post or perhaps his growing suspicion of the Countess of Huntingdon's irregularities made him prefer to regard the appointment as a sinecure.

In March Lady Smythe, widow of Chief Baron Smythe, who had presented Henry Venn to the living at Yelling, died. She left legacies to Henry Venn and to all his children; to John she bequeathed also the advowson of the parish of Bidborough, near Tunbridge Wells, where the Smythes had had a house. John Venn never had a presentation to the living but he knew John Brock, the incumbent, a Trinity man who had been appointed the previous year, and for the rest of his life encour-

[1] J. Venn to the Elliotts, Nov. 27, 1789 (MS.).

[2] J. Venn to Charles Elliott, Feb. 15, 1792 (MS.). All his children were inoculated for smallpox.

[3] J. Venn to H. Venn, March 27, 1792 (MS.).

aged him to visit him and seek his advice.[1] In 1813 Charles Elliott bought the right of presentation from him.

In November John Thornton died: Henry Venn felt the loss keenly, for Thornton was almost certainly his first friend "in Christ".[2] He was informed by Samuel Thornton, the eldest son, "My dear father has left you a legacy of £50. He had named you a trustee for his church patronage in a former will, but the change was made for your son, as a younger life."[3] "The younger life" was also thought to be in need of more money than his father and was left £100. This appointment, together with the recommendation to the Dowager Duchess's chaplaincy, shows the high regard John Thornton always had for his friend's son. The Thornton Trust amounted to eleven livings; these had been bought by John Thornton to ensure continuity of an Evangelical ministry in these parishes. Henry Thornton continued and extended his father's policy and on his death it was further extended by Charles Simeon with great shrewdness and much success.[4]

By the will the Thornton patronage was now shared by three clerical trustees, of whom the other two were Henry Foster and Roger Bentley. They were instructed in the case of a vacancy to appoint one of themselves or a man of similar views. In the case of the all-important living of Clapham, the patronage of which the Lord of the Manor had given over to John Thornton,[5] it was to be offered first to Foster; then, if he refused it, to John Venn.

Henry Foster was a bluff Yorkshireman, fourteen years Venn's senior, who had been nearly twenty years curate to Romaine at St. Andrew's-by-the-Wardrobe. Eventually he became lecturer at so many London churches that he gave up

[1] Brock remained at Bidborough till his death in 1830.

[2] *Life of H. Venn*, p. 489.

[3] S. Thornton to H. Venn.

[4] See C. H. Smyth, *Simeon and Church Order*, chapter V, especially pp. 231–247. Henry Thornton was sometimes as shrewd as Simeon was to be, as can be seen from this sentence in a letter to a nephew: "I have lately given £2,500 for an advowson at Ipswich, the present incumbent aged sixty-five" (Dec. 26, 1865, Wigan Book).

[5] C. Hole, *St. James Magazine*, August 1889.

his curacy, for there was little prospect of an Evangelical in London securing a benefice unless John Thornton bought it for him.[1] He seems to have been a somewhat prosaic character, though much respected as a pastor and a judge of character. With John Thornton he was a great favourite and he visited Little Dunham in Thornton's company in 1786. This was probably the first time that he and Venn met. They were to see much of each other in later years, not only through this joint patronage but also at the Eclectic Society of which Foster was one of the four original members.

Roger Bentley was ten years older than Foster and also a Yorkshireman. In 1769 John Thornton procured for him the living at St. Giles Church, Camberwell. Among his congregation were the Brasiers, the Edward Venns and the Gambiers. It was from his pulpit that John Venn had preached the sermon that made Parry consider offering him the living of Little Dunham. Roger Bentley died in 1795 and thus left the Thornton patronage to Venn and Foster.[2]

In August 1790 John Venn went to see the living of Bidborough as the new patron. On his way through London he met for the first time Charles Grant, who had arrived home from India with his family less than a month previously.

[1] Henry Foster (1745–1844) became Vicar of St. James, Clerkenwell, in 1804. His lectureships included St. Andrew's, St. Antholin's, St. Swithin's, St. Peter's Cornhill, Christ Church Spitalfields, and Long Acre Chapel. Romaine owed his appointment at St. Andrew's to his being elected by the parishioners, having made his name as a lecturer at St. George's, Hanover Square (see L. E. Elliott-Binns, *The Early Evangelicals* pp. 166–7). Cadogan, who held Chelsea Parish Church in plurality with St. Giles, Reading, was converted to Evangelicalism five years after his appointment. The only Evangelical incumbents in the London area were Roger Bentley of Camberwell, John Newton of St. Mary Woolnoth, and Richard Conyers, who had moved from Helmsley to Deptford in 1767: all were Thornton nominees.

[2] Bentley's place was taken by John King, Rector of Pertenhall in Bedfordshire. In the case of Camberwell either John Thornton cannot have purchased the perpetual right of presentation or the Trustees made a mistake, for Camden Chapel, Peckham, was founded "by those of his congregation who were dissatisfied with the preaching of his successor which was not of that evangelical character to which they had been accustomed" (Brayley, *Surrey*, Vol. III, p. 266, quoted in J. A. Venn, *Alumni Cantabrigienses* (1940), Part II, Abbey–Challis, p. 239). Here was a repetition of the case of Highfield Chapel, Huddersfield, a situation which constantly recurred until the Thornton-Simeon policy was successful and strong enough to counteract it.

Charles Grant, of whom much will be said in the next chapters, was a Scot of forty-four and outstanding among the servants of the East India Company. In India he and his wife had been converted to Christianity when God had spoken to them through the loss of their first two children, who had died of smallpox in infancy. Since his conversion, his one concern was the establishment of a Christian mission in India on a far more extensive scale than anything the S.P.C.K. had attempted. His twofold purpose in coming home was the restoration of his wife's health and the prosecution of his missionary schemes by personally advocating them at the highest level. It was his original intention to return eventually to India, but in fact he stayed in England for the rest of his life.

Meanwhile he was undecided whether to live in London or Norfolk. Edward Parry, whom he had known well in India, suggested his settling near him and placing his two sons, Charles aged twelve, and Robert aged ten, with John Venn. Grant was anxious to find them a good tutor as they were behind with their education. It was to discuss this that the meeting in London was arranged. Actually they met twice, and it was finally arranged that Venn should take the boys even if Grant took a London house, and Venn agreed to accept what Grant thought proper in the way of fees.[1]

Venn liked Grant from the first and Grant was delighted with him and writes of him to his sister as one "who has the most general and unequivocal testimonies of great piety and learning, who, being in easy circumstances, had no thought of undertaking anything of this nature, but out of regard to our friends, Mr. and Mrs. Parry, and to us through their long continued partial representations to him who is their neighbour, will for a time take our boys under his care." Parry seems to have exaggerated in no small measure to Grant the favour John Venn was doing him by taking his sons. Grant spent a few days

[1] John Venn did not know what he should ask for fees and wrote to his father, who had replied: "I can see no objections to your taking the children on trial—your dear mother thinks you may ask sixty for each, and ought not to take less" (H. Venn to J. Venn, Aug. 16, 1790, MS.). Jemmy Gambier, whom John saw in Kent to inquire whether he would take the Grants if they decided to stay in London, said he would ask £80 for each, which were the usual terms; few tutors took pupils for less.

at Dunham with Parry on his way to Scotland. He decided, however, to take a London house.[1]

The Grant boys were not Venn's first pupils at Dunham, though he had never contemplated taking such young boys. In 1786 a lad by the name of Mustard[2] came to live with him and prepare for the university, as already mentioned. The arrangement seemed to work well. Venn, who was feeling Nelly's departure a year previously, enjoyed both the companionship and the work.[3] It only became inconvenient in the summer of 1789, when the crisis in his relationship with Kitty demanded his presence at Hull a few months before Mustard was due to go up to Cambridge. The problem, as we have seen, was solved by his taking Mustard with him to Hull and combining tuition of Mustard with courting of Kitty.

The teaching and disciplining of this younger pair seems to have been beneficial for himself as well as for them. His father tells Nelly: "Now he is all alive and intent upon laying out his talents for good to the uttermost. Never in bed after six. His two pupils have made such a progress that Mr. Jowett, after a very strict examination in Greek, said, he did not think that there were more than two among his own pupils who could do so well."[4] Their parents were even more delighted: "On Tuesday evening Mr. and Mrs. Grant came on purpose to see me," John Venn tells Kitty, "I read to him his sons' exercises (the comparisons between Achilles and Hector, etc.). He could scarcely be made to believe they were their own and several times, then and afterwards, expressed a wish that if it were possible they might continue under my care at Clapham; this, however, I resolutely refused."[5] This was during the summer of

[1] For the next two and a half years Grant was living in Queen's Square from whence he moved to John Street, Bedford Row, presumably to enable him and his wife to attend St. John's Chapel, Bedford Row, where Richard Cecil was Minister.

[2] David Mustard, son of the Rev. D. Mustard of Copford, near Colchester, is recorded as being admitted to Magdalene in 1787. He presumably came back to Dunham each vacation.

[3] "I have much more happiness with my friend here than when alone. We daily pray together and you are not forgotten. I find my time passes pleasantly away in instructing him and going again over the same ground I trod so many years ago." J. Venn to Mrs. H. Venn, Aug. 4, 1787 (MS.).

[4] H. Venn to Mrs. Elliott, Jan. 30, 1792 (MS.).

[5] J. Venn to his wife, Sept. 27, 1792 (MS.).

1792 which the Grants spent at Dunham and during which he came to know them intimately. He tells his father in one letter, "I rejoice to have the opportunity of being so much in the company of so excellent and sensible a man",[1] and in another, after travelling in their coach to London: "The more I see of these excellent people the more I am charmed with them. I stand amazed to see a man of his abilities and attention to business, have his soul so much alive to God, and maintain so very low an opinion of himself. All our conversation was profitable, as it always was at Little Dunham. He gives the highest characters of Mr. H. Thornton and Mr. Wilberforce for their great seriousness."[2] Perhaps John Venn was looking ahead a little to the time when, from personal knowledge, he could write of Thornton and Wilberforce as he now did of Grant.

"About the latter end of next month," John Venn tells Charles Elliott, "I propose to have for the first time a meeting of ministers at my house. I hope we shall have six or seven, and a probability of more hereafter. Pray for us that this may be only the beginning of light manifesting itself in this land of darkness till the whole county is filled with the light thereof."[3] The first meeting of the Little Dunham Clerical Society was actually held on April 25, 1792. Clerical Societies were advocated by at least two bishops at the end of the seventeenth century: by Bishop Burnet in 1692 in "A Discourse on the Pastoral Care" in which he suggested the formation of societies of clergy in each deanery under the rural dean,[4] and also by Archbishop Tenison who had recommended them to the bishops of his province in 1699.[5] The first Evangelical clerical society was almost certainly Samuel Walker's Clerical Club formed in Truro about 1750.[6] Henry Venn heard of it while he was curate at Clapham from Risdon Darracott, a Nonconformist minister of Wellington, Somerset, who writes: "I find that

[1] J. Venn to H. Venn, June 25, 1792 (MS.).
H. Morris in his *Life of Charles Grant* (1904) says of Venn, "He must have been a first-rate scholar and a tactful teacher", p. 195.
[2] J. Venn to H. Venn, July 23, 1792 (MS.).
[3] J. Venn to C. Elliott, Feb. 15, 1792 (MS.).
[4] E. T. Vaughan, *Some Account of the Rev. Thomas Robinson* (1815), p. 263.
[5] G. C. B. Davies, *The Early Cornish Evangelicals, 1735–1760* (1951), p. 74.
[6] Davies, *op. cit.*, p. 74.

there are six clergymen who thus regularly meet together to strengthen each other's hands in the work of the Lord, and that the good effects of it have already spread through their several parishes and seems likely to diffuse its influence yet much further amongst the clergy and laity."[1]

Walker set an example and pattern that diffused its influence far beyond the borders of Cornwall. Henry Venn followed suit at Huddersfield and so did many others; Fletcher at Madeley, Jones at Creaton, Pugh at Rauceby, Riland at Birmingham, Haweis at Aldwinckle, Robinson at Leicester, Stillingfleet at Hotham, Newton in London (the Eclectic Society), and John Venn at Little Dunham. "Why may we not meet to pray when others meet to play at bowls?" asks Robinson; "Why may we not have our deliberative assemblies, when others of our brethren have their dancing and drinking assemblies? Why may we not seek to edify one another, whilst they care not if they corrupt one another?"[2] The clerical meeting became one of the chief means by which Evangelical clergy, isolated and despised as dangerous "enthusiasts" by other clergy, "strengthened each other's hands for the work of the Lord" and made their parochial ministries much more effective. An Evangelical moving to a new area was expected by his friends to try to start such a society. Henry Venn tells Mrs. Riland in 1775 that he supposes her husband "will soon establish a meeting of the clergy. I think I can reckon upon eight (possible members) within a tolerable distance."[3] And John Venn inquires of Brock at Bidborough: "Have you any meeting of Gospel Ministers in Kent? I think such a meeting as they have in Yorkshire and other places would strengthen your hands and be a means of much good."[4]

Henry Venn's society was formed in 1767 for Evangelical clergy in the north; in 1772, because Henry Venn's successor proved unsympathetic, it moved to Elland, where George Burnett, a former curate of Huddersfield Parish Church, was

[1] Risdon Darracott to H. Venn (MS.) partly quoted by Davies, *op. cit.*, p. 75.

[2] Quoted in Vaughan, *op. cit.*, p. 266. He also insisted that in starting a clerical meeting he was not guilty of canonical disobedience, of setting up an *imperium in imperio*.

[3] H. Venn to Mrs. Riland, July 8, 1775 (MS.).

[4] J. Venn to J. Brock, Aug. 1, 1791 (MS.).

incumbent; it has been known as the Elland Society ever since. At Yelling Henry Venn tried to repeat the experiment; in April 1786, Simeon, Coulthurst and Waltham[1] spent the day at Yelling in prayer, the ministry being the principal subject of their planned intercession. Though subsequent meetings were planned there is no evidence of their taking place; Simeon, however, became such a staunch advocate of these clerical societies that it is scarcely possible to find an account of an inaugural meeting of such without discovering there was at least one visitor present and his name, Charles Simeon.[2]

James Stillingfleet, who had been one of the founder members of the Elland Society, started his own society at Hotham, following very closely the earlier society. Another member was William Richardson of York, who had been also one of the original members of the Elland Society, and Joseph Milner. It was the Hotham meeting that directly influenced John Venn.[3] During the weeks of waiting at Hull to marry Kitty in the autumn of 1789 he attended the meeting at Hotham Rectory, "but alas my heart is indisposed".[4] Despite his preoccupation with thoughts that led away from the business of the meeting, the idea of attempting something similar in Norfolk soon germinated, and either then or later he obtained a copy of the rules of the Hotham Society, which, with some alterations became the rules of the new society at Little Dunham. "Your proposal of a meeting twice a year is from on high, and your usefulness is indeed increasing", his father tells him in January 1792.[5] He had written during the previous year to all the clergy within thirty miles of Dunham, whom he thought might support such a venture. There were six or seven of them; actually Hayward who was one of the first and most regular members came from Lakenheath, forty miles away.

John Venn was on his own for the first meeting of his society; his wife had taken the baby to Yelling because of whooping-

[1] Several letters allude to this occasion; the fullest is one from Henry Venn to Mrs. Elliott, April 15, 1786 (MS.), in the possession of Ridley Hall, Cambridge.

[2] There is evidence of Simeon being present at meetings at Little Dunham in 1792, Rauceby in 1795, at the Eclectic in 1799 and at Creaton in 1800.

[3] See Appendix B.

[4] J. Venn, Diary (MS.), Sept. 21, 1789.

[5] *Life of H. Venn*, p. 504.

cough in the village and the Grant boys had gone home for the holidays. Simeon arrived on April 24, the rest coming the next morning and leaving on the afternoon of the day following. "We had at our meeting," John Venn tells Kitty, "Mr. Edwards, Simeon, Hayward, Ivory, Webster Junior and myself."[1] Edward Edwards was a Fellow of Corpus Christi College and had just been appointed Lecturer at St. Nicholas' Chapel, King's Lynn; he was a great friend of Simeon, through whom he had met Venn a few weeks previously. Michael Hayward was Vicar of Lakenheath; he went there as a curate after leaving Magdalene and remained there till his death in 1818. Ivory of Hindolveston we have already met.[2] His poverty was no greater than that of Stephen Webster of Loddon[3] who, in spite of holding a vicarage and two curacies, received an annual income of £30 per annum. His reply to the original invitation reads: "Was I not in my own esteem so poor and despicable a creature and so mean an instrument (if instrument I may make so bold to call myself), I should rejoice more than I do at your proposal of a few ministers meeting now and then. I think the scheme eligible and shall not be a little glad to embrace the execution, if it can be put into execution."[4] For clergy like Webster a clerical society must have been a great blessing; he became a regular member.

Henry Venn, unable to be present, wrote his son a letter to be read at the meeting. In this he exhorted the members in their ministry to covet earnestly the gifts of the Spirit, to be diligently employing themselves "in some good work, either respecting the bodies or the souls of men," to consider themselves "the fathers of the poor and needy"; appointed not only to preach the Gospel, "but to be at much pains to supply their wants". He urges the ministers to value their time for much

[1] J. Venn to Mrs. J. Venn, April 27, 1792 (MS.).

[2] See p. 64.

[3] According to the *Alumni Cantabrigienses* Stephen Webster was Vicar of Claxton, Curate of Spexhall, Suffolk, and of Geldeston, Norfolk; perhaps he had given up Spexhall for Loddon by 1792. He is known as Webster Junior as his father Thomas Webster was also in Norfolk, and John Venn hoped he would come to the next meeting; his hope was disappointed.

[4] S. Webster to J. Venn, Jan. 10, 1792, quoted by H. Venn in his editorial notes (MS.).

reading and prayer and concludes: "I shall be with you in Spirit."[1]

Of the actual meeting John Venn tells his wife that on the Wednesday they met morning and afternoon, "in the afternoon we . . . determined the rules and laws of the meetings and the next morning we resumed our important business—very profitable indeed has it been to us all and will be I trust the foundation of much good to our souls and to our parishes".[2] The next meeting was in October and they met at the times they had laid down in the rules at the previous meeting. "The Ministers came on Tuesday evening and our meeting was continued till yesterday noon, with much life and I trust profit to everyone. Mr. Edwards mentioned his having a society formed of six or seven children of the age of twelve or thirteen, who appear to be under serious impressions. His dissertation was upon the nature etc. of these societies: mine upon the activity necessary in a Christian minister. The chief part of his will be published for the use of the societies. I was Director. Mr. Hankinson and Mr. Jowett were elected members. No new ones. The rest were all present."[3] Jowett was elected as Rector-designate of Little Dunham; he was not present. Robert Hankinson, who was only twenty-two and had just been ordained curate of St. Margaret's, King's Lynn, was a native of Lynn. Venn liked him and they became friends.[4]

At the third meeting, held on February 19 and 20, 1793, Jowett was present and two other new members, Hardiman and Ward.[5] John Venn took this opportunity of taking counsel with

[1] *Life of H. Venn*, p. 505. Henry Venn certainly cared for the bodies as well as the souls of his own parishioners. In times of unemployment and when bread was short at Yelling he appealed to his rich friends for money so that he could buy food cheap for "his poor". To Huddersfield he applied for clothes and blankets. Thomas Atkinson sent those woven at his own mill.

[2] J. Venn to Mrs. J. Venn, April 27, 1792 (MS.).

[3] J. Venn to Mrs. J. Venn, Oct. 19, 1792 (MS.).

[4] Robert Hankinson (1770–1863), Trinity College, Cambridge. Curate of St. Margaret's, King's Lynn 1792–1808. Vicar of Walpole St. Andrew 1808–1863. Honorary Canon of Norwich 1845–63. He endowed a wing in the West Norfolk and Lynn Hospital; this wing bears his name.

[5] Hardiman does not appear to have been a graduate of either Oxford or Cambridge. Ward may either be George Ward of St. John's College, Cambridge, who was curate of Waxham and Palling, or his brother William Ward of Trinity, who was curate of Little Cressingham.

his brethren with regard to his policy of preaching at Clapham and he raised the question: "In what way shall I begin to preach at Clapham; shall I follow Cecil's conciliatory advice or Mr. Wilberforce's?" Why this was an important question will become clear in the next chapter. Henry Jowett continued the society and John Venn came back occasionally as a visitor. The society is still in existence, though it has changed its name to the West Norfolk Clerical Society.

It is possible that one of the reasons why Evangelical Clerical Societies were so successful and multiplied so rapidly was that they met a deep-seated craving for friendship in the lives of many of their members. We can see examples of this first-hand in the relationship between Venn and Simeon, and between Venn and the friend Simeon introduced to him, Edward Edwards.

Venn and Simeon became more remote from one another after Venn left Norfolk. With the move to Clapham, Venn's visits to Cambridge became rarer; after his father's death in 1797 he did not see Cambridge again for more than twelve years; Simeon visited both Clapham and the Eclectic Society occasionally, but the part they played in each other's lives after 1793 was not great. Distance was not the only reason for the cooling in ardour of a friendship of which Henry Venn and Simeon himself expected so much. The key lies in the character of Charles Simeon, and John Venn's failure to understand that character. Max Warren in an essay gives this vivid portrait of Simeon:

> Simeon did not find himself an easy person to live with. "I have all my days," he once said, "felt my danger to lie on the side of precipitancy." Hot-tempered by nature, he found clumsiness and carelessness in others an easy spur to anger. Impetuous in his likes and dislikes, he found it hard to adapt himself to those who moved more slowly. Extravagant in his affections, he found the way of friendship often difficult. It is one of the marvels of spiritual history that a man thus tempered should have been able so to subdue his spirit as to face the years of opposition from parishioners, and the contempt and often hostility of the University, and in the end to win from all so great a regard. It was this triumph over his temper which was at once the proof of the depth

of his conversion, and the secret of his perseverance in his long ministry. Perhaps only a man who knew how to be abased could be trusted with the ability to abound. The same eagerness which led to temper led also to a readiness to seek forgiveness both from God and from those he had wronged. There was no pride in the man. Yet the deepest thing in Simeon was his humility. There could be no highmindedness in one who was humbled in thankfulness.[1]

This is an authentic portrait of the man as he was when John Venn knew him best and of the man who, at the time of his death in 1836, had so won the affection of Cambridge undergraduates that 1,500 of them thronged Holy Trinity at his funeral.[2] Conversion, however, did not make of him at once the humble and lovable saint of God which by grace he later became. Henry Venn saw Simeon's possibilities and nourished them; John Venn found him an angular and overbearing personality, aggressive, prickly in his personal relationships and lacking in sensitivity towards others "cast in a somewhat different mould". Henry Venn understood Simeon from the first in a way his children did not. "When Mr. Simeon paid us his first visit at Yelling," says Nelly, his eldest daughter, "it is impossible to conceive anything more ridiculous than his look and manner were. His grimaces were beyond anything you can imagine. So, as soon as we were gone, we all got together into the study, and set up an amazing laugh." But their father summoned them into the garden and, though it was early summer, asked them to pick him one of the green peaches.

[1] M. A. C. Warren, *Charles Simeon* (1949), pp. 12–13.
A similar picture is given by an ordinand who was at Cambridge in the 1790's who says: "He was naturally of a haughty, impatient, and impetuous temper, and these defects were sometimes exhibited in a way which was painful to the feelings of others. He was not always strictly observant of those rules of respect and courtesy which the conventional intercourse of life has prescribed and occasionally gave offence by an imperious mode of address. Being constitutionally of a very sensitive temperament, he has been known to express himself with undue severity on trifling and imaginary affronts; and, in the moment of excitement, would now and then redress his own grievances in a way which afterwards occasioned him pain and annoyance. He was fastidious in his attention to his person, dress and furniture, and over-punctillious in his observance of whatever he conceived to belong to the address and manners of a gentleman." *Memoirs of C. Jerram*, ed. J. Jerram (1855), p. 124.

[2] Smyth, *op. cit.*, p. 4.

When they showed surprise he said: "Well, my dears, it is green now, and we must wait; but a little more sun, and a few more showers, and the peach will be ripe and sweet. So it is with Mr. Simeon."[1] John Venn was doubtless at this time walking a little way with Simeon on his return journey to Cambridge but one wonders whether, like his sisters, he found "the singular gownsman of King's", whom he had first noticed in the University Church, always a little too "singular", and for that reason was never completely at ease with him.

Obviously the spiritual growth of Simeon was a subject that the Venns frequently discussed. After Simeon had been at Dunham on a three-day visit, John writes to his father: "Our dear friend Simeon came over to see me; very much improved and grown in grace; his very presence a blessing." His father replies: "Your account of Simeon is very just: my fears concerning him greatly abate. He appears to be much more humbled from a deeper knowledge of himself. He is a most affectionate friend and lively Christian." And a few months later: "Come by Cambridge, and pay some time with Mr. Simeon; he has the warmest love for you, and is the only one of all the Cambridge men who follows the Lord fully as Caleb did."[2] Affection on Henry Venn's side grew and grew: "My dear brother, Mr. Simeon, is as attentive to me as if he was my own son, and has paid us several visits",[3] he tells his daughter Kitty, whereas Simeon looking back on their first meeting says: "In this aged Minister, I found a father, an instructor, and a most bright example; and I shall ever have reason to adore my God to all eternity for the benefit of his acquaintance."[4]

With John Venn it was different. Though there is no sign of diminishing affection on Simeon's side at any time, only in the early years was John Venn able to reciprocate the warmth of

[1] The account of this incident is a conflation from two sources of a story Eling Elliott used to tell. It is to be found in the *Annals*, p. 119, footnote, and in H. C. G. Moule, *Charles Simeon*, p. 45.

[2] These letters are dated May 25th, June 9th, and October 16th, 1785. All are reproduced in Carus, *op. cit.*, pp. 68–9. He is wrong in saying that of May 25th is from J. Venn's diary. The diary reads "Mr. Simeon visited me for three days"; the quotation is obviously from a letter.

[3] H. Venn to Mrs. K. Harvey, August 23, 1793 (MS.).

[4] Carus, *op. cit.*, p. 23.

Simeon's lavish affection for him. Simeon loved Venn because he was his father's son and because he was "the first spiritual acquaintance I had in the world".[1] At the time of Venn's ordination, when they had known one another only three months, he wrote: "I used formerly to think that I had some idea of real friendship, but my acquaintance with you has convinced me that it was a very faint conception rather of what it should be than what it is. The Lord Jesus Christ, I trust, has given me to know something more of it now. I feel my heart glow with affection towards you and your dear father; may God increase and cement it more and more, and enable me to prove it in the whole tenor and conduct of my life! . . ." The opening and the postscript are characteristic of the writer: "My dearest friend, I most sincerely congratulate you, not on a permission to receive £40 or £50 a year, nor on the title of the Reverend, but on your accession to the most valuable, most honourable, most important, and most glorious office in the world—to that of an ambassador of the Lord Jesus Christ", and in the postscript he adds, "I suppose this is the first time of your being directed to as Reverend, but you will not find yourself half an inch higher for it."[2] John Venn's letters at this time were not lacking in intensity of feeling either. Before leaving Yelling for Dunham, he writes: "My heart is often with you and you are remembered cordially by many friends here who are much interested in your proceedings—May the Lord hear their prayers for you and cause you to grow more and more in grace and in the knowledge and love of God. . . . I am yours in the best of all bonds, J. V. Write me words soon how you go on."[3]

During the next three years Venn often came to Yelling by Cambridge in order to see Simeon and once or twice each year Simeon went to Dunham for a few days, and once at least for a whole week. They did not write often. "If anyone were to judge", writes Simeon, "of our friendship by our constancy in corresponding with each other, he would say that we were sworn foes: but be assured I do not weigh your love in so un-

[1] Carus, *op. cit.*, p. 368.

[2] C. Simeon to J. Venn, Sept. 23, 1782; quoted by Carus, *op. cit.*, pp. 28–30 but without the postscript which is to be found in the MS. alone.

[3] J. Venn to C. Simeon, April 10, 1783 (MS.).

certain a balance; and I trust that you do not come in the least behind me in ardour."[1] The letters that they did write were occasions for exchanging sermons, and, on Simeon's side, for passing on advice from the Yelling family when they were not writing, as for instance: "Mrs. V. desires you will take the yolk of an egg without any other mixture because it is that which mixes with the bile and carries it off."[2] Simeon also sent Venn some tracts he had written; in 1795, Simeon, visiting Clapham, brings with him Jenks'[3] Volume of Prayers that he has started to re-edit. If Venn approves he will complete his task; if not, someone else must do it.[4] A year earlier John Venn gave Simeon a colt as a present, which Simeon, after some protestation, accepted.[5]

Where, it may be asked, are there signs of diminishing enthusiasm on Venn's part for this friendship with Simeon? Of this unfortunately there is plenty of evidence, for the letters show that Simeon's temper, pride and enigmatical behaviour were a constant irritant. In the letter John Venn wrote just before leaving London to become Rector of Little Dunham, he takes Simeon to task over his temper, without complaining that he has felt its sting. He writes:

> I rejoice in the accounts I hear from Yelling that you go on successfully, for so I interpret what you have written to them, that the University pulpit thunders continually against Methodism. It is a good sign when the world begins to be alarmed and the prime advocates for the shrine of Satan cry out that their temple is in danger; but at the same time in such circumstances the Gospel is chiefly flourishing the minister by whom it is spread is in more than ordinary danger. If he is a man of warm temper, he is in danger of saying and doing rash and angry things; if of a meek character, the opposition he meets with may tempt him to soften and conceal the truth or may intimidate him from delivering it at

[1] C. Simeon, Sept. 29, 1784 (MS.).

[2] *Ibid.*

[3] Benjamin Jenks, Vicar of Harley, died 1724; some writers e.g. Henry Venn of C.M.S. believed that Evangelical preaching in the Church of England died with Jenks. His volume of Prayers was a devotional classic amongst Evangelicals, this new edition by Simeon being particularly popular. It went into several editions.

[4] C. Simeon to J. Venn, Jan. 8, 1795 (MS.).

[5] C. Simeon to J. Venn, April 23, 1794 and May 13, 1794 (MS.).

all. You are in no danger of the latter and I hope it will be an unnecessary caution in me to remind you that Satan will make his principal attacks upon you by the former. . . . Excuse me, my dear friend, in presuming to give advice to one so much my superior. But as I know you are in so critical a situation, I cannot help adding my whisper to the constant advice you have had from my father and the rest of your Christian friends.[1]

Twenty years later Simeon received a much more telling rebuke for the same vice from their mutual friend, Edward Edwards, the incidents showing the form Simeon's outbursts sometimes took. Simeon and Edwards were dining at Hankinson's house at Lynn, when a servant started poking the fire in a manner so "unscientific" that Simeon turned in his chair and thumped the man in the back to make him stop. On leaving, Edwards' servant put the wrong bridle on Simeon's horse; Simeon again lost his temper, so Edwards wrote a note from his servant, in which he said that in the kitchen they found it hard to believe that a gentleman who prayed and preached so well should wear no "bridle" upon his tongue. Edwards signed it "John Softly" and put it in a cloak-bag that was to follow by coach. When Simeon found the note he wrote a penitent and characteristic note to "John Softly" asking for forgiveness and signing himself "CHAS. PROUD AND IRRITABLE."[2]

It was "Charles the Proud" more than "Charles the Irritable" who upset Venn. Even in the early days at Dunham Venn felt constrained to write complaining of Simeon's lack of love; Simeon apologizes, suspects self has got in, which is "like a cork exceedingly light and ever uppermost".[3] Two months later Venn complains that Simeon has written sarcastically and out of turn. Simeon says this is untrue—the real cause of friction seems to have been Simeon's refusal to come to Dunham to preach for Venn. This happened more than once. Venn seems somewhat unreasonably discontented that the only time Simeon addressed his flock was at the large meeting in the Rectory in 1785, and in 1790 he pressed him again to come to Dunham and preach. In July Venn supped and slept at Simeon's rooms

[1] J. Venn to C. Simeon, April 10, 1783 (MS.).
[2] Carus, *op. cit.*, pp. 194–5.
[3] C. Simeon to J. Venn, July 15, 1783 (MS.).

at King's, hoping to dispose of the coolness that existed at that time in their mutual relations and to gain an affirmative answer to his request for Simeon to preach for him. While Simeon was out of the room, another guest told Venn that Simeon was unlikely to accept the invitation. Venn's comment to his wife on this is: "I bless God I feel no such reluctance to preach in a small place."[1] Simeon may later have become aware of the pain he caused Venn, for in 1820 Henry Venn of the Church Missionary Society heard him say: "I thank God, it does not *now* give me any concern who come to church or who stays away, whether there is a large congregation or whether there be a dozen. The consideration that God has sent me to preach to the congregation, be it what it may, engrosses every other feeling."[2]

There were other incidents; perhaps the most revealing was one that provoked the following letter from Simeon to the new Rector of Clapham:

> You will pardon readily the intimations which I suggested; they arose only from a deep-rooted attachment which my soul has ever felt towards you from the first day that we were introduced to each other, and which I hope and trust will continue not only with unabated but with increasing fervour. Years have now evinced that I was not mistaken in the opinion which I had formed of you: on the contrary the Lord has so enabled you to make your light shine that I covet, exceedingly covet, a closer intimacy with you than ever. We are indeed cast somewhat in a different mould; and I am sensible that my complexion necessarily induces a conduct sometimes which needs forbearance, particularly from those whose natural dispositions do not altogether accord with mine. . . . I now assure my dear friend that (D.V.) I will never more misconstrue his natural shyness into any declension of love towards me; I heartily beg his pardon that in his last visit to Cambridge I was in some measure guilty of it. But from henceforth adieu to such evil surmising for ever. If my dear brother will let me know when he comes next to Yelling I will fly over if possible to meet him, and to enjoy sweet conversation with him.[3]

[1] J. Venn to Mrs. J. Venn, July 22, 1790 (MS.).
[2] H. Venn's Editorial Notes (MS.).
[3] C. Simeon to J. Venn, April 23, 1794 (MS.).

This letter tells us a great deal of both men; Simeon, headstrong, clumsy, passionate, penitent; Venn, shy, over-sensitive, resentful of a slight which was repented of almost as soon as it was inflicted. Although Venn came to Yelling twice within the next twelve months and on both occasions Simeon "flew over" to "enjoy sweet conversation with him", the closer intimacy, that Simeon coveted, Venn denied him, and their meetings after 1795 were few. It must be asked whether Venn really tried to understand Simeon, but it must be said, as Simeon himself admitted, that others found him difficult. When Kitty Venn was staying at Yelling in 1792 and heard from her husband of the Clapham offer she says she and Henry Venn had discussed the matter but "I have not dared to ask Mr. Simeon",[1] which suggests that Simeon had visited Yelling but Kitty had been too frightened of him to talk about the problem which deeply concerned her, her husband, and—had she known it—Simeon himself.

On Simeon's side his affection for Venn was never quenched. He once offered to stand as godfather to any child the John Venns might have, an offer which does not seem to have been taken up, but he was not discouraged. During the course of a long letter written in 1805 Simeon says:

> A little time ago I went to preach at Everton; and, according to custom, consecrated the time when I was in view of Yelling Church to the special remembrance of those who ought, both for their father's sake and their own, to be ever most dear to me. I began with your dear and much-honoured father. . . . I then proceeded to offer up my poor thanksgivings for you; for the graces and gifts with which He has mercifully endowed you; for the little family with which He has blessed you; for the use He has made of your ministry; for the increased life and energy with which He has favoured you by means of your late heavy afflictions;[2] and to my thanksgivings I added my poor prayers for still richer and more abundant blessings, that all which God has already done for you may be only as the drops before the shower. I then endeavoured to remember your dear children and to implore all needful blessings upon their heads.[3]

At the beginning of 1807 overwork told severely on Simeon's

[1] Mrs. J. Venn to J. Venn, May 1, 1792 (MS.).
[2] Kitty Venn died in 1803.
[3] C. Simeon to J. Venn, Dec. 12, 1805, quoted in Carus, *op. cit.*, pp. 206–9.

health and he was persuaded to take several months off, which he spent partly in London and partly on a long ride west with Edwards to Cornwall, to plead with Lydia Grenfell for Henry Martyn,[1] who was hoping she would join him in India as his wife. On Simeon's arrival in London he "received a very kind and sympathizing letter from Mr. Venn, who had heard of my weakness, and announced his intention of coming to see me".[2] Two days later they met at the Eclectic; "Mr. Venn was there, and expressed all the kindness imaginable."[3] Simeon was overjoyed and hopes of the deep friendship he had always desired revived; the next day he wrote to Venn as follows: "I feel most sensibly the tender concern which you have expressed for my welfare, and the kind attention which you have shown me in my present debilitated state, and I hope it will be the means of reviving the sentiments of most endeared affection, which once glowed in our bosoms and knit us together as David and Jonathan." He then says he is hoping to spend "Passion Week in quiet retirement and meditation at Clapham with Dr. Fearon",

> But I look on the kindness you have shown me, as a kind of call from God to give you preference, if you can give me a tolerably warm room to myself; having been habituated to a warm room, I feel that the want of it would take from that entire attention which I wish to give to things that do not relate to the body; . . . a tinder-box, a little wood to kindle the fire speedily, a few roundish coals, to prevent a whole house being occupied in stirring and blowing the fire, are but small matters in themselves; but to one who rises early, and longs to serve his God without distraction, they are of some importance. Give me but a warm room and all my wants (with the exception of a little bread and cheese) are supplied. . . .
>
> I remain your old friend, your father's friend, and your truly affectionate friend,
>
> C. S.[4]

[1] Henry Martyn had written from India asking Lydia Grenfell, whom he had courted in England, to come out and join him. The whole story is beautifully told in C. E. Padwick, *Henry Martyn* (1922). Simeon's visit, which did not succeed in its purpose, is referred to on pp. 189–90.

[2] Simeon kept a diary during the time he was away from Cambridge from which Carus quotes extensively: Carus, *op. cit.*, p. 217.

[3] *Ibid.*, p. 218.

[4] C. Simeon to J. Venn, March 10, 1807; quoted in Carus, *op. cit.*, pp. 231–3.

Whether Venn replied welcoming Simeon we do not know, but we do know that he was suddenly called away on March 17th to his sister Kitty Harvey, who was dangerously ill at Caldecot.[1] He did not get back to Clapham till Easter Eve, ten days later; as Dr. Fearon went to Caldecot as well, Simeon must have stayed elsewhere in London. On Easter Monday he walked to Clapham and called on James Stephen. He does not appear to have seen Venn at all.[2]

In the spring of 1810 John Venn visited Cambridge on his way to and from Norfolk, and called on all his Cambridge friends including Simeon for whom he preached twice; Simeon and Farish accompanied him as far as Ely on his journey north. A year later Venn hastened to Cambridge because Farish was ill; again he saw something of Simeon and preached on two Sundays at Holy Trinity. During the same year Simeon visited Clapham three times and on the last occasion preached for Venn. The following year Venn took his second wife to the Isle of Wight for their honeymoon. They found Simeon staying with his brother at St. John's; Venn called on him and they went out in a small open boat together. During Venn's last illness, Simeon, who was staying in London, visited him thrice, and on one of these visits he promised to complete the "Life of Henry Venn" which John Venn had begun; Simeon undertook the task but finding insufficient documents he wrote to the family saying he was unable to do it, and proceeded to write his own autobiography.[3]

Although unable to perform this particular service he did much for John Venn's family. Henry and John Venn found him a wise and affectionate friend during their time at Cambridge, where both were enthusiastic "Sims". It was to John that Simeon paid particular attention, giving him special instruc-

[1] After his curacy at Dewsbury, James Harvey never held any preferment but moved to Caldecot near Sandy in Bedfordshire, where his family owned property.

[2] Carus, *op. cit.*, p. 222.

[3] *Ibid.*, introduction XIX, XX. Simeon says "on examining the papers which were to form the groundwork of his life, I find that there are no documents to serve as the substratum for my work, nor any facts whereon to found my comments and observations". Having seen the papers mentioned I think it more likely it was their bulk as much as anything that would have deterred a busy parish priest like Simeon. The autobiography is included in Carus's *Life of Simeon.*

tion in sermon delivery, and presenting him to one of the Simeon Trust livings at St. Peter's, Hereford.[1]

The rich friendship which Simeon desired Venn to share with him, Venn bestowed without stint on their mutual friends, William Farish and Edward Edwards. Of Venn's affection for Farish there is plenty of evidence but no letters that passed between them have survived. On the other hand most of the letters that have been preserved were written to Edwards.

Edwards was Norfolk by birth and seven years junior to Venn and Simeon. He was a scholar of Corpus Christi College and in 1788 was elected Fellow. In December 1791 he came to King's Lynn as Lecturer at St. Nicholas' Chapel,[2] and on January 7, 1792, Venn met him at a breakfast party at Lynn where he had come with the Grant boys for the day. The same day Henry Venn wrote to him: "You are going to have a very excellent Christian preacher at Lynn: Mr. Edwards is his name and he is Fellow of Benet[3] and chosen Lecturer at Lynn. Dear Simeon is to bring him to see me and by letter to introduce him to Dunham."[4] A week later Simeon's letter arrived; in it he committed Edwards to Venn's pastoral care. It seems that Edwards' conversion was recent, and although Simeon had been impressed by what he had seen of his humility, it is as yet too early to tell how permanent the change might be.[5] On the strength of this letter Venn wrote almost immediately to Edwards, welcoming him, and saying:

> It has been almost the only inconvenience to which my present situation has been subject that I have been removed from the society of Christian ministers. Often have I wished for the company of but one near me, from whom I might receive advice, by whom I might be quickened, in whose joys and trials I might bear a share, and who might also partake of mine. For in the road in which we travel, and in the work in which we are engaged, difficulties continually occur which call for faithful advice,

[1] See *Annals*, p. 187. See also Warren, *Charles Simeon*, pp. 17, 18.

[2] St. Nicholas' Church was and is the daughter church of St. Margaret's, King's Lynn.

[3] Corpus was sometimes known as St. Benet's College.

[4] H. Venn to J. Venn, Jan. 7, 1792 (MS.).

[5] C. Simeon to J. Venn, Jan. 13, 1792 (MS.).

and burdens are daily to be borne which require the kind assistance of a friend.[1]

It is not surprising, therefore, that Edwards received a more than usually warm welcome when he came to stay at Little Dunham Rectory during the following month.

> This week [John Venn writes to Elliott] I have enjoyed a feast such as I never expected to enjoy in this place. A Mr. Edwards has just got the Lectureship at Lynn. . . . He is a man of great abilities, exceedingly serious and deeply humble, well acquainted with the truth and earnestly labouring to make others acquainted with it. Though we have been but two days together yet our hearts were as much united as they would have been in the ordinary friendship of the world for many years.[2]

Henceforward John Venn gave himself to Edwards as he gave himself to no other man. After the move to Clapham, only a year later, John Venn, usually a bad correspondent, wrote more letters to Edwards than to anyone else. In this correspondence[3] it was Edwards, not Venn, who was the laggard. For Venn, Edwards could not write too frequently nor visit him too often. There was an extreme tenderness in their friendship, something almost "passing the love of women", which we, who have been brought up to feel squeamish about deep male friendships, find hard to understand. Perhaps the figure of the Duke of Wellington as "the strong silent man", whom all good Englishmen are taught to admire, cuts us off from the days when men were more spontaneous and emotional in their attachment to one another.[4] Few men would, or even could, write some of the letters Venn wrote to Edwards, but a study of them can hardly fail to convince the reader that something exquisitely delicate and beautiful has been lost. "I count my friends as a miser does his jewels", John Venn wrote once to Edwards,[5] and Edwards

[1] J. Venn to E. Edwards, Jan. 17, 1792 (MS.).

[2] J. Venn to C. Elliott, Feb. 15, 1792 (MS.).

[3] John Venn was notorious among his family and friends for being a bad correspondent. He himself told Edwards on one occasion, "You and William Farish, I always consider as the dearest friends I have in the world, and yet I correspond with neither of you" (April 3, 1807). Farish, it is true, received few letters, Edwards a never-ebbing stream.

[4] I owe this point to Canon Charles Smyth.

[5] See p. 102.

must have known he was himself reckoned by the keeper of the collection as the richest jewel of them all.

The time the two friends had together in Norfolk was extremely brief. In April 1792 John Venn knew that the move to Clapham was imminent; by the following March he had left Dunham. Edwards was one of the founder members of the Little Dunham Clerical Society and attended all three meetings held at Venn's Rectory. In August Edwards came to stay for another couple of days, and in October Venn took "ship with my intimate friend Mr. Edwards" to Hull to spend a few days with Kitty and the Stillingfleets at Hotham. No letters from Edwards to Venn have been preserved, which makes information concerning him difficult to come by, but John Venn's letters and the glimpses given in Carus's *Life of Simeon* do suggest an attractive personality, rich in humour and Christian understanding, who unlike Simeon and Venn never took himself too seriously. Venn says he was something of an artist and had made a sketch of Little Dunham Rectory and Church. In 1799 he became Rector of St. Edmund's, North Lynn,[1] and remained such till his death in 1849. Some years before his death he was made an Honorary Canon of Norwich.

John Venn had been away from Norfolk only four months when he writes impatiently to Edwards: "When, my dear friend, shall I see you at Clapham? I long for an interview. Do come if you can."[2] Next summer from Yelling he writes:

> I have been calculating that it is but eleven miles from Lynn to Downham, eighteen from Downham to Maypole, seventeen from Maypole to Yelling, in all forty-seven miles, just a day's journey. What should hinder Edwards from coming over and spending a few days with me. I cannot go to Lynn as I could not leave my father, and I must go to Little Dunham if I went into Norfolk at all. I cannot therefore go to Lynn, but Edwards may come to Yelling and gladden the hearts of Mrs. Venn, Miss Venn, Mr. Venn Senior and Mr. Venn Junior, surely he will be glad to have this opportunity of giving so much pleasure, and doing so

[1] This may have been a sinecure, for North Lynn was washed into the sea in the sixteenth century.

[2] J. Venn to E. Edwards, July 29, 1793 (MS.).

much good as he may do. I hope that you neither can nor will make any objection to the propriety of this reasoning.[1]

This letter is typical of Venn's playfulness and affection for Edwards; he is always trying to woo him into a visit.

In 1796 Edwards married Anne Pead, also of Hull. John Venn chides him for allowing his honeymoon to last seven months, eighteen days, which is the time that has elapsed since the wedding and during which time Edwards has not written. "However, joking apart, I feel much impatience to have a long and full account how you are going on as a man and a minister. I want to hear of your health, your happiness, your plans, your societies, your friends, your labours, your sermons, your everything, and I know not how it comes that I never knew so little about you as since your marriage when I wanted to know the most, and positively I should have been half-angry if I had not loved you so much."[2] A month later he writes again: "Pray write to me often. Let me know your views—let me share your pleasures and let me bear as well as your dear Anne the burthen of your heart. She will not, I know, be jealous, and true love like flame loses nothing by communication, nay the more our affections are drawn out in fervency of friendship and benevolent feelings, the more are they fitted upon the principal object of their choice."[3]

"It is eight years since we parted," John Venn writes in 1801, "and during that period, a long one in a short life, I have formed no friendship like that which I enjoy with you."[4]

The theme of friendship is one to which Venn constantly returns in his letters to Edwards:

I have a heart I think formed for friendship and affection and the further I advance in life the more warm is my affection for my friends. I am often with you in spirit and in my intellectual enjoyment of your company, your conversation, your affection, your prosperity and welfare, anticipate that time and state in which probably actual intercourse will actually be carried on

[1] J. Venn to E. Edwards, Aug. 1794 (MS.).
[2] J. Venn to E. Edwards, Sept. 26, 1796 (MS.).
[3] J. Venn to E. Edwards, Nov. 11, 1796 (MS.).
[4] J. Venn to E. Edwards, March 31, 1801 (MS.).

with nearly as much ease as the spirit now travels over mountains, hills, seas and continents to a beloved friend.[1]

In 1810 their friendship was further enriched by John Venn spending a fortnight at Lynn following attendance at a meeting of the Little Dunham Clerical Society. At Lynn he stood godfather to John Francis Edwards, preached at St. Nicholas' Chapel, and had long walks and conversations with Edwards and Hankinson. Edwards and his wife took him over to Hunstanton to see Mrs. Birkbeck, a Quaker, but left him behind when they went to Earlham to visit the Gurneys.[2] However, John Venn paid a shorter visit the following year and dined with John Gurney, Elizabeth Fry's brother, at Lynn. The first visit John Venn remembered with particular pleasure; it was on this occasion that he wrote to Edwards: "I count my friends as a miser does his jewels . . . I would not part with the recollection of my visit to Lynn for much gold."[3]

In a sermon on "Intercession for Others" John Venn says that prayer for friends will induce in them, as well as in the intercessor, "the spirit of love". "Intercession", he says, "enlarges the exercise of friendship; it opens a new source of love."[4] Christian friendship has a depth and a consistency that is lacking in all other friendship. When Venn preached that sermon he may well have had Edwards in mind, and possibly Farish as well, for although Venn had a genius for friendship only Edwards and Farish knew the full extent of it. Simeon, ardently as he desired it, never approached this place in Venn's affections. It is a little disturbing to find Venn, after he had received Simeon's gentle protestation of friendship along with his request for a room at Clapham Rectory for Passion Week 1807, writing to Edwards: "You and William Farish I always consider as the greatest friends I have in the world", and continuing: "Dear Simeon has informed me of your proposal to accompany him

[1] J. Venn to E. Edwards, April 11, 1798 (MS.).

[2] The Gurneys of Earlham are the large and famous Quaker family of which Elizabeth, later Elizabeth Fry, is the best known. Another sister, Hannah, married Thomas Fowell Buxton, and J. Gurney was well known as a Quaker with strong Evangelical leanings and thus thought by many of his fellow Quakers to be unorthodox.

[3] J. Venn to E. Edwards, Jan. 19, 1811 (MS.).

[4] J. Venn, *Sermons*, Vol. III, p. 312.

into the west, and that you will be in town on Tuesday. Where will be your home? It must of course be partly at Mr. Pead's, but may I hope to have a share of it? I will not say you do not know how happy it will make me for I believe you do know. Let me enjoy that pleasure. I have room, and I have a heart larger than my room."[1]

We only hope that he answered "dear Simeon's" letter with similar affectionate enthusiasm, even if Venn did not count him amongst his greatest friends. Perhaps Venn would have felt more warmly towards Simeon had he known that it was entirely to Simeon he owed the appointment to Clapham, which was to give him an even more important opening than Huddersfield had given to his father; but he never knew, for Simeon never told him.

John Venn was by no means an outstanding success as rector of a small country parish; rather the reverse was true of his ministry at Little Dunham. He was too remote from his people; his only real friends in the parish were the Parrys, and the only people whom we know he influenced permanently came to him from outside the parish boundaries. However, the consequent discouragement did no permanent damage to a spirit prone to morbidity, nor did his isolated position have disastrous consequences on his character. In John Venn's case comparative isolation helped him to develop a healthy independence, and made him long for and then give himself entirely first to the wife he married and later to the friend who came to stand next to his wife in his affections. The offer to become Rector of Clapham came to the right man at exactly the right time—there he achieved both maturity and a considerable measure of success in his work for God.

[1] J. Venn to E. Edwards, April 3, 1807 (MS.). Mr. Pead was Edwards' father-in-law.

3

CLAPHAM

On April 14, 1792, the Reverend Sir James Stonhouse, Rector of Clapham, died. In accordance with John Thornton's will the living was offered first to Henry Foster and there seemed every possibility of his accepting it. Parry wrote to John Venn almost immediately from London, "I have seen Mr. Foster and though I could not get his determination yet I think he is determined to take Clapham",[1] and Kitty from Yelling where she is awaiting the birth of their second child, "Your father and sister appear as easy as you do respecting Clapham, and as certain of Mr. Foster's accepting it."[1] Neither Parry nor Henry Venn had reckoned on Simeon, who many years later told the younger Henry Venn that "as soon as he heard of the vacancy he told Foster that he was convinced it would benefit the Gospel for Venn to be moved from his obscurity, that he thought him admirably suited and that if Foster would forgo this he (Simeon) would make over to him the whole of his private fortune to make up his sacrifice. Mr. Foster declined compensation,"[2] without complaint or bitterness, and stood down. "What an honour and lustre is thrown upon Mr. Foster's character",[3] wrote Henry Venn when he heard that Foster had declined, but neither he nor his son ever knew the real reason for his self-sacrifice.[4]

[1] Both quoted in Henry Venn's Editorial Notes (MS.).

[2] H. Venn's Editorial Notes (MS.). Foster's income was only £200 according to Samuel Thornton, *Yearly Recollections*, (1891) p.76.

[3] *Life of H. Venn*, p. 509.

[4] Stillingfleet gave Kitty a reason which may be true, but is only part of the story. She says: "Mr. Stillingfleet gave me a reason I never heard before for Mr. Foster refusing Clapham, he says he went over, made many enquiries and fixed in his own mind to accept it, that upon this determination he lost his peace of mind,

Venn received the news during the course of the first meeting of the Little Dunham Clerical Society on April 25th. Simeon doubtless came to that meeting, not only because of his zeal for clerical societies but because he was anxious to persuade his friend to accept Clapham. He arrived the night before and after the final session on April 26 Venn rode with him and Edwards to Lynn, most probably to seek their counsel. Venn then came back as far as Swaffham and wrote to his wife: "My mind, you will naturally suppose, has been very agitated, my dearest K., by the information of Mr. Foster's having declined Clapham." He tells his wife that he has heard already from Samuel Thornton offering him the living, from Bentley enclosing Foster's resignation, and from his cousin John Brasier congratulating him. Foster's resignation, he says, is couched in terms which show his great humility and amiableness.

> With respect to my own feelings, you my dear partner of my life and friend of my bosom, who know all that is in my heart and to whom I cannot use any reserve.[1] I am almost overwhelmed with the sense of the many and great difficulties I can foresee. To others I could not speak fully. They would look upon it as the affectation of humility and laugh at those things which appear to me matters of most serious concern. And to you I am almost afraid of speaking for fear of distressing you. . . . I see it matters little where we are, provided we are useful, and if I accept Clapham it will be only under the idea of being called by God to be of use there. . . .[2]

John Venn's diffidence and hesitancy is very apparent in this letter. It was only overcome by much persuasion from his wife, his father and several friends, and by his own growing conviction that Clapham was the place of God's appointment for him.

At the beginning of May John Venn went to London with his father. He saw Grant, who "told me that he thinks of build-

and could get no rest—when he came to the resolution to refuse his peace was restored and he was happy." Mrs. J. Venn to J. Venn, Oct. 8, 1792 (MS.). Others have sought explanation in the unwillingness of Foster to leave his successful lectureships at Long Acre Chapel and elsewhere, e.g. L. E. Elliott-Binns, *The Early Evangelicals*, p. 246. The fact that Foster also closely kept the secret throws further "lustre" on his character. He worked happily with Venn in the Eclectic team.

[1] The letter also contains the alternative "I need use no reserve"; neither reading is crossed out.

[2] J. Venn to Mrs. J. Venn, April 27, 1792 (MS.).

ing a house at Clapham, and Mr. Henry Thornton, he says, is also going to buy one there. This intelligence gives me concern rather than otherwise. I would almost forgo the pleasure of their company and friendship that they might enjoy the benefit of another person's ministry, indeed let them hear anyone but myself."[1] This is the first inkling he had of Henry Thornton's plans for a Clapham Sect, and the prospect of being their chaplain made him even more hesitant to accept the living. "On Friday morning", he tells his wife, "I breakfasted with Mr. S. Thornton at Clapham and viewed the Parsonage house. It is a large old building with many rooms in it, but extremely out of repair. There is a garden about as big as ours at Little Dunham and in it a fine mulberry tree."[2] Samuel Thornton said that the living was worth £650, which included rent from a house built on the twelve acres of glebe. The same evening he joined his father and their relations in Camberwell, but returned to Clapham on Sunday.

> On Sunday morning I came here and attended divine service but did no duty except that in the evening I expounded to Mr. R. Thornton's family. I am now more discouraged than ever after I have seen the congregation and made inquiries. I have almost come to a determination to relinquish the offer of Clapham, for indeed I clearly see myself to be totally unfit for such a sphere and I am sure nothing hinders me from it but the fear of contradicting the call of God. I am afraid of being like Jonah, whose character suits my own, oh pray for me without ceasing for I am almost overwhelmed with a sense of my own insufficiency.[3]

But this Jonah's wife before she received this letter wrote to try and shake him out of his double-mindedness.

> I send you [she says] two letters—our dear friend Stillo's to comfort and encourage you—R. Jarratt's by order—observe there is not one dissenting voice, ought not this to encourage you? I begin to think we do wrong in being so cast down and not sufficiently thankful for the honour God has put on you by calling you to so important a sphere . . . you seem to have no will of your

[1] J. Venn to Mrs. J. Venn, May 8, 1792 (MS.).
[2] J. Venn to Mrs. J. Venn, May 14, 1792 (MS.).
[3] J. Venn to Mrs. J. Venn, May 14, 1792 (MS.).

own either in accepting or refusing Clapham. Could you go contrary to the opinion of all your friends?[1]

Kitty knew her husband and his weaknesses, so did his father, who also wrote to her from town,

> A great door of usefulness is opened and a full scope for the ministry of J. Venn; and much exercise there will be for patience, self-denial, faith and prayer. I, on Tuesday, sat an hour with Mr. Thornton who feels tenderly the diffidence of your husband, and wishes him not to be discouraged. He assured me, the name of Venn, old and young, was held in very great respect.[2]

By mid-May John Venn had definitely accepted and he was instituted Rector of Clapham on June 8. On June 25 he read himself in "with less agitation than I expected"; he says he was pleased "to find it a very easy church to speak in".[3]

However, he did not move permanently to Clapham till March in the following year. There were several reasons for this: Jowett found it would inconvenience Magdalene if he left college for Little Dunham before April or May 1793 and asked Venn to stay at least till Lady Day. Grant would be at a loss for a tutor for his boys if there were a long interregnum and Parry was anxious that Venn should stay in Dunham one more winter. Meanwhile duty at Clapham was taken by Richard Lloyd, curate at Camberwell, who not only took the Sunday services but came over in the middle of the week to visit the sick. He was a popular preacher; although decidedly Evangelical, his sermons did not cause offence to a congregation suspicious of "enthusiasm" and were a good preparation for the more solid expositions of John Venn. Some of these were prepared whilst he was still at Dunham.

> Yesterday morning [he writes to his father on July 23] I preached at Clapham Church for the first time before the three Mr. Thorntons, Mr. Wilberforce, and Mr. Clarke, Vicar of Hull,[4] who is here also on a visit. I did not consider myself as their pastor opening his commission, because it would not be so suitable while I do not come to reside among them. I only preached therefore as

[1] Mrs. J. Venn to J. Venn, May 15, 1792 (MS.).
[2] H. Venn to Mrs. J. Venn, May 17, 1792 (MS.).
[3] J. Venn to H. Venn, June 25, 1792 (MS.).
[4] The Rev. Samuel Clarke, Wilberforce's brother-in-law.

Mr. Lloyd's friend upon an indifferent subject. My text was Luke 9: 56,[1] from whence I took occasion to dwell upon the benevolent character of Christ manifested in the ends for which He came into the world, and the manner in which He fulfilled them. My sermon was only twenty-five minutes long. I considered in everything the prejudices they entertained against me which I understood were very strong. I thought it therefore most prudent to begin at first with subjects on which we did agree, that they might be disposed to assent more readily to those on which we did not. The effect, I understood, was that they were extremely surprised. Mr. Wilberforce thanked me in a very affectionate manner. I am aware that many serious people would blame me, and I think I was not unfaithful, but as far as I know my own heart I think my conduct was conducted by prudence of a Christian kind not inconsistent with even a zealous attachment to the name of Christ. I wish, however, to have your opinion upon the subject, and I hope the Lord will in all things and at all times direct me how to work for the glory of his name. I think that had I not preached with caution many would have left the church, or have heard afterwards with such prejudice as would have prevented their receiving any benefit.[2]

The ordeal of facing a large congregation known to be, in the main, hostile to his views made him more than usually nervous and prevented him from giving of his best; he tells Nelly that "extreme dryness of mouth", to which "I am subject when my spirits are hurried, embarrassed my delivery a good deal".[3] In the circumstances his father's reply to his request for advice must have been particularly disheartening; in it he said that he deprecated caution and wanted him "explicit as a confessor and preacher of Christ crucified"; he disapproved of the text for the occasion and thought the sermon too short by five or seven minutes.[4] However, he was told later that although John had respected his audience, yet he was much approved of, and "there was no doubt after your residence begins you will grow bolder".[5]

[1] "And they went to another village". Presumably he expounded the account of our Lord's attitude to the Samaritan village in the preceding verse. Benevolence was, of course, the keynote of the prevailing theology.

[2] J. Venn to H. Venn, July 23, 1792 (MS.).

[3] J. Venn to Mrs. Elliott, Aug. 4, 1792 (MS.).

[4] H. Venn to J. Venn, July 26, 1792 (MS.).

[5] H. Venn to J. Venn, Aug. 27, 1792 (MS.).

The experience of this first encounter with his congregation made John Venn consider carefully how he might prepare himself for his future work.

> I propose [he tells Nelly] to give myself to close study that I may be better prepared for the important sphere to which I am called. For indeed it is not a common situation. To preach before such men as Mr. Thornton, Wilberforce, Grant and others in a high station in life. To direct those whose pride and wealth renders them jealous of religious authority: to dwell amongst some of the most determined enemies of Christ and the Church of England, Socinians; to have the care at the same time of a great number of poor people, and to be myself encompassed by the snares of wealth. All these circumstances (and I might add others), do not meet in every situation, and where they do, require no common watchfulness, prudence, faith and zeal.[1]

In September he paid a second and longer visit to Clapham at Henry Thornton's suggestion, preaching in the church on two Sundays; he reports to his wife: "On the whole I am very much pleased with my visit to Clapham; it has tended more to reconcile me to my situation than anything else."[2] It also did much to reconcile the waverers in his congregation to him, for he told his father that there was no more talk in some quarters of leaving the church when his real ministry began.[3] This happier state of affairs was increased by Henry Thornton's hospitality and the opportunity it gave for both men to get to know one another. Venn must have been one of the earliest guests at Battersea Rise; he writes to his father: "Slept at Mr. H. Thornton's, who has got into his new house. . . . Mr. Wilberforce was not there being on a visit to a friend in Hertfordshire."[4]

On February 19 he attended the last of the meetings of the Clerical Society as Rector in Little Dunham, on the 28th his society met at the Rectory with him for the last time, and on March 17 he preached his farewell sermons, following them up by a farewell letter to his parishioners, reminding them of

[1] J. Venn to Mrs. Elliott, Aug. 4, 1792 (MS.).
[2] J. Venn to Mrs. J. Venn, Sept. 27, 1792 (MS.).
[3] J. Venn to H. Venn, Oct. 11, 1792 (MS.).
[4] J. Venn to H. Venn, Sept. 26, 1792 (MS.).

two points in his preaching; faith-union with Christ and the sanctifying influence of the Spirit of God.[1] The next day the Venns finished packing and began their journey south. His sister, Jane, who had come from Yelling to help, gives this rather sentimental picture of the scene. "The people all came to their doors with tears in their eyes, lifting up their hands to heaven, recommended him and his family, and begged the best of blessings might be showered upon him."[2] They reached Thetford the first evening and London next day, going to the Elliotts' new house at Paddington; Henry Venn was very concerned that they did this journey in a day, for Kitty was well advanced in pregnancy.[3]

When John Venn left Clapham as a babe in arms in 1760, it was a large village of about a thousand inhabitants, most of whom were wealthy; when he returned in 1793 it had grown into a popular and populous London suburb. Suburb may not be quite accurate as a description, for Clapham was still separated by country from London, but it was only four miles from Westminster Bridge and five from the City via Stockwell, Kennington and London Bridge. With better roads and a good coach service running four times a day before 1800,[4] the number of business men living in Clapham and going up to town every day increased annually. Besides these, as John Venn had told his sister, "a great number of poor people" had come to live at Clapham. In 1791 the population was 2,700 and it increased every year he was there; in 1811, two years before he died, it was just over 5,000; Lysons reckons that no other place on the outskirts of London grew so rapidly.[5] Part of the reason for the change was that a local magistrate had drained the Common and improved the roads, which before had been almost impassable; that was in 1751, but the effect was not fully felt till later. Not only was the Common drained but it was made more picturesque by the planting of a large number of trees, some of

[1] This open letter has been preserved in manuscript.

[2] Reported by H. Venn to his daughter, Mrs. J. Harvey, March 20, 1793 (MS.).

[3] Jane Catherine was born at Clapham on May 16, 1793.

[4] J. Telford, *A Sect that moved with the World* (1907), p. 78. Telford says that by 1827 there was a ten-minute service from Clapham to London.

[5] Daniel Lysons, *The Environs of London* (*Additions*), 1814. The account in this book on Clapham is partly based on information given to Lysons by John Venn.

them known as "cotton trees"; rumour had it that Captain Cook had brought them to Clapham from the Pacific Isles he had discovered.[1] There were also a number of ponds, two of which were filled in during the nineteenth century as they were thought to be a danger to health.

The church where Henry Venn had served as curate was the old church, dedicated to the Holy Trinity, situated on a hill on the London–Kingston road. It was far too small for the needs of the growing population and the vestry decided on "a new strong church"; this was built at a cost of £11,000, and opened on June 10, 1776.[2] The initiative came from John Thornton, who was chiefly responsible for the planning and building of the new church at a considerable cost to himself.[3] This is the church that stands on the Common to-day; it suffered severe damage in 1940 but has since been restored. The first organ and the portico were added in John Venn's time. The church was built in the style of the period of which it is a notable example. Lysons gives this description of the building as he knew it:

> Like most modern churches it had neither aisles nor chancel; the communion table is within a recess at the east end. There are spacious galleries on the north, south and west sides; the pews are all of foreign oak. The whole structure has a pleasing appearance, and is devoid of all unnecessary ornament. The length of the church is about a hundred feet, the breadth sixty-six; at the west end is a small dome and turret.[4]

About the aisles, Lysons was mistaken; there were three. Facing the centre aisle stood a tall three-decker pulpit which completely obscured the Holy Table. Stretching down the centre aisle were rows of upright benches for the poor. These were increased in number by Venn, as were the pews in the

[1] Henry Whitehead, *The Oldest Inhabitant*, a lecture given to the Clapham Literary and Scientific Institution in 1859, p. 7. Whitehead was curate of Clapham. His oldest inhabitant was an imaginary figure, through whose eyes he relates the changes that took place in Clapham over a long period.

[2] *Annals*, pp. 127–8; the old church was pulled down apart from one aisle and was used as a mortuary chapel till 1815, when it was finally demolished and St. Paul's Church was built on the site, *Annals*, pp. 176–7.

[3] J. C. V. Durell, *The Clapham Sect* in Clapham Guide, ed. J. Battley, 1938, p. 66.

[4] Lysons, *op. cit.*, p. 163.

galleries, all of which were let.[1] The entrance at the east end leads into a spacious vestry and committee room, "the latter of which has a fire-place and having a large door opening into the church, which one let at half a year each to those who prefer that accommodation to seats".[2] Venn possibly allowed this worship in additional comfort, for the rest of his church, which held 1,400 people, was usually full and an extra beadle had to be employed to superintend the parking of carriages.[3] Such large numbers gave considerable work to the trustees of the church committee whose responsibility it was to allot the seating. The system was that gentlemen could hire their own pews. A certain number of seats were reserved for servants and provision was also made for the children from the Charity School.

What his policy was to be as Rector of Clapham was a matter which, as we have seen, exercised John Venn's mind considerably. In this he was not wanting in good advice from good friends. Stillingfleet writes with real insight on the value of his experience at Dunham and on what seems required of him at Clapham:

> Your talents have been comparatively dormant in the very circumscribed situation of Little Dunham, and though God has not been wanting in making use of you for good there, yet this was designed but as a place of initiation to lead you on and gradually to overcome that timidity which is so interwoven with your constitution, and might have been unable to have stood the shock of such a call as the present at an earlier period.

With regard to his approach to his "educated and worldly congregation" at Clapham, he advises:

> Be direct and simple—speak the truth and error will be clear. Be true to the Church especially as you may be sure you come under the disadvantage of a character suspicious here, though most unjustly. But so it is and must be expected to be from your connexions. Take care of all innovations at first, otherwise they

[1] "We go on but poorly at Clapham. A considerable increase of congregation, another row of pews in the galleries, quite round the church and all of them let, fresh benches put up for the accommodation of the poor and sometimes well filled." J. Venn to E. Edwards, Aug. 1, 1794 (MS.).

[2] R. de Rudolph, *Clapham and the Clapham Sect* (1927), p. 15.

[3] R. de Rudolph, *The Churches of Holy Trinity, Clapham*, in Clapham Guide, p. 59.

will think you have come to turn all topsy-turvy. Let them know your sound principles before you proceed to these things and then you will be able to make such alterations as you see necessary with the assistance of the more intelligent. Another thing I beg leave to suggest is be yourself the dispenser of your own Gospel. By this I mean don't let any stranger into your pulpit for some time.

If Venn has some week-day services let them be devoted to expounding the Homilies or the Catechism or some part of the Liturgy.[1] Robinson also warns him that not every minister is a suitable preacher for Clapham and that substitutes must be chosen carefully. He also saw that chief difficulties would come from "your opulent parishioners"; these should not be offended needlessly but visited occasionally, and he is to be afraid of lowering his standards to theirs: "be afraid of too familiar intercourse, and never forget your character and office when in their company. Let them at least be convinced that your religion is not confined to the pulpit."[2] In his father's letters the critical spirit of the reply to the questions raised by the first sermon completely vanishes. In January 1793 Henry Venn visited Clapham on a Sunday; later in the week, writing "in a coffee house, amongst Jamaica captains, and in a great din",[3] he put on paper some thoughts to encourage his son. "I beseech you", he writes, "to understand how very plainly has the choice and appointment of you to this service appeared. The judgement of all who consider it is but one—that you are, if ever man was, called and chosen to the work. Moreover, all agree you are eminently fitted for the situation."[4]

The cautious tactics which Venn had adopted while preaching to his congregation before he had come into residence as their Rector, Richard Cecil advised him to continue after his induction; it was necessary, Cecil thought, to win the complete confidence of the congregation and gradually to lead them to "clearer views of the Gospel". Wilberforce on the other hand advocated an outright challenge from the start. Venn sub-

[1] J. Stillingfleet to J. Venn, Aug. 27, 1792 (MS.).
[2] T. Robinson to J. Venn, July 27, 1792 (MS.).
[3] *Life of H. Venn*, p. 517.
[4] *Ibid.*, p. 514.

mitted the question to the Little Dunham Clerical Society on the eve of his departure in the following form: "In what way shall I begin to preach at Clapham; shall I follow Cecil's conciliatory advice or Mr. Wilberforce's?" Only one thought Cecil's approach the right one, the other seven were in favour of Wilberforce's. It was this latter that he adopted, as his first sermon preached on his induction clearly shows.

His text was 1 Corinthians 2: 3, "I was with you in weakness and in fear and in much trembling" (a very apt description of the nervous preacher as he stood before his new congregation). His subject, "The importance and difficulties of the Christian Ministry". The sermon is lucid and well-reasoned, but there is no diluting of its Evangelical theology; had Henry Venn been in the congregation he would have been fully satisfied. The exercise of the Christian ministry, Venn maintains, has effects both on the nation and on the congregations of the Church; in both it is a case of like priest, like people. In the case of individuals

> The Gospel is the great remedy supplied by God for the disorders introduced into the world by sin; and the dispensing of this remedy is entrusted to His Ministers. They are the stewards of His mysteries, the shepherds of His flock, and labourers together with God. He has chosen to commit the treasure of His Gospel to "earthen vessels". He communicates spiritual health by the hand of their fellow-sinners in the same manner as He healed the sick by the hands of His Apostles and Prophets. Wherever, therefore, His Gospel is faithfully delivered, His blessing may be expected to attend it. The sinner will be awakened, grace will be imparted, faith will be strengthened, and hope enlivened. The fruits of love to God and of cheerful obedience to His law will be produced, and a spirit of benevolence and charity to man will be diffused. These, even if estimated as referring to this life only, are important benefits; but they become invaluable when referred to eternity. They constitute the purest and most perfect happiness of this world, and are the earnest of glory in the next. But to point out the value of these blessings is to show not only the importance of the office of the Minister, by whom they are dispensed, but his responsibility and his danger. Let him ponder upon eternity, let him estimate the value of the soul and the worth of spiritual

> blessings, and he cannot enter upon his sacred office without fear and trembling.[1]

As the sermon gathers pace the preacher spares neither himself nor his hearers; this is what he has to say of the difficulties of the Christian Ministry:

> It is a difficult service in its own nature. Were the work of a preacher indeed confined to the delivery of a moral discourse, this would not be an arduous task. But a Minister of the Gospel has much more to do. He will endeavour, under Divine Grace, to bring every individual in his congregation to live no longer to himself, but unto Him who died for us. But here the passions, prejudices, and perhaps the temporal interests of men combine to oppose his success. It is not easy to obtain any influence over the mind of another; but to obtain such an influence as to direct it contrary to the natural current of its desires and passions, is a work of the highest difficulty. Yet such is the work of a Minister. . . .
>
> We have to convey unpleasant tidings; to persuade to what is disagreeable; to effect not only a reformation in the conduct of men, and a regulation of their passions, but, what is of still higher difficulty, a change in their good opinion of themselves. Nay, further we have not merely to "wrestle against flesh and blood but against principalities and powers, against the rulers of the darkness of this world, against spiritual wickedness in high places". "Who is sufficient for these things?" For this office the Christian Minister may in himself "have no resources above those of any of his congregation", their weaknesses are his weaknesses, he must therefore undertake his work in weakness, fear and much trembling, but knowing that it may yet be effectual, for it is in weakness that Christ's strength is always made perfect.[2]

The sermon was well-received and by some well-remembered; when, after his father's death in 1813, Henry Venn sought Henry Thornton's help in selecting sermons for publication, Thornton begged him "to seek for this one particularly".[3] As he began so he continued. "As to the success of my preaching," he tells Edwards in July, "I can say little. I am told it meets

[1] J. Venn, *Sermons,* Vol. I, pp. 4—5.
[2] *Ibid.*, pp. 8–9.
[3] H. Venn's Editorial Notes (MS.).

with universal approbation and the church is evidently better attended."[1] In November Henry Venn writes to Kitty: "Don't tell J. V. unless you feel it right, that his preaching is very acceptable. His brother, Elliott, thinks he is amongst the best preachers."[2] Indeed the three volumes of the sermons that have been preserved show that as a preacher he was quite outstanding, and the directness of his challenge seems to have won him hearers rather than driven them away. In the early summer Henry Venn was in Clapham. He reports to Kitty Harvey: "Your brother is become a good speaker and is heard from one end of the church to the other. What is best of all, he deeply feels the weight of the charge of near three thousand souls."[3] According to another letter, written about the same time, over a thousand of these were in church.[4]

In the first ten years of his ministry at Clapham John Venn paid considerable respect to the intelligence of his congregation and some to their suspicion of his Evangelical views. His sermons, although retaining their distinctive Evangelical emphasis, were mainly apologetic in character, attempting to demonstrate the reasonableness of faith in Christ. In 1804 he informed Henry Jowett that he was contemplating a change of tactics; henceforth he intended to appeal to the will and consciences of his people as well to their intellects.[5]

The church was well attended and, as we have seen, congregations increased from the start of his ministry. After he had been in the parish two months he gave Edwards this impression of the situation he had inherited and the task before him.

> My congregation is pretty large, but I am extremely sorry that scarcely any of the poor come to church. The poor are very numerous here and extremely dissolute. They have lost even the form of religion and though their wages are very high[6] and the benevolence of the rich great, yet many of them live in a state of

[1] J. Venn to E. Edwards, July 24, 1793 (MS.).
[2] H. Venn to Mrs. J. Venn, Nov. 1793 (MS.).
[3] H. Venn to Mrs. K. Harvey, May 16, 1793 (MS.).
[4] H. Venn to Mrs. King, June 1793 (MS.).
[5] J. Venn to H. Jowett, July 21, 1804 (MS.). This policy was obviously adopted, judging by some of the published sermons; unfortunately these are not dated.
[6] Wages in the London area would seem high to anyone coming from rural Norfolk.

extreme wretchedness by reason of their drunkenness and other vices. What can be done to reclaim them? They are almost too hardened to be softened by speaking to. However, I do not speak in my own strength, nor my own words; and the Lord will work I trust upon some of them to their good. I am more pleased with the children. I catechize them in the manner I saw you do yours, and am much pleased with their proficiency. This takes up an hour or upwards at the school every Sunday evening, and I shall continue it throughout the year.

With respect to the rich, I yet meet with nothing but respect; this however will not, I think, hold long. They are very regular and punctual in their attendance at church, and as far as the outside of religion goes, very exemplary. But alas, here they rest, and I fear that it will be very hard to convince them that the power of religion must be felt in the heart, as well as the form of it kept up in their lives.[1]

Opportunities for convincing the rich of "the power of religion" came to Venn the same way as they come to any other parish priest. "Thornton Astall", Mrs. Henry Thornton tells Hannah More, "seems now to be reaching the close of a luxurious, prosperous life. It is a great comfort that he sees Mr. Venn every day."[2] To meet the general situation outlined in his letter to Edwards, Venn increased the number of services, or, it might be more accurate to say, the opportunities for instruction and evangelistic preaching. When he arrived at Clapham there was a morning service taken by the curate for an absentee rector, and an afternoon service taken by the lecturer, the Reverend John Sharpe.[3] To these Sunday services Venn added what he called "a parlour lecture" on Friday nights in the Rectory; this was the Clapham successor to the similar institution at Little Dunham.

However, this week-night meeting did not do much to solve his most obstinate problem, that of reaching the poor. To this end Venn gradually introduced what in fact became a third Sunday service. Such an innovation was unheard of and was

[1] J. Venn to E. Edwards, May 24, 1793 (MS.).

[2] Feb. 2, 1799, quoted in Thornton Wigan Book (MS.). Thornton Astall was a relation of the Thornton family; like John and Samuel Thornton he was a member of the Russia Company.

[3] See p. 131.

only established in the teeth of opposition. Because of pluralism and non-residence in the Hanoverian church only about half the churches in England were able to make provision for Matins and Evensong each Sunday;[1] further, in many of the churches where Evensong was read in the afternoon there was no sermon.[2] For a parish which already had two services both with sermons on a Sunday to be required to have a third was revolutionary in the extreme and smacked of Methodism; hence, to achieve his purpose, Venn moved with caution. After a year of catechizing the children in the school on Sunday evenings, he decided to hold the class in church. This could not be done in the recently-built parish church because, there being no expectation of evening services, there was no adequate provision for lighting the building. However, it was possible to use the old parish church. Here John Venn started on Sunday evenings what he called his "catechetical lectures", which were intended for parents as well as their children.

> I hear [he reports to Edwards] of some good being done by my preaching. The church is well-filled and my catechetical lecture is crowded. My plan is to ask the children questions in the Church Catechism or rather to speak to them in a familiar manner about it, and to explain and to enforce the truth it contains. This I intend as much for the instruction of the parents as for their children. I then ascend the pulpit and read a lecture in the plainest manner with very close addresses to the conscience. Walker's Fifty-Two Sermons[3] are my model, and I often make considerable extracts from him. The place generally contains, I should suppose, two hundred people, as it is as full as it can hold. Some of the higher class attend. . . . Henry Thornton has been three times. I have great hope that this will be more useful than an evening sermon in the new church.[4]

Increasing attendance made Venn change his mind, and within a few months he had a chandelier set up in the new church and announced his intention of holding his Sunday evening lecture there. It was this that caused the uproar. A

[1] N. Sykes, *Church and State in England in the XVIIIth Century*, p. 239.

[2] *Ibid.*, p. 243.

[3] S. Walker, *Fifty-Two Sermons on the Baptismal Covenant* (1763). These were intended for adults rather than for children and are deeply theological.

[4] J. Venn to E. Edwards, May 20, 1794 (MS.).

protest meeting was held at the Plough Inn by members of a card club which met there on Sunday evenings and who felt their vested interests threatened by a rival attraction; they said that they were "shocked to think that a matter so pernicious to the morals of the place, so favourable to the system of intrigue and debauchery, so subversive to good order in families, and so likely to spread amongst the lowest orders of society a factious, zealous spirit, etc. should be proposed,and especially that it should be proposed to be done by me without the consent and against the will of the parish."[1] This protest shows the way that ordinary middle-class people thought that Evangelical "enthusiasm" would produce the same undesirable results as Jacobinism; it also suggests that John Venn was getting "the lower orders" to church on Sunday evenings.

Venn therefore resolved to refer his case to the Vestry the following Sunday in this letter:

To the Inhabitants of the Parish of Clapham assembled in Vestry.

Gentlemen,

Your attendance has been requested to-day for the purpose of considering the propriety of my establishing a Sunday evening lecture in the parish church.

It will not, I hope, be censured as pertinacious in me, if I maintain the right of the rector of the church to establish such a lecture by his own authority, since I am supported in it by the best legal information I could obtain on that subject; but the expediency of exercising that right at the present time is a different question, and it is this which I now willingly submit to your decision, being well assured that an entire harmony between a minister and his parishioners is the best foundation for that general good which it is the object of his labours to produce.

I am aware that objections have frequently been made to evening lectures, and I am ready to acknowledge that some particular bad effects have sometimes taken place in consequence of them: but I still think after mature consideration, that those effects may be prevented by prudent precautions on the part of heads of families and of the minister; and that, allowing them still to exist to some degree, they are more than overbalanced by the

[1] J. Venn to E. Edwards, Jan 3, 1795 (MS.). The fact that the chandelier had been erected without a faculty gave further grounds for complaint.

general good which a greater degree of religious instruction and the formation of habits of piety are likely to produce.

The morning and afternoon services may perhaps be thought sufficient but when it is considered how many are prevented by necessary avocations from attendance upon these; and how much among the lower classes especially, the misspending of the evening more than balances the advantages of the day, I think the establishment of an additional evening service will not appear to be precluded.[1]

The letter concludes by saying "expenses will be defrayed by a few persons" who are not going to allow the afternoon Lecturer to suffer from diminished subscriptions and also that his own decision to have such a lecture in no way binds his successor.

Venn was not present at the meeting, which lasted three hours, but his wise and restrained letter secured him a majority of forty-three to five. The Clerk was asked to inform the Rector that the Meeting approved of his proposal, wished it good success and thanked him "for exonerating the parish from the expenses attending it".[2] There the matter closed. Venn began his evening lectures in the new church the following spring and his congregations, morning and evening, according to the report he gave Edwards eighteen months later, were "manifestly increasing".[3]

Venn's successful use of the Catechism at this service for children and adults alike was very much in line with a recommendation of some of the earlier Hanoverian bishops. These urged that in those churches, fortunate enough to have Evening Prayer read each Sunday, but where a sermon was not customary, an exposition of the Catechism should be given in the place of a sermon; this was in fact required by the 59th canon.[4]

[1] Clapham Vestry Minutes, Vol. 6, pp. 293–5; quoted in *Annals*, p. 133.

[2] *Ibid.*

[3] J. Venn to E. Edwards, Sept. 1796 (MS.).

[4] Sykes, *op. cit.*, p. 243. The 59th canon requires "every parson, vicar, or curate upon every Sunday and holy-day before Evening Prayer" for the space of half an hour or more, to "examine and instruct the youth and ignorant persons of his parish in the Ten Commandments, Articles of Belief, and in the Lord's Prayer," and to "hear, instruct and teach them the catechism as set forth in the Book of Common Prayer."

Some clergy adopted this practice for Lent, but nowhere does it seem to have been used throughout the year.

In an article written for the *Christian Observer* Venn urged the revival of "this excellent custom" which "gave the children an interest in the worship as a part of the congregation: afforded to the minister an excellent opportunity of familiarly instructing the elder part of his audience, while he addressed the younger, and . . . served to constitute a direct and visible pastoral relation between him and the 'lambs of his flock', which was calculated to inspire them with reverence for him, and to give him an interest in their welfare."[1]

How long John Venn used the Catechism as the framework of his evening lecture we do not know, but we do know that for six years, beginning in 1800, he devoted each Sunday morning in Lent to "catechism lecture for young people"; he then moved this lecture to Friday evenings in Lent and preceded it by catechizing the younger children in the school at 4 p.m. on the same day. In 1806 the titles of the first four lectures were (1) The Grand Principle of Religion, (2) Duties of Children to their Parents, (3) Dangers and Snares of the Young, (4) Necessity of Self-Command.

It is not surprising that a clergyman so careful in the instruction of children and young people should have shown the same care in preparing candidates for Confirmation. Venn refused an invitation to attend a May meeting of the Little Dunham Clerical Society, saying, "we have about that time a Confirmation and I have found no seasons so profitable to us as those in which I have prepared my young people for that ordinance".[2]

The preparation he gave was extremely thorough even by modern standards; in the eighteenth century it was quite remarkable. Every Friday for seven weeks he gave a Confirmation lecture in church; on the Monday following the Confirmation itself he gave a further lecture. He was usually able to present two hundred to two hundred and fifty candidates to the bishop; these vast numbers were partly occasioned by the rare occasions on which the Bishop of Winchester was in the

[1] J. Venn, "On the Proper Mode of Conducting Charity Schools", *Christian Observer*, Sept. 1804, Vol. 3, p. 541.

[2] J. Venn to E. Edwards, April 4, 1808 (MS.).

north-east area of his diocese administering Confirmation. As far as the records show, John Venn only had five opportunities of presenting candidates during the twenty years he was at Clapham.[1] At what age most of these candidates were presented it is difficult to say, but infrequency of opportunity must have made for considerable variety. Venn's own children give some indication. Henry was confirmed in 1811 when he was fifteen; his three elder sisters three years earlier, when Catherine was seventeen, Jane fifteen and Emelia fourteen. Confirmation in their cases was not followed promptly by first Communion, for it was not till Christmas Day 1810, that their father's diary records: "This day introduced my dear daughters, Catherine, Jane and Emelia to the Lord's table. May the great Head of the Church receive them as members of His mystical Body."

John Venn's ministry at Clapham meant not only a revival of Evangelical preaching and teaching, but of sacramental life. The Holy Communion was celebrated every second Sunday morning in the month and on Good Friday. The registers show that usually more people communicated on Good Friday than on Easter Day, and that the number of communicants on those days was not much in excess of those on the other Sundays.[2] The records do not go back beyond 1800 but between that date and 1813 communicants rose steadily from about a hundred to over one hundred and fifty. Cunningham says that Venn "enlarged" the "altar" for his increasing flock of communicants. It was to meet the problem of regularly communicating such numbers that John Venn adopted the practice of saying the words of administration to two people at a time instead of one, as was done formerly. He sets out his reasons for doing this

[1] J. Venn, Diary (MS.).

[2] We should not be surprised at the absence of Communion Services on Saints' Days or even on Ascension Day. Few churches in the 17th and 18th centuries had services of Holy Communion more frequently than once a month. It seems that there was such a demand for the Easter Sacrament that there was a tendency to spread its celebration over three days: Good Friday, Easter Day and Low Sunday. In such circumstances it is not surprising that in Evangelical churches the service on Good Friday should be particularly well-attended. There is no reason to think, as Overton suggests, that the 18th century church lapsed into the practice of Good Friday communions (*The English Church in the Nineteenth Century*, p. 129), but that few, if any, questioned the propriety of what the Prayer Book provided till the Oxford Movement when Roman custom was invoked.

in a long letter to John Owen, the first Secretary of the Bible Society.

> I think there can be no doubt whatever in the mind of any person that in the original institution of the sacrament the words "This is my body, take and eat", "Drink ye all", etc. were delivered only once, generally to all, and not repeated individually to each disciple, when the bread and wine were delivered. It appears equally clear, I think also, that the practice of the primitive church was to repeat the words to each table and then to break the bread and give a piece of it to each communicant, and thus they being many by being partakers of one loaf (ἄρτος) were one. The repetition of the words came in with and naturally followed the doctrine of transubstantiation, and the nature of the Lord's Supper was in some measure changed by it. It was no longer considered as a communion but as a sacrifice. It was not the communion of saints with their common Lord, but the solitary reception of pardon through the sacrifice of the Mass.
>
> We, however, it may be said, who are ministers of the church have nothing to do with primitive usage, but must confine ourselves to the prescribed ritual of our own church. It is true—but wherever a slight deviation may become necessary, it is well that this deviation accords with the primitive and scriptural mode, and it is in that view only that I mention the ancient usage. It appears to me to be vastly more solemn and proper to deliver the words only once to each table in a loud and impressive manner and then to administer the elements in common rather than to whisper the words to each and give the elements as it were in private. I have known this done in several churches with a most impressive effect but the prejudice of the people will not bear it in many cases, and in them we must give way to those prejudices, or accommodate as far as we can in a point in which the usage and the directions of the church are generally against us.
>
> The experiment was tried in Mr. Daubeny's church I think, but the people would not bear it, and the bishop being appealed to, I understand, said that he approved it in his judgement yet he could not sanction it as not being according to the Liturgy. I might, however, have asked his Lordship why he and all the rest of the bishops lay their hands in Confirmation upon six or eight, or even more at once, repeating the form only once, when the rubric is express that the bishop should lay his hand upon the head of every one severally saying "Defend, Oh Lord, this thy child, or this thy servant". Another clergyman was also compelled

to abandon this practice in consequence of the clamour of the people.

There is, however, a middle way which has been more frequently adopted, against which the prejudices of the people have not been so strong, namely, to administer to *two* at once, and this shortens the labour one half which is a very material saving. I adopted this at Clapham first submitting it to a vestry who made no objection to it; and when thus sanctioned I did not hear of any objection being made to it afterwards, but on the contrary all were pleased with it, as all had felt the inconvenience of waiting so long before. My mode is to give to two at once saying, "the body etc." which was given "preserve your bodies and souls". The same is done at all the parishes in Hull, and everybody is, I believe, satisfied with this mode. Possibly three might receive it at once in this way without exciting too much opposition.

You see that I rest the whole matter upon the degree of accommodation which we ought to give to prejudice and the degree of strict conformity in letter, which we ought to use, to the ritual. Your friend must take care lest, by gaining this point, he should not lose much more in essential ones.[1]

Here we can see the origin of the mode of administration more or less as it is practised to-day in most Anglican churches. As we notice from this letter, it was adopted to meet the practical problem created by a large increase in the number of regular communicants occasioned by the Evangelical Revival. It is significant that it should have been believed on historical and theological grounds by John Venn and also by a strong High Churchman like Archdeacon Daubeny that the words of administration should be said to each row together and not to each individual communicant. Modern research would not substantiate this.[2] It is pleasing to see that when making "deviations" from Prayer Book rubrics Venn should try to make certain that they conformed to primitive and Scriptural

[1] J. Venn to J. Owen (undated letter in MS.).

[2] See Gregory Dix, *The Shape of the Liturgy* (1945), pp. 136–7.

John Venn of Hereford adopted Archdeacon Daubeny's practice, but came into conflict with his bishop, Dr. Grey. When Venn used his father's argument with regard to the analogous case of Confirmation, the bishop replied he always confirmed each candidate separately. Consequently Confirmations in the Hereford diocese lasted for hours and Communion Service at St. Peter's, Hereford on one occasion took from 11 a.m. to 4 p.m. *Annals*, p. 202.

practice; and also that he should go no further with alterations than he could carry his congregation with him. It is also worth noting the way he criticized any idea of "the solitary reception of pardon" whether it came from Catholic or Protestant sources. The little dig at the bishops for their failure to adhere to the Confirmation rubric is delightful, although the problem of large numbers created at Confirmations the same problem as Venn is discussing with regard to Holy Communion.

The impression gained from this letter is that at Clapham Parish Church the Holy Communion was celebrated with a reverence and care which would commend itself to any High Churchman. In this revival of careful and regular Communion services John Venn was not alone among Evangelical clergy; the same high standard is evident amongst his friends, especially Simeon at Holy Trinity, Cambridge, and Daniel Wilson at Islington.

In John Venn's published sermons, teaching given on the Holy Communion is incidental and extremely sparse, but sometimes on Sacrament Sundays he devoted some of his address to the subject.[1] Henry Venn writes to Edward Venn: "What pleasure did I feel in reading that, when you were at Clapham on Sunday, you were well instructed before you met at the table of the Lord. My prayers had been warmly presented that the name of the Lord Jesus might be magnified, and many might eat the flesh of the Son of Man and drink his blood."[2] Was it Venn's instruction that led Henry Thornton to write in his diary in Holy Week 1795: "I am now preparing to receive the Sacrament, which for various causes, I have for a long time not done"?[3] John Venn's diaries bear eloquent testimony to his diligence in taking Communion to the sick. In 1812 John Bowdler was taken ill at Battersea Rise; Venn called twice during the week. On the second occasion he made this note in his diary: "Tea at Mr. H. Thornton's and administered the Sacrament to Mr. J. Bowdler."[4]

There are other signs of a reinvigorated Anglicanism showing

[1] See *Sermons*, Vol. 3, pp. 55, 165–6.
[2] H. Venn to E. Venn, Nov. 12, 1793, quoted in *Life of H. Venn*, p. 524.
[3] Thornton Wigan Book (MS.).
[4] Diary, June 16, 1812 (MS.).

itself in the parish of Holy Trinity, Clapham, during the incumbency of John Venn. Like his father he dearly loved the Liturgy and devoted at least one course of sermons to the exposition of it. Further than this, he found the writing of an article for the *Christian Observer* on Charity Schools[1] a suitable place for showing how much more was required of the Anglican parson than preaching and reading prayers, and in another article in the same journal on the observance of Lent he extolled the virtues of the Christian Year.[2] In the former he writes:

> I would not undervalue the benefit of preaching: it is one part, if you please, the most important part, of a clergyman's duty; but it should not therefore supersede the rest. A clergyman with cure of souls is a public instructor set apart by God and man for the instruction and improvement of his flock. He is responsible to God and to his country for the morals of his peculiar charge as it is in his power to influence them; and this obligation surely requires him to use every endeavour in his power for their religious improvement. It is the chief advantage of an establishment of religion in any country, that in every district into which the country is divided, there will be an individual regularly appointed to superintend the moral state of the persons in that district, to devote himself to their religious improvement, to watch against all the inroads of vice and corruption. In the discharge of this duty, it surely is not enough to read the appropriate prayers and deliver a weekly sermon. Far more active exertions should be made; every probable means of improvement should be tried, and the spirit of the law as well as the letter should be fulfilled.[3]

In the other article, which he entitles "On the Observance of Lent as Preparatory to Good Friday and Easter", he writes:

> The value of the Christian Year is that it draws us away from the preoccupations of a busy life to better things, and helps to fix the attention . . . at certain seasons on certain events. The six Sundays in Lent show how truly evangelical our Church is, ever placing before our view the Redeemer in His sufferings or triumphs, as the only hope of man, the centre of all His thoughts, the ever-present object of faith, of desire and of love. Most people

[1] *Christian Observer*, May 1805, Vol. 5.
[2] *Ibid.*, September 1804, Vol. 3.
[3] *Christian Observer*, Vol. 3, p. 541.

> will disregard this season, the respectable will find excuse for not keeping it, the formalist will regard the letter but not the spirit. A few will gladly embrace the opportunity of improvement which is afforded to them, and endeavour, to the best of their power, to profit by the excellent advice of the Church.[1]

He says that some might question the right of the Church to appoint seasons; to which his reply would be that a man might devote a day in quiet meditation in preparation "for the better celebration of the death of the Lord"; he might ask others to join him; there could be no objection to this; this is exactly what the Church does. "The ordinances of the Church are not placed on the same footing as divine appointments, yet it is evident, that there is due to them, when not in themselves unreasonable, a degree of reverence and obedience, which no good man will refuse to pay."[2] (This latter sentence reveals the limits of Venn's conception of the Church, which is further shown in his description of the Church as "the highest conceivable human authority".)[3]

Further, he was concerned that the observance of Lent had declined within his lifetime: "The pulpits in many churches, during my own remembrance, were hung with black: many persons put on mourning: all public amusements were suspended: a restriction which even yet in part prevails: on Wednesday and Friday salt-fish was the principal diet at most tables, and a man would have been esteemed profane who did not regulate his conduct in some degree by a conformity to the customs of the Church. Probably in all this there might be too much attention paid to outward forms; but if this were the case at that period there is evidently too little paid at present."[4]

[1] *Christian Observer*, May 1805, Vol. 4, p. 143.

[2] *Christian Observer*, Vol. 4, p. 145.

[3] *Christian Observer*, May 1805, p. 145.

[4] C. J. Abbey gives a similar picture though different in some of its detail; he says that there was a "tolerably general feeling throughout society that Lent was not quite what other seasons are, and ought not to be wholly disregarded. There were few marriages in Lent, comparatively few entertainments, public or private; in some cathedral towns the music of the choir was silent. And just as Sunday is sometimes honoured by the putting on of a better dress, so the fashionable world would often pay that easiest show of homage to the sacredness of the Lenten season, not by curtailing in any way their ordinary pleasures, but by going to the theatre in mourning". C. J. Abbey and J. H. Overton, *The English Church in the Eighteenth Century* (1878), Vol. 2, p. 449.

Venn suggests that his readers should not only be regular at their attendance at public worship during Lent, but that they should lengthen their daily devotions, giving time to self-examination, writing down their sins and keeping in view Christ's death which they "will celebrate on Good Friday". Abstinence in food and drink may help some but not others; each must discover what form of discipline will help him most, and "chiefly direct his efforts to subduing his besetting sin; for the covetous this will mean giving lavishly to the poor, for the lazy an attempt to overcome love of ease, and for others the avoidance of company and frivolous conversation, and the curbing of vanity". Venn suggests that private prayer should begin with the Confession taken from the Communion Service; this should be followed by a prayer for pardon and a petition for grace to use Lent to strengthen repentance and enliven faith in Christ.[1]

There is every indication that by the beginning of the nineteenth century clergy were making a minimum use of the Christian Year.[2] How far Venn went against the stream in his own practice is difficult to determine apart from this careful observance of Lent, but we know that towards the end of his life he makes references in his diary to saints' days on which prayers were said, presumably in church, and at least on one occasion he devoted a series of sermons to expounding the Liturgy. Even if his practice with regard to the frequency of the celebration of the Holy Communion was not in advance of other conscientious clergy of his day, he was one of the creative forces in the movement which threw up Daniel Wilson who, at Islington in 1828, had "three full services in the church on Sundays and great festival days, and one in the week, besides morning prayers on Wednesdays, Fridays and Saints' Days", together with the Sacrament at eight and noon each Sunday.[3]

The use of the Psalter in worship was another matter that

[1] *Christian Observer*, Vol. 4, pp. 147–8.

[2] J. H. Overton and H. M. Relton, *A History of the English Church from the Accession of George I to the end of the Eighteenth century* (1924), p. 296.

[3] Bateman, *The Life of Daniel Wilson* (1860), Vol. I, p. 266. Wilson's parish was larger than Venn's and the problem of accommodating communicants correspondingly greater. For instance on one Sunday in 1827 there were 238 communicants at the morning service.

engaged Venn's attention. Several writers have described the antics of the parish clerk whose duty it was to lead the singing of the Psalms, and of the pathetic attempts of a few of the congregation to follow his singing of the doggerel of Sternhold and Hopkins' metrical version of the Psalter. Venn, who derived much of his own spiritual strength from the Psalter, decided to publish his own version and in 1800 there appeared "Select Portions of Psalms extracted from various versions and adapted to Public Worship, with an appendix containing Hymns for the principal festivals of the Church of England (for the use of Clapham Church)." On March 1st the following year he introduced this version to his congregation. An innovation he owed to Methodism was a watch-night service on New Year's Eve.

Although in the eighteenth century less attention was paid to the Christian Year than to-day, the number of days appointed by the State to be observed by the Church were more frequent; these were generally days of national thanksgiving and fast days devoted to humiliation and prayer. During the French Wars one day in Lent was set aside for a general fast day, which was the equivalent of the National Days of Prayer familiar to us; at Clapham they were diligently observed. In the autumn of 1803, when Napoleon was assembling invasion barges on the coasts of France and the Netherlands, George III ordered that October 19 should be set apart as a special day for "humiliation and prayer on account of the present circumstances of our country". In addition to this the first Friday of each month was to be observed as a fast day "on account of the national sins and our share in them", and every Sunday evening "some part of the time between 7.30 and 9.30 should be allotted to the office of intercession for the security and prosperity of our country".[1] This latter time was fixed to allow those who had been to church the opportunity of including special intercessions in their private and family prayers at home. John Venn wrote an article in the *Christian Observer* on the duty of keeping these days and composed this prayer for family use:

O Lord, be favourable to our land. Save us from the evil designs of all our enemies. Let no foreign foe be suffered to invade

[1] *Christian Observer*, September 1802, Vol. 2, p. 574.

our coasts—to spread amongst us the evils of anarchy and despotism. Suffer no internal enemies to sow the seeds of domestic strife; or by kindling the flames of rebellion to overthrow our happy constitution and subject us to religious or civil tyranny.[1]

An example of a thanksgiving service is to be found in the entry for December 5, 1805 in the Clapham Register which reads: "J. Venn. General Thanksgiving for Lord Nelson's Victory off Cape Trafalgar in which he and Sir Richard Strachan took and destroyed 24 Sail of the Line. A collection made afterwards for the wounded and the widows and orphans amounting to £189 - 4 - 6."[2]

Typical also of the "age of benevolence" was the preaching at Clapham of annual charity sermons; some of these were for Bible distributing societies or the parochial schools, but more often they had as their object some society with a title more typical of the generous spirit of the eighteenth century such as the Charity Schools, societies for the deaf and dumb, the indigent blind and the lying-in charity. Sometimes there was an attempt to meet a special emergency as in 1809 when £125 was given, after a charity sermon, to the "distressed Swedes",[3] or in 1813 when £65 was given to "distressed manufacturers"; probably the society helped in the latter case was the "Association for the Relief of the Manufacturing Poor" which had been founded by Wilberforce the previous year.[4]

Most of the distinguished Evangelical divines appeared in Clapham pulpit during the twenty years of Venn's incumbency. Isaac Milner and Thomas Gisborne were frequent guests of Wilberforce and their names appear in the register on several occasions. Other names that occur there are Richard Cecil, Robinson of Leicester, Dikes of Hull, Legh Richmond, Basil Woodd and John Owen, and of course, very frequently, Edward

[1] *Christian Observer*, September 1802, p. 577. The fear of internal enemies is most significant. It shows how widely the middle class shared Pitt's views of a revolutionary rising in England of "the lower orders".

[2] Clapham Parish Register (MS.).

[3] This would be as a consequence of the war that Czar Alexander I of Russia made on Sweden, 1808–9, following his alliance with Napoleon at Tilsit. Peace was signed by Russia and Sweden in September 1809; the sermon was preached in February.

[4] Halévy, *A History of the English People in the Nineteenth Century*, Vol. 2, *The Liberal Awakening* (1949 edn.), p. 12.

Edwards. Farish and Simeon both preached for Venn, the latter on at least three occasions. In June 1805 Henry Martyn occupied the pulpit two months before he sailed for India; Thomas Thomason, who followed Martyn out to India as a chaplain, was another visiting preacher. A significant entry is that of Henry Campbell, late Rector of St. John's Church, Antigua, which suggests that John Venn's friendliness to the S.P.G. extended further than public pronouncements. John Jebb,[1] while still an Irish country rector, preached two Sundays at Clapham in August 1809. Amongst visitors towards the end of Venn's time two are noteworthy: G. C. Gorham, then Fellow of Queens' College, Cambridge, and William Dealtry, Professor of Mathematics at the East India Company College at Haileybury, who succeeded Venn as Rector of Clapham.

Frequent and recurring illness kept John Venn out of his pulpit, and often out of his church, for months at a time. It was for this reason alone that he came to employ his two curates, Hugh Pearson from 1803 to 1805, and John Cunningham from 1809 to 1811. At other times Venn considered he had no need of a curate as he regarded his lecturer, John Sharpe, as a member of the staff. Venn had originally offered Sharpe the curacy, but he refused it. Nevertheless he seems to have done work in the parish other than on Sundays. He and Venn were on excellent terms; he retained the lectureship after Venn's death and as a sign of the family's affection was given the Rector's robes. Sharpe was one of the earliest subscribers to the C.M.S.

Pearson was engaged when Venn was recovering from his long illness (1802–3); the original arrangement was that he should stay six months, in fact he stayed two years. Hugh Pearson was an Oxford man of considerable ability, who had been curate in Cecil's country parishes of Chobham and Bisley. While at Clapham he married Charles Elliott's eldest daughter[2] and earned John Venn's praise as an "excellent preacher". At the beginning of 1805 he resigned, and Venn, apparently feeling fitter, seems to have taken no immediate steps to find a successor. Pearson had a distinguished ecclesiastical career and was one of the first Evangelicals to hold high office; he was appointed

[1] John Jebb became Bishop of Limerick.
[2] This was by his first wife, not Eling, John Venn's sister.

Dean of Salisbury in 1823. Pearson and Cunningham shared their Rector's missionary concern, for in 1807 Pearson gained the Buchanan prize at Oxford and Cunningham at Cambridge;[1] later Pearson wrote lives of Buchanan and Schwartz.

John W. Cunningham came to Clapham in January 1809. A year previously it had become obvious that a curate was a necessity to the sick Rector; John Venn had written to Edwards asking if he knew of a possible candidate who might be engaged on a six-monthly or annual basis at a salary of £100 per annum. "Chief business would be to preach twice on the Sunday and to read prayers once, besides taking a week of parochial duty alternately with Mr. Sharpe."[2] Cunningham had for a time been a pupil of Henry Jowett at Little Dunham along with Robert and Charles Grant; it was doubtless through Jowett that Venn came to know him. He went up to St. John's College, Cambridge and became Fifth Wrangler and Fellow of his College. He had already served a curacy at Ripley and Ockham in Surrey, before coming to Venn. He was married and the Cunninghams, like the Pearsons, became close friends of John Venn.

Cunningham on his side found in Venn the model of a Church of England vicar. Venn appears under the name of Berkely in Cunningham's book *The Velvet Cushion* which was published the year after Venn died.

Venn's portrait hung in Cunningham's room at Harrow, where he was appointed Vicar in 1811; he stayed there till his death fifty years later. He exercised a powerful and influential ministry, making many friends and some enemies; amongst the latter was Anthony Trollope's mother, Frances Trollope, whose favourite pastime was baiting "Velvet Cunningham", whom she satirized in her novel *The Vicar of Wrexhill.*[3] At Clapham, however, there seems to have been no doubt either of his success or his popularity. "What friends have I lost in the Cunninghams", Venn writes to Pearson. "Their affection for me has been shown in the most lively manner. The whole congregation

[1] Buchanan gave Oxford and Cambridge £500 each for prizes for the best English prose work on specified missionary subjects.

[2] J. Venn to E. Edwards, Sept. 26, 1808 (MS.).

[3] See M. Sadleir, *Trollope* (1945), pp. 56–8.

will have cause deeply to lament Mr. Cunningham's loss."[1] In another letter about the same time he writes: "Mr. Cunningham likes Harrow very well, though he pants and sighs after Clapham friends and Clapham congregations."[2]

The Clapham congregations had gone on growing and, even at the beginning of Cunningham's curacy, Mrs. Henry Thornton told Hannah More: "Cunningham is now preaching away at Clapham with much spirit and originality, and the church is as full as it can hold."[3] As early as 1806 Venn discussed the need for a chapel of ease with the Bishop of Winchester, but there must have been delays on one side or the other, for it was not till the last months of his life that Venn was able to write to Edwards: "I am busy about a Chapel of Ease which I hope to get erected in this place. The applications for seats at the parish church are so numerous that such an additional accommodation is absolutely necessary and I hope to get a Bill for that purpose through the House this season."[4] St. Paul's, Clapham was opened in 1815, two years after Venn's death.

Cunningham said that Venn's parish "was only his larger family, and his family his smaller parish. Those who had seen him in the one could determine what his conduct would be in the other."[5] Such consistency is to be envied. No doubt in the parish as in the home he was attempting to put into practice that pattern of fatherhood he had admired as a boy. Some people thought him over-credulous, but this fault was outweighed by the corresponding gentleness and understanding which all who sought him, as a pastor, found. In his study hung a picture of Mary anointing our Lord's feet; this expressed Venn's attitude to the penitent sinner as it did his Master's. A letter survives that he wrote to a Magdalene who had been living with a soldier.[6] He tells her not to despair, if she turns to Christ there is hope of restoration to friends and happiness on earth and joy in Heaven. It is a very kind letter, but lacking in

[1] J. Venn to H. Pearson, 1811 (MS.).
[2] J. Venn to Miss Dring, Oct. 11, 1811 (MS.).
[3] Mrs. H. Thornton to Miss H. More, April 17, 1809. Thornton Wigan Book (MS.).
[4] J. Venn to E. Edwards, Dec. 25, 1812 (MS.).
[5] Cunningham, *op. cit.*, pp. 177–8.
[6] March 3, 1795 (MS.).

practical suggestion as to what the girl should do next. The same tenderness is apparent in the many letters written at times of illness and bereavement to parishioners, relations and friends. These betray a sympathy made all the deeper by his own wife's death. He wrote to the Pearsons when their son, who was also his godson, died:

> I think the most substantial relief which I experienced was not so much from distinct arguments proving the reasonableness of resignation but rather an endeavour to turn the channel of the affections into a pious course. Five minutes' fervent prayer gave me more substantial relief than an hour's meditation on topics the justice of which could not be questioned. In prayer I conversed with God—I appealed to God—I humbled myself before God—I loved Him—and a holy tranquillity of mind insensibly stole upon me. God was with me whilst I was with Him, and if God be with us we need not mind what we suffer. God was with the martyrs in the flames and they undauntedly sang praises in the fires.[1]

A man whom sorrow had brought as close to God as that was likely to be able to succour others in time of need.

John Venn's worst enemy, as we have already seen, was a natural indolence increased by constant illness. His sister, Jane, used to say that if Sunday morning's sermon was half-completed before he went to bed on Saturday night she was satisfied.[2] In his parish work he was continually driving himself to do more and his letters are full of resolutions to this effect. He tells Edwards in 1807: "I feel it much easier to indulge a mere carnal apathy than to obtain a spiritual deadness to the world"; nevertheless, he goes on, "My life is now one continual hurry without intermission, and unavailing endeavour to keep up to duties which I am continually behind-hand in performing . . . the care of my family, educating my children engrosses my first hours; then I have to visit the school, to make necessary calls on my friends, and to take exercise on horseback which is absolutely necessary for my health. After dinner I am again occupied in various ways till either I go out to tea, or till bedtime at home.

[1] J. Venn to the Rev. H. and Mrs. Pearson, April 7, 1811 (MS.).
[2] *Annals*, p. 135.

My secular employments consume a great part of my time and in these I am much behind-hand."[1]

The diary reveals that most of his invitations out to tea were from special friends in the parish, often from one member of the Clapham Sect to meet Babington or Gisborne or some other visiting friend. After Cunningham left in 1812 he told Pearson: "It is my full intention to make a new sermon every week, and to labour diligently by visiting the poor daily and the school weekly. I deeply feel the responsibility that now lies upon me. Thank God I was never in better bodily health and this gives me reason to hope that I shall be enabled to fulfil my duty."[2] The following January he notes in his diary: "Began this week to visit my parish from house to house to inquire into their state and to furnish them with Bibles and Prayer Books where wanted."[3]

It would be interesting to know in how many parishes in England in 1812 the incumbent practised house-to-house visiting. It is also significant that John Venn was not just content to leave the Bible only; if the family were without a Prayer Book that too must be provided. His younger son says that his father boasted before his death that every child could be taught to read and write gratuitously; that every family could be supplied with a Bible, and that every inhabitant could find accommodation to worship God. The Bibles were supplied by the newly formed British and Foreign Bible Society, of whose Clapham Auxiliary[4] Venn was the enthusiastic chairman. The claim about accommodation for worship was not really fulfilled till the chapel of ease was built, but the boast about facilities for education was by no means extravagant.

A school had been built in Clapham by voluntary subscriptions in the middle of the seventeenth century. Its curriculum in the early eighteenth century was that of a grammar school, and one Vicar of Wandsworth sent his son there as a preparation for Eton. However, by Venn's day it had become a Charity

[1] J. Venn to E. Edwards, April 3, 1807 (MS.).
[2] J. Venn to H. Pearson, 1811.
[3] Diary (MS.).
[4] "Our Clapham Bible Society flourishes. The subscriptions amount to upwards of £1,400, so mightily grows the word of God and prevails." J. Venn to E. Edwards, Dec. 25, 1812 (MS.).

School for young children. The change probably took place in 1781 when the school was rebuilt to accommodate a hundred boys and forty girls. During the last five years of John Venn's life he further enlarged the buildings so that the school could take two hundred pupils, raising the necessary funds by asking those people who already subscribed to the school to increase their subscription. As superintendent he had the school under his direct control, though the fact that he frequently attended a "school meeting" suggests the existence of some sort of committee to help him. When well, Venn visited the school regularly, taught Scripture and the Catechism; he also chose and distributed the prizes himself.[1] Venn must have been one of the earliest exponents of Bell's new methods, which, in a letter to Edwards, he contrasts very favourably with those advocated by his rival Joseph Lancaster:

> Of Lancaster I entertain no very high opinion. He is very conceited and has been spoiled by public favour. He is besides very imprudent and most of his plans are, I think, not well conceived. But the great objection I have to his plan is that it does not embrace religious instruction, or inculcate these principles on which alone a true system of good education can be founded. As a system of discipline it is excellent. The scholars are all drilled pretty well, and there the matter ends. I approve much more highly of Dr. Bell's system from which Lancaster originally obtained all his improvements, as he calls them, in education.[2]

John Venn had been asked to write for the *Christian Observer* an article on the rival systems of Lancaster and Bell, but had to refuse because of lack of time. However, he had four years earlier written an article on Charity Schools which tells us something of the ideals and methods in education which he himself advocated. In this article he criticizes the practice of some Charity Schools where the children are taught "to read, to write and to repeat the catechism by rote". Such "mechani-

[1] Venn tells Edwards that he proposes to publish "some scriptural questions for schools". Whether he ever did so is not known. J. Venn to E. Edwards, Dec. 1804 (MS.).

Venn believed there was a place in education for reward, though he discouraged emulation as being worldly. "Teach children to love knowledge, not to strive to surpass others." Eclectic Notes, p. 400.

[2] J. Venn to E. Edwards, April 9, 1808 (MS.).

cal operations" are not, in his judgment, education. "Education properly defined is that series of means by which knowledge is obtained, proper dispositions acquired, and a right character formed."[1] This means teaching children to think as well as to read. Before being taught reading, the children should be told interesting stories and asked to repeat them. The lesson should be broken into by asking the children questions; for religious instruction the Church Catechism should be used. "*Mrs. Trimmer's*[2] *Teacher's Assistant* should be in the hands of every teacher and visitor of a charity school." Venn considers choice of the right teachers essential; the master of a school should be a good disciplinarian but not over-severe.

He considers education as a *preparatio evangelica* for two reasons. For the clergyman it will produce "a rising generation of young persons disposed to listen with a lively interest to his sermons, qualified by a stock of religious knowledge to understand them; prepared by good habits to attend regularly the ordinances of worship; accustomed to revere him as their guide and attached to him as their friend".[3] But, more important than that:

> Man is almost universally what he is trained up to be. Man, it is true, cannot by education be made a real Christian; but by education he may be freed from prejudices and delivered from the dominion of dispositions highly favourable to temptation and sin. He may, by education, be endued with qualities friendly to the growth of Christianity. His mind may be enlightened by knowledge instead of being darkened by brutish ignorance. His conscience may be awakened instead of being seared by insensibility. He may be made attentive, docile, submissive, rational; instead of being thoughtless, obstinate, intractable, void of understanding. The soil may be cultivated and prepared for the reception of the heavenly seed.[4]

With most of the points he makes, a modern writer on Christian education would probably agree; but he would cer-

[1] Charity Schools, *Christian Observer*, September 1804, p. 542.

[2] See essay on "Good Mrs. Trimmer" in W. K. Lowther Clarke, *Eighteenth Century Piety* (1945), pp. 118–125.

[3] *Christian Observer*, 1804, p. 542.

[4] *Ibid.*

tainly not agree that part of the purpose of educating the poor was to make them "docile and submissive". Nevertheless much of the article is devoted to an exposition of this principle. Venn says that some have said that education of the poor is a source of "democratical poison", but the education he advocates is the antidote of Jacobinism for it teaches children to be "industrious and frugal, sober and moderate, faithful and obedient", fitting them to become "useful servants, good husbands, and careful masters of a family".[1] He says that the school should be run "like a regiment of soldiers . . . at all times, but more especially in these days when democratic opinions have been so widely and so fatally diffused; when they have loosed the bonds of just subordination throughout all the various ranks of society, it becomes especially necessary to promote a spirit of obedience to lawful authority." Elder children should be taught "that they are accountable to God for their behaviour to their parents, their masters, their magistrates and their king".[2]

In his attitude to the poor and to the education of the poor, John Venn identified himself with his friend Hannah More, whom he defends against contemporary critics in this article.[2] Hannah More was criticized in her own day for making the attempt to educate the poor and give them a better opportunity in life: this, it was thought, was the gateway to Jacobinism. To-day the criticism is that her attempt was patronizing and unjust. John Venn having praised both the teaching methods and the character of his pupils he had found in the Somerset schools, adds:

> It is but a piece of justice due to the excellent Mrs. H. More[3] to say, that the writer principally alludes . . . to one of the schools under her patronage. He had the opportunity of learning some very striking facts corroborative of the above remarks. These facts will one day loudly speak to the character and designs of this much-injured lady, who has devoted talents and learning, calculated to instruct and delight the highest circles of society, to the improvement of the lowest; and whose benevolent labours, like those of her great Master, have been rewarded with calumny and reproach.

[1] *Christian Observer*, 1804, p. 661. [2] *Ibid.*, p. 543.

[3] Unmarried women after middle age assumed the title "Mrs." at this period.

In modern times criticism of Hannah More's attitude and principles has become sharper; John Venn is open to the same line of attack. However deplorable their attitude may be by modern standards, we have no right to condemn it until we have at least made an attempt to comprehend it.

In the eighteenth century there was a rigid stratification of society; men believed that rank was ordained by God, Henry Venn, in his "Prayer for a Student Educating for Holy Orders", puts this sentence into the young man's petition: "May I be respectful to my superiors, amiable to my equals, meek towards my inferiors."[1] He believed, in fact, in a three-tiered society.[2] As this society was thus arranged by Almighty God it was blasphemous to attempt to alter it. God did indeed "make men high or lowly and order their estate";[3] the idea that it was right for a man to "better himself" came with Bentham. During the early years of the Industrial Revolution men like Richard Arkwright did rise from bottom to top of the social scale, but it was not till the twenties and thirties of the nineteenth century, when Utilitarianism became fashionable as a social philosophy, that the attempt to climb from one class to another gained wide approval. In the static society of the eighteenth century, it was cruelty to educate a child beyond its station.

Dr. M. G. Jones in her recent biography of Hannah More has carefully explained the attitude of mind considered here along similar lines. Her explanation is as valid for John Venn as it is for Hannah More. Further, as we shall see in the next chapter, Hannah More, Venn and the rest of the Clapham Sect for that matter were prepared to do anything for the poor—they really loved them, they really cared for them, body and soul; but, because of their belief in a rigidly defined society, they would not work with the poor, or directly encourage them to produce their own leadership. This was their limitation: two generations

[1] *The Complete Duty of Man*, Appendix A.

[2] It might equally be well termed a "five-tiered" society when classification was by function and social responsibility, in which case the classes would be: nobility, gentry (including clergy), yeomanry (including large independent manufacturers), tenant-farmers, and labourers.

[3] Mrs. Alexander wrote her hymn in 1848. However, it is not surprising to find the wife of an Irish archbishop writing in terms of an earlier day: many upper-class people in England in 1848 would share this view, but many would challenge it.

later Maurice and Kingsley, living in a more fluid society, were prepared not only to work in Christ's name for the poor but to work with them as well.[1]

Another factor which may be even more significant comes out in Henry Thornton's description of the baptism of his third child, Lucy. Venn baptized the child of a pauper at the same service. The contrast struck Henry Thornton very forcibly, for there were the Thorntons and the Wilberforces in their Sunday best, with Lucy Thornton resplendent in "a full, flowing, white christening robe", whereas the other child was "scarcely covered by a wretched coloured old frock and a course ragged little towel", supported only by her parents and a godfather. Mrs. Thornton obviously felt uncomfortable and gave the mother a few shillings, while her husband, after some thought, wrote in his diary: "It is only for a few fleeting days that the difference really exists." For the Thorntons and the Venns, class distinctions mattered but they were not going to matter for long. This may seem to us a wrong way of looking at things *sub specie aeternitatis*, but again we have to remember that along the lines of philanthropy both Venn and Thornton did a great deal for the Clapham poor and it is to the credit of both of them that there was no question of a separate service for the wealthier family.[2]

A new school was started in Clapham for the Sierra Leone boys, whom Zachary Macaulay brought home from Africa. It was continued as a private school under the same master when the Africans departed.[3] There were several other schools in the district, including a girls' school where Venn was a regular visitor and where he also distributed the prizes. In this school a Young Ladies Society met, which was probably the equivalent of the Girls' Bible Class to-day. In addition to this there was a Friendly Female Society and a Female Club. The latter was run by Mrs. Henry Thornton in her own name: it is difficult to tell whether it was more like a Women's Fellowship or a Women's Luncheon Club: on occasion John Venn was invited to give a devotional address. There was also a Book Club which

[1] M. B. Reckitt, *From Maurice to Temple* (1947), p. 35.
[2] Thornton Wigan Book (MS.).
[3] See chapter 5, pp. 241–2. The master was William Greaves.

met monthly at the Rectory; the only surviving entry in Venn's diary which gives any clue as to the composition of this Club reads: "December 11, 1806: Book Club at my house. Fourteen gentlemen present": this suggests that women were excluded. By schools and clubs something was done for most of the children in Clapham and the adults were by no means neglected.

As for the poor, what Venn did for them in practice was considerable. From the time of his arrival he showed an active interest in poor relief at vestry meetings. It had been decided to extend and enlarge the existing workhouse. In 1796 Venn was chairman of the committee which inspected the building and recommended that it be whitewashed throughout and several structural changes made including "the alteration of the fireplace in the lying-in room to be altered according to Count Rumford's plan". This latter proposal was undoubtedly Venn's, for we know him to have been an ardent advocate of Rumford's methods. However, although the poor rates at Clapham were 2s. 6d. in the pound in 1793, Venn found that they were inadequate to provide for the needs of the large number of poor parishioners he now discovered under his care. Previously there had been a fund, built up through private subscription, which had done something to relieve destitution. This Venn revived as the Clapham Poor Society, which provided subsidies to enable the poor to buy bread, coal and potatoes at cheap rates. In 1797, meat stew was also made available at a penny a quart. To make this "soup" as it was called, a certain Mrs. Jones was paid three shillings each time. In a bad year the Poor Society might spend as much as £400 in relief, in a good year no more than £60.

Nevertheless John Venn was not satisfied that all that could be done for the poor in Clapham was being done; he felt that on the one hand the Overseers of the Poor were restricted in the assistance they were authorized to give, and on the other that there were better ways of helping the poor than through the charity of the Clapham Poor Society. In February 1799, he formed the Society for Bettering the Condition of the Poor at Clapham. It took its title and some of its leading ideas from a new society that Thomas Bernard had formed two years previously in partnership with Wilberforce and the Bishop of Durham.[1]

[1] See next chapter.

By means of this more ambitious organization Venn was able to provide his parish with its own social services. He maintained that Clapham was a small enough community for the rich to perform their "proper duty of knowing and looking after the poor".

The new society was formed of more than thirty persons who agreed "to drink tea together in each other's houses" once a month and to execute the business of the society. A substantial fund was built up from private subscription and from the "Sacrament money";[1] the latter brought in about £100 per annum. Venn himself was appointed treasurer; he shared the chief work of organization with a layman, Robert Barclay. The parish was divided into eight districts. Each district had its own treasurer and two or three other visitors. The aim was to give each visitor care of eight or ten families and thus to attain "the familiarity of a small village". They were to work in co-operation with parish officers and doctors; the latter were urged to become honorary members. Among the names listed as visitors in 1805 are those of Lady Teignmouth, Mrs. Robert Thornton, Mr. Sharpe, the Lecturer at the church, and John Venn's sister, Eling Elliott and her husband. The visitors and treasurer of each district met whenever convenient to discuss their cases. At the monthly meetings of the whole society the visitors made their reports, suggesting ways and means of assistance; the treasurer of each district read out his accounts and grants were made from the general fund where required; in certain respects these general meetings resembled those of the local committees of the Charity Organization Society.[2]

Special attention was given to the sick. They were regularly visited and in special cases a nurse was supplied. Where quiet was required children were boarded out in a neighbour's house. The same precaution was taken in cases of infectious diseases, where the successful isolation of the patient prevented the spread of infection. In such cases the visitor informed the treasurer, who called in the doctor. Communication with other

[1] John Venn was doubtless mindful of the Prayer Book Rubric which says that the alms at the Communion Service are "for the poor".

[2] Formed in 1869; became Family Welfare Association in 1946.

houses was then stopped, the clothes of the entire household were fumigated by being exposed to vapour of burning brimstone, all linen was put in cold water to which vinegar had been added. Where possible all doors and windows were left open in the sick person's house. Steam of boiling vinegar or the vapour from burning tobacco was occasionally introduced to refresh the air of the room. Blankets which were lent to sick people were thoroughly fumigated by the same methods. The walls of a house where there had been serious infection were washed with hot lime. In days before the importance of hygiene in maintaining public health was generally recognized, these drastic methods were highly commendable. In all this the Rector was the driving force.

In 1800 a smallpox epidemic was stayed by vaccinating the parish. Venn's diary reads: "1800, September 1, Caroline and Maria vaccinated. October 7: Agreed upon a plan of vaccinating the parish; vaccination just introduced."[1] Venn thus showed himself to be a precursor of slum parsons like Champneys of Whitechapel, and of medically-minded country parsons like Charles Kingsley who marched round his parish at Eversley with bottles of gargle to ward off diphtheria.[2] For keeping supplies of all the things that were needed for maintaining this health service, the Society found it necessary to employ an agent, who looked after the stores; she also had a register of nurses and "charwomen" who could be recommended. In addition she had supplies of sago, oatmeal and wine, which she could issue on receipt of a note from the committee requesting relief. She also had the blankets and the unslaked lime. The agent had to be a single woman who did not go out to work; she was also required to be clean, honest and a good cook. Her stores were bought for her by "three ladies of the Society", to whom she was responsible. She was paid only three shillings a week.[3]

[1] Quoted in *Annals*, p. 122. Samuel Thornton adds "The cowpox has been introduced with success as a substitute for the smallpox, and been generally successful, except in one instance at Clapham." Samuel Thornton, *Yearly Recollections*, p. 111.

[2] M. B. Reckitt, *op. cit.*, pp. 71–2.

[3] Thomas Bernard, *Reports of the Society for Bettering the Conditions and Increasing the Comforts of the Poor* (1800), Vol. II, p. 342.

The Society ran two small schools, one where older children were taught spinning in flax and wool and another for children under six who were taught to read and knit. This school was used on Sundays as a Sunday school: in it there were about twenty children.

To relieve hardship and destitution the visitors could in the first instance do something on their own initiative if they considered the case urgent, but a second application for assistance had to be submitted to the committee. Direct financial assistance, however, was strongly discouraged; the Society did not give alms to the poor or distribute charity indiscriminately. The main criticism of the aims and methods of John Venn's society is that it discriminated too carefully between the deserving and undeserving poor, probed too deeply into the lives, behaviour and beliefs of the recipients of its bounty, and demanded too much in the way of proof of industriousness and reform of character. His attitude to relief of the poor was very much akin to his attitude to their education. This comes out very clearly both in the rules of the Society and also in the report he made as treasurer when the Society was a year old. Rule IV reads:

> Before any relief is granted information should be particularly sought concerning the moral character of the applicant, particularly if he is accustomed to attend public worship; whether he sends his children to school, and trains them in the habit of industry. An account is also taken of his weekly earnings and expenses and debts; and the particular cause of his distress is to be investigated. This information will serve as a basis on which to found both the kind and quality of relief which it will be proper to administer.[1]

In his first report he affirms that "bettering means more than the relief of immediate wants, which may be done by any person who possesses the money; it means to extricate him from future want, to cut off the sources of his poverty, to instil into him good principles, to elevate his mind to a state of independence, to raise him to a higher tone of character. This is a work worthy of the talents and knowledge which a society founded on the

[1] *Rules and Regulations of the Society for Bettering the Condition of the Poor at Clapham, Surrey* (1817), p. 16.

principle of bettering the conditions of the poor ought to display."[1]

He then goes on to speak of the damage that indiscriminate charity can do to the character of those who receive it. "There is a spring and energy in an independent spirit which is capable of great exertions. Nothing damps, nothing extinguishes that independence of mind so much as the habitual reception of alms. The very character of a man who subsists on charity is changed. He has lost his boldness, his fortitude, his openness, his manliness, and is become mean, abject, pusillanimous and often deceitful."[2] This meant that in the few cases where alms were given it was always less than what a hard-working man could earn, and it was stopped as soon as work could be provided; it also meant that an expectant mother was asked to save up to five shillings a week towards the expenses of her confinement, which the Society doubled and returned to her to meet expenses. In every way the Victorian gospel of self-help was instilled. As Venn says in the closing paragraph of his report:

"In a word, let it be the aim of this Society to say, not merely this man was hungry and we fed him, but this man was naked and behold he is clothed by his own industry; this man was a drunkard and his family in rags, behold him sober and see him decently clad. This man was idle, and poor, and miserable; now he is industrious, prosperous and happy; and above all this man was a wretched profligate and now he is moral and religious. Where the Society can appeal to these proofs of its utility it will have deserved well of mankind, and may justly rejoice in the success of its labours."[3] Reform rather than relief was the primary aim throughout. "In vain a man is relieved if he retains a corrupt principle which will again lead into debauchery, idleness or gaming. More than the mines of Peru can supply is required to rescue that man from misery and want; he must be reformed. . . . To give without reforming is but to pour water into a broken cistern."[4]

But what of those who refused to be reformed? In such cases re-

[1] *Clapham Poor Society Rules and Regulations*, pp. 25–26.
[2] *Ibid.*, p. 27.
[3] *Ibid.*, pp. 31–2.
[4] *Ibid.*, pp. 28–9.

lief was withheld, or, if they could be moved back to the parishes from which they originate, this should be done so that it might be said that "Clapham is no place for the idle and worthless."[1]

Clapham under John Venn and his tea-drinking committee in some ways resembled Geneva under the rule of the saints, in others the rule of the Benthamite administrators of early Victorian England. 1800 is an early date to find utilitarian principles being applied to social welfare; it is certainly a far cry from the idea that social benefits must be earned and that those who do not earn them are penalized, to the Evangelical concept of free grace. Nevertheless it must be admitted that many who, like John Venn, stand fast in theology by the doctrine of justification by faith, do in fact demand justification by works in other spheres of life; such works are the fruit of the reform Venn so much insisted upon. Perhaps already in 1800 Evangelicalism and Benthamism, which were to become so influential in the life of Victorian England, were already influencing one another albeit unconsciously.

There was one other matter in which Venn made an attempt to introduce a godly discipline to the holy village of Clapham, namely, Sabbath Observance.

Although he did not follow his father's practice at Huddersfield of having "Venn people" patrolling the streets to encourage Sunday quiet, he did write a forceful address to the people of Clapham on the subject.[2] In this he urges that Sunday be regarded as a day of rest to which every man has a God-given right; it should also be observed as a day for the pursuit of religion. He therefore asks shopkeepers not to open their shops on Sundays and to come to mutual agreement on the matter; further, "if it is the duty of the tradesman to keep the Sabbath, it must be equally the duty of customers not to tempt him to break it". Parents should encourage children to attend school[3] and church; they should read their Bibles with them and above

[1] *Ibid.*, p. 29. By the Act of Settlement of Charles II's reign, each parish was allowed to send a man back to his native parish in case at a future date he should become chargeable on the rates.

[2] "Address to the Inhabitants of Clapham on Hallowing the Sabbath", printed in the *Christian Observer*, July 1805, pp. 402–4.

[3] The term "school" here is ambiguous; it undoubtedly means Sunday school but the teaching given would not necessarily be exclusively religious.

all set an example by observing the Sabbath themselves. Moreover an example should be set "to the lower orders"; this involves abandoning usual occupations and avoiding "improper pursuits" such as "travelling, visiting, diversions, reading secular books, writing letters or settling accounts".

In a sermon on the same subject Venn advances a novel argument for keeping the Sabbath. He says that for six days men are concerned with providing for their bodies and "engaged in the petty concerns of this transitory life", however, "the proper life of man is his eternal life; here he is in his infancy, in his cradle—but on the seventh day we lay aside our trifles, our occupations are those which respect the life to come. . . . Then we live. Every other employment, however splendid, is but the play of children—on the seventh day we become men."[1]

From all that has been said so far it can be seen that John Venn's influence in local affairs was immense. There is further evidence to show that few parsons have been more involved in the secular affairs of their parish than John Venn was during his first ten years at Clapham. There was hardly a committee or subcommittee of the local Vestry on which he did not sit, usually as chairman or treasurer. It was only his long illness in 1802–3 which enabled him to reject finally the plea of the Vestry that he should allow himself to be selected as a magistrate for the county.

It is almost true to say that though Clapham was by the end of the eighteenth century a suburb of considerable size, it was very much still a village dominated by squire and parson. The squire was Samuel Thornton, who was Lord of the Manor and patron of the living; in 1801 he moved to Albury Park near Guildford and thus brought the partnership to an end. Venn's illness the following year gave him an opportunity to consider whether public affairs were engrossing too much of his time and attention.[2] On this decision not to take such an active part, he wrote to Edwards two years later:

[1] *Sermons*, Vol. III, pp. 349–50.

[2] Venn remained Chairman of the Poor Committee till 1813 when Charles Elliott took his place. In that year he was still being asked "to make inquiry about the different articles for preparing the soup".

> I hope I was doing some temporal good and certainly I had gained a very great influence which was in some cases very usefully employed. But on the whole it was clear I ought to decline entry into such occupations again. And this resolution I have now kept for two years and with increasing comfort and conviction of its propriety. A minister in a public situation may do good, but this will be more than balanced, I think, by the loss of time, by hurry and fatigue and frequently by the collision of those interests in which a great part of the odium and dislike will attach to him in spite of all his prudence, integrity and mildness. I once foolishly imagined that by openly stating my reasons, enlightening the people and taking much pains to do them good, I could secure their approbation. But, alas! I found I was most abused for the things which were evidently most for the advantage of the people. However, the chief objection was the secularization of my thoughts and the drawing me from my proper employment to which I had solemnly devoted myself and which was surely of importance and difficult enough to require every particle of my time and thoughts. We should esteem our employment infinitely the most honourable and most useful employment in the world and devote ourselves to it accordingly.[1]

The significance of this letter is not that here is a clergyman who discovered that his spiritual work leaves little time for an active public life; but that here is an Evangelical clergyman who for ten years undertook responsibility in local affairs as a Christian duty, and withdrew only when he realized that his pastoral work would suffer if he did not do so.

In nothing was Venn's concern in public affairs more remarkable than in the part he played in the formation of the Clapham Armed Association in April 1798. This was the time of the first invasion scare following the appointment by the Directory of Bonaparte as Commander of the Army of England, and preparations were being made along the coasts of France and the Netherlands: "The crisis which has long been threatened," Venn tells Edwards, "is in appearance soon approaching. All this neighbourhood will probably soon be in arms. We are to have a meeting in the parish on Friday to consider some plan for that purpose."[2] Bonaparte, however, switched his forces to

[1] J. Venn to E. Edwards, Feb. 7, 1806 (MS.).
[2] J. Venn to E. Edwards, April 11, 1798 (MS.).

the Mediterranean soon after this was written, and the Army of England became the Army of Egypt.[1]

The Armed Association was the Home Guard of its day; it replaced the Supplementary Militia and the Cavalry Association which had been formed on Venn's initiative the previous year. He too was the prime mover in the formation of the new organization. He was Chairman of the Committee, Treasurer and, later, Chaplain. He drew up the rules, solicited subscriptions, generated the necessary patriotic fervour both from the pulpit and on the parade ground. He told Edwards that he intended to be present on all drilling days to address the men "as Mr. Riland, The Chaplain of the Volunteer Corps of Sutton, always does. He is the first on the field and the last to leave it." Neverthless he himself was opposed to a clergyman bearing arms: "I think all men ought now to fight against the French as they would against devils, and were I not a minister I would do it in person, but I think my whole congregation would be shocked at the impropriety of seeing me in a red coat and a grenadier's cap."[2]

Within a year the Association had received 270 offers; 40 cavalry, 190 infantry "to be armed with firelocks" and 42 to be issued with pikes. The uniform was a blue cloth jacket with scarlet trimmings, a white Russian duck waistcoat, white pantaloons, gaiters and white buttons with a crown in the centre and *Clapham Volunteers* round the edge, bear-skin hats, with a scarlet feather and a black cockade. Appended to the rules was a paragraph which made the purpose of the Armed Association quite plain, namely "to defend our liberty and property against foreign invasion or internal commotion".[3] Venn, who was a violent Pittite, feared internal rebellion as much as a French invasion; his sentiment was shared by most of the middle classes at the time.[4] When the Association was formed Samuel Thorn-

[1] The French reached Egypt in July. It was the Directory's idea to invade England; Bonaparte preferred to strike first at English trade.

[2] J. Venn to E. Edwards, May 4, 1798 (MS.).

[3] *Rules and Regulations of the Clapham Armed Association*, Vestry Committee Book (MS.).

[4] Venn once told the Eclectic Society that he believed that there was a marked connection between democracy and error in religion. He instanced Muir and Palmer, two advocates for Reform, who were sentenced to transportation. Muir was a Scottish lawyer, Palmer an Anglican clergyman living in Dundee who presumably held views Venn considered heretical.

ton was asked to become its Colonel. The colours were kept in Clapham Church, and for a time the vestry was used as an armoury. On the occasion of Church Parades, the men were first paraded on the cricket field and then marched to church. On more than one occasion the committee asked Venn to publish at their expense the sermon he had preached on the Association: unfortunately none of these have been preserved.

After his resignation from all offices save that of Chaplain, Venn still rallied the Volunteers in church. When Napoleon was making his second and more serious preparations to invade the country in the winter of 1803–4, Venn wrote to Edwards: "You seem to be more alarmed about the French than I confess I am. Indeed some time ago I preached a sermon holding out the language of encouragement and hope, which the Military Committee and Vestry of this place requested into print. . . . I believe in Norfolk you have been rather neglected but I have no fears of this wicked and cruel man being able to do any hurt to us, united and armed as we are."[1] He told the Eclectic "Bonaparte is Satan personified".[2]

How much time this public and parochial work allowed John Venn to give to his wife and young family, it is difficult to ascertain, but it cannot have been very much. It is unfortunate, though not surprising, that whilst there is ample information available concerning his public activity during his first ten years at Clapham, the family records covering the same period are disappointingly meagre: even the long letters to Edwards give only an occasional glimpse here and there.

When John and Kitty Venn reached Clapham in March 1793, their one child, Catherine, was just over a year old. The family, however, was quickly enlarged: Jane was born two months after their arrival, Emelia the following year, Henry in 1796, Caroline in 1798, Maria in 1800, and finally John in 1802. Emelia was called after Parry's first wife and Parry himself became her godfather: Henry, of course, owed his name to his grandfather.[3] Jane Venn wrote to her brother from Yelling:

[1] J. Venn to E. Edwards, Jan. 1809 (MS.).

[2] *Eclectic Notes*, p. 331.

[3] Their first child who only lived a month had been named Henry. John Venn complained to his sister, Eling, when she called her first boy Henry Venn Elliott.

"Tell my sister we wish her in her little Harry all the joy a mother can receive from a son. My dear father talks of him and this day told me that he presented him early this morning to that God to whom he dedicated his own son, as soon as he received him."[1] Though unable to be present at the christening Henry Venn drank his health and offered prayers for him. Meanwhile Stillingfleet wrote from Hotham desiring that Henry should be more like Jesus Christ than his father or his grandfather.

Henry Venn came to live at Clapham the same year that his grandson was born. John Venn had rented the house next to the Rectory for his father and his sister, Jane, who had been looking after the aged Rector of Yelling since his second wife died four years previously. The move took place just before Christmas. In the following month Samuel Thornton noted in his Yearly Recollections, "Old Mr. Venn is almost in the last stage, like a shock of corn fully ripe, and promises to end his course triumphantly."[2] By June he was dying but the prospect made him so jubilant and high-spirited that his doctor said that the joy at dying kept him alive a further fortnight. In his will he left £50 to Ruth Clarke, the old family servant,[3] and £5 to Simeon to buy a mourning ring by which their great friendship might be remembered. Jane received his property and John his effects. Thus was the earthly link between father and son broken. Their relationship, as we have seen, had been remarkable. In Henry Venn's latter years, as his own powers were declining, he rejoiced to see his son's manifestly increasing, and John Venn's occasional visits to Yelling left fragrant memories. "My son's sermons, the two Sundays before last, collected a more numerous congregation yesterday than, I think, has been in our church for years. We had eighty at the table. I read the prayers. . . . After service, with a triumphant voice, we made the church ring with Hallelujahs—'Lives again our Glorious King'. It was a glorious feast indeed! Glory be to God!"[4]

John Venn writes to Edwards a few days after his father's

[1] Miss J. Venn to J. Venn, Feb. 10, 1796 (MS.).

[2] Samuel Thornton, *Yearly Recollections*, p. 94.

[3] John Venn visited her in London in 1806.

[4] H. Venn to Charles Elliott, Oct. 7, 1793, quoted in *Life of H. Venn*, p. 525.

death, saying that during the last weeks his mind became deranged and his memory deserted him. "You did not know him in his best days when he was himself, yet you saw enough of him to admire his uprightness, his zeal in the service of God, his incipient endeavour to do good, his sweetness of manner and his interesting talents. I hope one day to be able to give some sketch of his life, for his was a life not fitted by Providence to be obscured in a corner."[1]

There is little in John Venn's letters of family affairs, except holidays. Seaside holidays for the upper and middle classes were just becoming fashionable.[2] John and Kitty Venn went, without the children, to Broadstairs one year and Brighton another. The family holiday consisted of an almost annual visit to Hull to stay with Kitty's mother. John Venn's favourite form of relaxation was a long excursion on horseback. These "tours", as he called them, were often undertaken as a form of convalescence after a bout of illness. He sometimes took a friend with him and usually made for the west country. The way John Venn galloped round the country became a standing joke among his friends. "Venn is on his travels", Henry Thornton tells Hannah More, "and will, I hope, come home loaded with useful information."[3]

The longest and most successful of these tours were those in South Wales in 1801, in Yorkshire, Lancashire and the Potteries the following year and the Devon tour of 1811. While Kitty was living he wrote almost daily, and on all occasions kept a full diary himself, making observations not only on people and places but also on ecclesiastical and economic developments. A new world was springing up at the turn of the century and an inquiring traveller like John Venn was determined to see and learn all that he could. Venn went to South Wales to visit Henry Bewicke, the son of a wealthy Clapham parishioner. Bewicke met him in Cardiff where Venn noticed that most of the women had blue serge dresses and petticoats but were without shoes or stockings, though some had men's round hats. Beyond Cardiff they saw a number of coal-mines round Caer-

[1] J. Venn to E. Edwards, June 27, 1797 (MS.).
[2] G. M. Trevelyan, *English Social History* (1945), p. 402.
[3] H. Thornton to Miss H. More, Sept. 17, 1802. Thornton Wigan Book (MS.).

philly and visited Crawshay's iron works at Merthyr Tydvil, which Venn describes as "the first place in the kingdom for iron works".[1] He gives an account of the huge furnaces and forges "and shafts dug in the mountain through which coals are brought from the mines or iron ore". His letter home is illustrated with diagrams for the children and there is a brief lesson in economic geography explaining how the manufacture of iron requires an abundance of coal, limestone and iron in close proximity; then follows a description of the process of manufacture and he concludes with a note that at Merthyr a canal comes close up to the works for transport. Another letter contains drawings of the new bridge at Pontypridd with illustrated explanations of why the old bridge fell in.

The next year Venn and Charles Elliott[2] were admitted as friends of Wilberforce's to Benjamin Gott's[3] woollen mill at Leeds and Wedgwood's potteries at Etruria. In Leeds and Huddersfield Venn revisited many of his boyhood haunts, including his father's vicarage.

From Huddersfield he went on to Manchester and Liverpool by coach. The coach arrived at Liverpool to the accompaniment of drums beating and bells ringing. He found himself a witness of one of the greatest city fires since the Fire of London. A warehouse was ablaze and, as it was twelve stories high, the fire-engines were unable to bring the uppermost floors in range of their hoses before the fire spread to neighbouring warehouses. The fire was not brought under control till 5 a.m. and seventeen warehouses were destroyed.[4] Next day John Venn toured the city, whose public buildings he describes with great enthusiasm.[5]

[1] J. Venn to Mrs. Venn, Sept. 1801 (MS.). Richard Crawshay, the second owner, was an ironmaster to be compared with John Wilkinson of Broseley. During the French Wars he employed a staff of 2,000; by 1830 there were eight furnaces. Later in the century the works were closed because of labour troubles and the invention of Bessemer steel.

[2] Charles Elliott, son of John Venn's brother-in-law by his first marriage.

[3] Though there were no "woollen kings" to compare with "cotton kings", like Arkwright and Peel, there were some important woollen manufacturers, chief among whom was Benjamin Gott of Leeds.

[4] Troughton, *The History of Liverpool* (1810), pp. 232–4.

[5] "Liverpool is a splendid place and without a shadow of comparison superior to every other place but London in England. The public buildings are many of them much superior to those in London. Their libraries and newsroom make yours at Hull appear contemptible." J. Venn to Mrs. Venn, Sept. 1802 (MS.).

As we shall see shortly, he paid dearly for what he saw that night.

On these journeys John Venn sometimes put up at hotels or ale-houses, but just as often at the homes of Evangelical clergy and laity; whether it was returning through Devon and Somerset from Plymouth, or going to visit the Rilands at Birmingham via Oxford, or the Edwards at Lynn via Cambridge, there were always friendly parsonages and country houses where he was welcomed. Like the leaders of the primitive church, Evangelicals were "given to hospitality", and from this anyone who travelled as much as Venn greatly benefited.

While John Venn was at Little Dunham he seems to have had some recurrence of the feverish attacks he had experienced at Cambridge. However, when he moved to Clapham the trouble grew more serious. In June 1802 he was taken so seriously ill that, apart from two Sundays in October, he was out of his pulpit for fifteen months. The tour of Yorkshire and Lancashire in the summer of 1802 was an attempted, and, as it proved, a disastrous remedy; from his couch he wrote to Edwards in November as follows:

> I was taken ill at the latter end of last spring, though indeed I had long been far from well, having grown very unwieldy[1] and not knowing that it was occasioned by disease. After a long and serious discipline from the doctors I recovered, and a long and pleasant journey on horseback in the month of August seemed to restore me to a degree of health and vigour I had been a stranger to for years; but, as man would say, unhappily, I arrived at Liverpool on the night of the dreadful fire and was at an inn in the neighbourhood. The fatigue and anxiety I suffered together with other imprudence brought on my complaint with hectic fever which still continues and wears away my strength. I have done no duty now except twice for twenty Sundays. I cannot see my friends except at short intervals. I have no prospect, according to Dr. Fraser's report, of doing anything except lying on the sofa for six months to come. He gives me hopes that I shall then recover.[2]

[1] It is possible that the increase of weight was due to some defect of the liver which made it difficult for him to digest his food, but the evidence he gives about his condition is too scanty for us to say for certain what his chronic complaint was.

[2] J. Venn to E. Edwards, Nov. 9, 1802 (MS.).

His friends at Clapham were very kind, especially Henry Thornton and his wife. Henry Thornton made it possible for him to employ Hugh Pearson as a full-time curate and through his wife made an offer of money to assist John Venn and his family. This Venn refused.

The task of nursing her husband through this long illness placed a severe strain on Kitty's delicate physique. In February 1803 she fell from a high stool and evidently damaged herself internally. However, with a sick husband to nurse she carried on till the beginning of April, when she was suddenly taken ill while returning from church with Mrs. Edwards. Although she did no more than complain of extreme fatigue, her husband was alarmed and either took her or sent her to Cheltenham for a few days. She came back apparently better, but quickly caught a cold which developed into influenza and a raging fever.[1] Three days later she was dead.

When she knew that she was dying she summoned her husband and with amazing composure took leave of him. A few minutes later he came out and called "the whole household in to prayers",[2] after which she spoke to each of the servants individually, thanking them for their kindness to her. The short obituary that appeared in the *Christian Observer* speaks of her abiding sweetness of character, her sincerity, her humility and her freedom from pious affectation. The writer speaks of her devotion to God, her family and the parish and says "she was valued in proportion as she was known", and adds, "she was more especially the friend and patroness of the destitute and afflicted in her parish, for whom she felt an almost parental sympathy, and towards whom she exercised a parental care."[3] As for her husband, he wrote to Edwards: "What should I now feel were it not for the Gospel of our Lord Jesus Christ."[4]

This faith and the sympathy and help of his many friends sustained him, though Samuel Thornton writing at the end of the year can only describe him as "a disconsolate widower",

[1] The doctors were unable to decide whether the final cause of her death was fever or an abscess on the liver.

[2] We owe this detail to the governess, Sarah Winsor; the other accounts make no reference to the children, which suggests they were not included.

[3] *Christian Observer*, April 1803.

[4] J. Venn to E. Edwards, May 23, 1803 (MS.).

and observes: "His ministerial usefulness has for a time been dried up."[1] On the other hand Henry Thornton said Venn had accepted Kitty's loss, and was "not at all out of humour with the world because of it".[2] Kitty's death was not only something he felt as deeply as any man who has known married happiness and suddenly lost his young wife, but from his experience of God in his desolation he was able to comfort and help others, and, as we have seen, was quite prepared on occasion to speak about it. In letters written immediately after his wife's death John Venn speaks of his "dear departed friend" holding that our Lord's words about the Resurrection forbid his calling her "wife".[3]

In June, Jane Venn came to Clapham to look after her brother and his seven children. Thus for the second time did this remarkable woman take the place of a Mrs. Venn.[4] Remarkable she had to be, for the eldest of the seven children was only ten and the youngest just a year old. Her own health, though not as precarious as her brother's, was not then good and she was ill several times while she was in charge of her nephews and nieces. Nevertheless according to Marianne Thornton, Henry Thornton's eldest child, the Venn children did not much like their Aunt Jane, but they adored their father. He made the Rectory she says "the most hospitable house on the Common". She was often dumped there for a day when her mother was going out, and shared in the Rector's "instructions and in his hospitalities". "As a little child I can recollect how his entrance into the room seemed to brighten everybody and everything in it."[5]

This is all the more remarkable because during the last ten years of his life, when Marianne Thornton knew him best, he was seldom well. Some part of every year he was confined to his house or forced to take himself off on one of his tours. He

[1] Samuel Thornton, *Yearly Recollections*, p. 123.

[2] H. Thornton to Miss H. More, Sept. 9, 1803. Thornton Wigan Book (MS.).

[3] St. Mark 12: 25.

[4] An eloquent testimony to her ability and character is contained in the *Annals*, whose author remembers her as an old lady verging on ninety. She lived with her unmarried nephew and niece, John and Emelia Venn, first at Pinner, then at Hereford. She died in 1852. *Annals*, pp. 109–110.

[5] E. M. Forster, *Marianne Thornton* (1956), p. 39.

gave up his prominent place in local affairs, he resigned from the C.M.S. Committee in 1808 and took on John Cunningham as curate in 1809. The following year he preached twice on a Sunday for the first time for two and a half years. For the next two years he imagined that he was improving in health, so he tried to do more work, but he had many relapses. By 1813 the symptoms of first jaundice and then dropsy became unmistakable. Periods of enforced parochial inactivity gave him time for his work on the *Parentalia*, which consists of an account of the Venn family from the reign of Elizabeth I;[1] it also gave him time to devote to the children who so much appreciated him.

There can be no doubt at all that the family at Clapham Rectory was an extremely happy one, as happy as the homes John and his sisters had known at Huddersfield and Yelling, and theirs was no exception amongst the families of early Evangelicals in general or of those of Clapham in particular. Henry Venn had four children and John Venn six who reached adult life. Of these not one kicked over the traces or rebelled against the religion of the home. The change came in the next generation and is best exemplified in Leslie Stephen, a grandson of James Stephen and John Venn, who became a prominent agnostic and forms the chief link between the Clapham Sect in the early nineteenth century and the Bloomsbury Sect in the early twentieth.[2]

The reasons for this rebellion in certain Victorian families were not only intellectual. It was also a revolt against the pressure that Evangelical discipline placed on children in the home, and which made it a gloomy place. While it is true that a much larger proportion of Evangelical homes in Victorian England than is usually conceded were happy homes,[3] it is very noticeable that this pressure increased as the nineteenth century

[1] John Venn's grandson of the same name used the MS. book in two volumes as the foundation of his *Annals of a Clerical Family*.

[2] N. Annan, *Leslie Stephen* (1951). In this book, especially in Chapter III, "Evangelicalism", Mr. Annan traces the revolt in the Clapham families through to their Bloomsbury descendants. He maintains that in each generation there is a move away from the beliefs of the previous generation, e.g. the Wilberforce sons turning to Rome. On the whole the Wilberforces were exceptions, together with T. B. Macaulay, for the children of the Venns, the Thorntons and the Stephens themselves remained firm in the second generation but rebelled in the third.

[3] E. L. Woodward, *Short Journey* (1943), p. 13.

advanced. An example of this growing strictness with regard to what they called "the world" is to be seen in the Venn family itself. John Venn once received a letter from his friend, Edward Edwards, asking for advice as to whether he should allow his children to be taught dancing and to be allowed to attend parties. Here is John Venn's reply (his eldest child was fifteen):

> Your question about the education of children is very important. With respect to parties, they never go to any where cards and dancing are introduced, neither do they learn to dance. About the latter point I have had some doubts, my father had me taught to dance Minuets and the dancing master of his own accord chose to add country dances. My sister has had her children taught and several of my religious friends, others have not. I do not condemn those that do, but, on the whole I think it right to lean on the safe side. . . . I have seen so many instances of children of professors by indulgence in this respect, enter into the vanities of the world, that I am afraid of giving them any liberty beyond the bounds of strictest prudence. With respect to the children themselves I make them my friends in the case and frankly tell them these my views and my desires, to arm their minds beforehand and I hope I shall teach them to bear the reproach of singularity and imputation of folly. . . .[1]

The next generation were even stricter, and the problem of whether children were sent to dances just did not arise. John Venn's grandson writes of his own father, Henry Venn of C.M.S.: "He shared to the full the old-fashioned distrust and aversion to 'worldly amusements'. Theatres, novel-reading, dancing, cards, etc., were never, to the best of my recollection, named or denounced, but the understanding was none the less clear that such things were not for him or his."[2] He adds that there was only one novel in the house, *Quentin Durward*. "How it had effected an entrance I cannot say." The answer is simple, John Venn of Clapham ordered and read all Scott's novels as they appeared and recommended them at least to his daughters. *Quentin Durward* must have escaped the Victorian purge, or may be one of Henry's sisters had the rest.

Another reason for the loyalty of the Venn family to the Evangelical tradition was the positive approach to religion in

[1] J. Venn to E. Edwards, Feb. 7, 1806 (MS.).
[2] *Annals*, p. 169.

the home. Two months before he died John Venn said to the children: "You can all bear me witness that I have never represented religion to you as a gloomy thing, I have never said you must do this or you will go to Hell, but I have set it before you as a scene of joy and happiness unspeakable."[1] This did did not mean that the dark side of their father's beliefs was kept from the children. John Venn believed in Hell, original sin and total depravity, as this letter to a former curate on the birth of a daughter reveals: "May the dear infant who is just come into this corrupt world with a body of sin be washed and sanctified by the blood of Christ and the Spirit of God",[2] words that are reminiscent of a letter he had received from his father on his twentieth birthday: "On this day, when the news was brought to me, I was called up to see you—a mere animal conscious only of hunger and thirst, pain or ease, warmth or cold, light or darkness; without any power to tell explicitly your wants; and to me, as every new-born babe always is, a living demonstration of the Fall."[3]

However, there is one side of the Venn family religion which cannot but seem morbid to us; that is what could almost be called the cult of a holy death-bed. When Maria Venn, John Venn's youngest daughter, died at the age of nine, Henry Thornton's children were invited to attend family prayers and to follow her "to her grave".[4] More significant, the Venn Family Papers contain full accounts written by three of his daughters of John Venn's own last illness and death. In two of these there is a full report of two visits paid by Simeon a month before Venn died, and of the conversation which seems to have been chiefly on the subject of death; one of these reports comes from Emelia who was only nineteen. She, her two elder sisters and their stepmother were present throughout the visit.[5] Perhaps it was thought that the words of one about "to depart and be with Christ" were of special value and needed to be treasured.

[1] This is recorded in the Notes on the Illness and Death of John Venn by more than one of his daughters.

[2] J. Venn to J. W. Cunningham, April 28, 1813 (MS.).

[3] *Life of H. Venn*, p. 270.

[4] H. Thornton, Thornton Wigan Book (M.S.).

[5] Marianne Thornton did the same for her parents. See E. M. Forster, *Marianne Thornton*, chapter 2, "The Death Beds".

Other features in family life at Clapham Rectory had in common with other Evangelical families of the day included early rising, keeping of diaries and family prayers. "Excellent is your purpose", John Venn is told by his father, "to rise early and study hard. I pray God to give you resolution and perseverance. Be sure to keep an account of yourself in order that you may know your own heart."[1] John Venn did both. The keeping of the diary was neither for the purpose of memoranda nor for the compilation of an interesting chronicle, but as a means of spiritual examination at the end of each day. Wilberforce and Henry Thornton[2] did the same. In this way they continually reminded themselves that they were vile sinners constantly in need of God's grace.

Family prayers themselves were the real hall-mark of the true Evangelical family. It was within the family circle at worship that John Venn first learnt the power of corporate worship; it was here too that six months before his ordination he preached his first sermon. Henry Thornton has left this account of family prayers at the Rectory: "Breakfasted yesterday with Venn. . . . Attended his family prayer—was pleased with the attentions and good behaviour of Mrs. Venn. If there be happiness in this world this is it."[3] To remark on Kitty's good behaviour, as if he were surprised by it, is strange, but at the time of the visit he was still a bachelor. Soon Battersea Rise was to be filled with a young family and the daily happiness of family prayer experienced. In fact, the prayers Thornton used were published after his death and their use in Victorian households became "a distinctive sign of true Evangelicalism".[4]

Family prayers were attended by the entire household: parents, children and servants. Servants attended as members of the family and as such were treated without condescension. Henry Venn had set the example in this, for in his own home

[1] H. Venn, Sketch of Life of John Venn of Clapham (MS.).

[2] Thornton began this practice on January 7, 1795, after Venn had preached a sermon at his house in Battersea Rise on self-denial.

[3] Thornton Wigan Book (MS.).

[4] G. W. E. Russell, *The Household of Faith* (1906), p. 241. Thornton's *Family Prayers* were edited by R. H. Inglis after his death. At Battersea Rise before his marriage there would have been prayers for Thornton, Wilberforce and the servants, but family prayers in their proper sense they could not be called.

he had put into practice what he had written in *The Complete Duty of Man*: "Servants are not upon a level with cattle, fed and kept only for work. They are fellow creatures capable of knowing God equally with their masters, and in his sight as good as themselves."[1] How refreshingly unlike the patronage with which many Victorians treated their domestic staff![2] The same spirit pervaded Clapham Rectory and Battersea Rise, "where", in the words of E. M. Forster, "the nursery could visit the schoolroom, the schoolroom the library, and all of them the pantry without self-consciousness."[3] In the Rectory pantry there were, at least during Kitty's lifetime, two servants, William and Betty, who lived in; there was also a gardener who lived out. As the children grew in number and age there was occasionally a nurse in the nursery[4] and a governess in the schoolroom, though not necessarily at the same time.

The names of the governesses were Miss Winsor and Miss Dring. Sarah Winsor left in 1804 to marry Peter Hartwig, one of the two German missionaries the C.M.S. employed as pioneers in Sierra Leone. She does not seem to have been satisfactory, for on her departure Venn and his sister undertook the entire education of the five elder children apart from French, for which they found a master. After three years and with seven children to be taught Venn told Edwards he was looking for another governess who on the one hand must be God-fearing, on the other "Free from affectation and cant phrases".[5] Perhaps Edwards was successful in procuring the services of Miss Dring, who proved more satisfactory than her predecessor and became herself a valued member of the family.[6] She took the girls off their father's hands except for Latin which she

[1] H. Venn, *The Complete Duty of Man* (1779), p. 323.

[2] G. W. E. Russell, *op. cit.*, p. 241.

[3] E. M. Forster, *op. cit.*, p. 35.

[4] The Thornton's Nurse Hunter told a story of one of "Mr. Venn's nurses", who was so preoccupied with her knitting when out with the children that she let Maria fall into the water. *Ibid.*, p. 31.

[5] J. Venn to E. Edwards, Aug. 7, 1808 (MS.).

[6] That Miss Winsor was employed as nursery-maid and then governess seems hardly likely. In 1798 Venn had complaints about a new nursery-maid that he voiced at the Eclectic: "My children's tempers become altered from a change of nursemaid. . . . Above all a nursery-maid is the devil's instructor for vanity." *Eclectic Notes*, p. 74.

began to learn together with Catherine, Jane and Emelia from the Rector himself. When these three were too old to require a full-time governess, Miss Dring was sent on to the Edwards family with high commendation from Venn who asked Edwards to continue the instruction in Latin.

John Venn, as we know, had strong views on education; he also proved himself a zealous and imaginative teacher of his own children. While they were very young he composed a spelling-book for them himself. When either he was away from Clapham, or one of the children was staying with friends or relations, he used to write letters like this one written to Jane, aged twelve, who was staying with her Aunt Eling Elliott at Brighton:

> Write every Monday to me in a middle-sized hand, taking as much pains in your writing as you can, but taking care that your style is perfectly natural and easy. That is, write to me as you would talk to me if I were with you, only leaving out the vulgar expressions. You should also avoid beginning any two sentences with the same word. This is not agreeable to the ear.[1]

He is very pleased with the letters she has already written but can trace signs of her cousin's help; the cousin must be asked to desist, "these are to be exercises". He complains that the last letter written in French contained many faults and Anglicisms. He says that her sisters are now studying Fontaine's *Fables* with him.[2] Jane is evidently studying English History and is now sent a Latin Grammar. She is also to learn five verses of the Bible by heart daily. In another letter, written to all the children from Bath, he writes on the training of their consciences:

> Do not do anything because you see other children do it, but ask yourselves is it right to be done? What would God who made me have me to do? If you reason in this manner you will find an inward monitor always present with you who will direct you what

[1] J. Venn to Miss J. C. Venn, May 23, 1805 (MS.). After their father's death his daughters copied out a large number of letters their father had written; those written to themselves and Henry fill one thick notebook.

[2] From these references to French it seems that either the French master was not employed after all, or if he was, he did not keep his post long.

to do. It will tell you, for instance, to be diligent, to improve your time, to resist an idle and trifling spirit, to be obedient to all your superiors, to be kind to everyone, and to study the welfare and advantage of others rather than your own.[1]

From the letter to Jane it can be seen that the curriculum was wide. To the usual subjects John Venn added those in which he had become interested; for instance, shorthand, in which the girls became so proficient that they habitually used it when corresponding with each other, and also employed it when copying some of their father's letters.[2] After Miss Dring's departure there is an entry in the diary for January 1811, "Girls began Euclid"; which girls is not explained. However, about the same time to mathematics was added some simple astronomy, Venn giving a series of lectures on "Globes" for the benefit of his own and his friends' children. The first lecture was held at Battersea Rise, when Venn hoped to use the heavens themselves as a visual aid, but a cloudy night frustrated his purpose. More successful was a picnic in the garden of the same house one afternoon when "about twenty children ate some strawberries under the tulip tree", Henry Thornton reports to Hannah More, "and Mr. Venn gave us an animated lecture on the duty of parents".[3]

So far nothing has been said of the education of his sons, Henry and John. With Henry, who was seven when his mother died, he intended to take the same care as his own father had taken with his education. From 1805 he took Samuel Thornton's son, Samuel, together with his own boy. They spent term time at the Rectory and the holidays at Albury. It may well be that John Venn favoured having two pupils about the same age rather than giving his own boy his sole attention, but another factor may well have been financial pressure, for Venn discovered that each year he had been at Clapham his expenditure had exceeded his income; although he was not prepared to accept monetary gifts from his wealthy friends, he was not

[1] J. Venn to his children, 1805 (MS.).
[2] The Gurney system they used is now extinct.
[3] H. Thornton to Miss H. More, June 5, 1801, quoted in Thornton Wigan Book (MS.).

averse to earning fees from them.[1] In an autobiographical fragment Henry gives this account of what happened under this arrangement.

> In the year 1805, Samuel Thornton, a year younger than myself, came to be my father's pupil and to be educated with me. Then, I suppose, plans of instruction were adopted, such as my father's wisdom was well calculated to devise; but he was overwhelmed with the business of his important ministerial charge, and could only hear our lessons in the morning from eight to nine. The rest of the time we learnt our lessons alone in a schoolroom which opened out on a playground, and two windows looked into the street. I have a more lively recollection of transactions at the door and window than at the table. . . . I cannot but in some measure deplore the idle and desultory habits of reading which I thus acquired. That habit of strenuous application and exact attention which boys get at a good school, and under the excitement of emulation, I never had, and when I went to college I grievously felt the want of it and was forcibly discouraged by that feeling far beyond the reality of the case.[2]

In spite of this Henry Venn became a Fellow of his College and Samuel Thornton an Admiral of the Fleet. The reason for their success is possibly contained farther down in the same paragraph where Henry adds:

> My father gave me the wisest instructions about my studies, set me a high standard of accuracy, excited a desire to excel in composition and style of writing, and to enter into the spirit of an author; he encouraged me also to seek the acquisition of all kinds of knowledge—mechanical knowledge, astronomy, electricity, gardening, and heraldry.[3]

In 1812 John Venn took on two additional pupils, Thomas and John Baring, sons of the banker. They had previously been Cunningham's pupils but, when he left, required six months' further coaching before going on to Winchester. John Venn

[1] J. Venn wrote to Edwards in Dec. 1804: "As my family increases my expenses have increased also, and indeed during the whole of my residence at Clapham my expenses have every year exceeded my income, which has, God knows, been a source of disquiet to me and embittered my rest many a night" (MS.).

[2] Quoted, *Annals*, pp. 148–9.

[3] *Annals*, p. 149.

was sufficiently pleased with his own son's progress to allow him, in some measure, to act as a pupil-teacher. The following March Henry went up to Cambridge with Charles Baring to read with Farish for a year or so before entering college, and John Venn, now within three months of his death, went with him to Cambridge to introduce him to all his old friends. In his son's progress he took the same sort of active interest his father had taken in his studies in the period just before entering the university:

> I have borrowed a Wood's Algebra that I may follow you page by page, and on Monday I shall expect a register of the fortnight's work. . . . You must do innumerable examples and set yourself many to do. . . . I would send you Bonnycastle's Algebra if I could find it . . . he abounds in examples. . . . Do you assist the Professor to take down his models and to put them up? Make yourself well acquainted with this principle of machinery, which a little practice in this way will soon teach you.[1]

Whether Venn, had he lived, would have given the same sort of education to his younger son John is uncertain. At the age of seven John was sent to Mr. Greaves' school. To this school the Macaulays had sent their own son Tom, who although two years older than John Venn became as frightened of him as the dissenting minister's son at Barnes had been of John Venn's grandfather.[2] Whenever Zachary Macaulay brought his son to the Rectory "to play with Johnny Venn, he generally contrived to slip away into a cloakroom or cupboard with a book. If found, he was routed out on to the common and harried by his companions. Thence he would endeavour to escape, and if discovered would generally be found hidden among the furze bushes declaiming poetry."[2] During the last year of his father's life John was sent to a school at Bewdley, Worcestershire, kept by the Rev. John Cawood, an Evangelical clergyman.[3]

In 1808 Kitty's mother, Mrs. King, died and John went to Hull for the funeral. He stayed there for three weeks visiting

[1] Quoted, *Annals*, p. 123.

[2] *Ibid.*, p. 176.

[3] John Cawood was one of the many Evangelical clergy educated at St. Edmund Hall, Oxford. It would have been his religious principles that made John Venn choose his school for his son. Cawood was perpetual curate of Bewdley 1814–1852

various friends, through whom he met Miss Frances Turton, a young woman in her early twenties, whom he was asked to look after on the journey back to London. George King crossed the Humber with them; it would be interesting to know whether he guessed that Frances Turton would eventually become the second Mrs. John Venn.

John Venn courted her for four years—why he delayed so long before he married her it is difficult to say; it may have been his uncertain health or his equally uncertain finances, or there may have been a temporary rift between them, for Frances Turton's name disappears from his diary for a whole year at one stage. Some letters have survived: these are usually on debatable theological topics such as predestination; some, however, reflect the purpose of the writer, but they are treatises on affection rather than love-letters. In 1809 Frances Turton moved with her parents from Turnham Green to Clapham and John Venn helped them prepare the garden. There follow entries in the diary of visits to art galleries and the British Museum with the Turtons, an occasion on which he explained the workings of the thermometer and the compass to the Turtons and one or two references to sitting with Miss Turton "in the summer-house, etc.". In 1811 he had vast alterations made to the Rectory, so vast that the family had to take a house temporarily at Carshalton; he had his portrait painted by Slater and on August 25, 1812, they were married at St. George's, Bloomsbury, by Sharpe.

He was fifty-three and she was thirty when John Venn had decided that circumstances were at last propitious enough to make his second marriage more than probable. He wrote to his children explaining the whole situation fully and frankly, saying that it would make no difference to their fortunes or to their relationship with himself. "Few families, my beloved children, have been as happy as we have been."[1] They seem to have accepted the situation calmly, but John's sister Jane, who had been in reality their mother for nine years as well as manager of her brother's household, was extremely upset. This should not have surprised John Venn, but evidently it did, for we find him writing to one of his other sisters: "Undoubtedly

[1] J. Venn to his children, March 24, 1812 (MS.).

the shock which she received from parting from my house was very great, and had I known how great it could have been, I should, I think, have sacrificed every prospect of my happiness to hers."[1] The arrangement was that she should stay with her sisters and friends for part of the year but return to the Rectory for most of the time.

John and Frances Venn were married less than a year, and after John Venn's death Jane returned to look after the children till they were grown up. Mrs. Venn lived on till 1870. Long before her death her mind had become deranged.

It is difficult to form much of an estimate of the character of Frances Venn, for none of her letters have been preserved. The only thing we know for certain does not redound to her favour. On Kitty's death her mother had sent John Venn a full-length portrait in oils of Kitty as a girl of sixteen dancing. Frances Venn had the portrait cut so that only the head remains. Whether the motive was jealousy or bigotry, or a mixture of both, it is difficult to determine.

Cunningham's remark about John Venn's parish being his larger family and his family being his smaller parish is illuminating. It suggests that his parishioners were surprised by his gentleness and humility and his children perhaps a little awed by his firmness and authority in the home. In both parish and home he was attempting to exercise that parental care which he himself had experienced at Huddersfield, Yelling and Cambridge. Like his father, he had many of the qualities that make a great parish priest. He possessed the ability both to preach and to teach: he had by now learnt the secret of identifying himself with his people.

In every department of his life there is evidence of a strong imagination and the power to put thought into practice. This can be seen in his ordering of Church life and worship, in his conduct of local affairs and in his ideas for the education of both other people's children and his own. The poor of the parish he regarded as his children and took the responsibility of doing what he thought was best for them. His powers of organization and leadership flowered at Clapham: the first Chairman of the Church Missionary Society owed a debt of gratitude to the

[1] J. Venn to Mrs. Kitty Harvey, 1813.

founder and organizer of both the Clapham Armed Association and the Society for Bettering the Condition of the Poor in Clapham. Added to these qualities he possessed a judgment on which others could absolutely rely—this quality, which was noted by his friends in his undergraduate days, achieved maturity at Clapham.

4

WORDS AND DEEDS—A CHAPTER ON THE CLAPHAM SECT

IN the previous chapter we saw John Venn at the centre of the civil as well as the ecclesiastical life of Clapham; in this he stands with others on the circumference of a circle of friends whose centre is one of his parishioners, William Wilberforce.

It was this group of friends that made Clapham during the twenty years of John Venn's ministry the most important parish in England. Never have the members of one congregation so greatly influenced the history of the world. The effect of their prayers and actions not only profoundly altered the religious and social life of this country, it was also felt in Africa, in the West Indies, in India and in Australasia; in fact wherever freedom was given to slaves, wherever the ideal of trusteeship in colonial affairs was implemented, wherever the Gospel was preached by Chaplains of the East India Company, by missionaries of the Church Missionary Society or by colporteurs of the British and Foreign Bible Society. It is the purpose of this chapter to see John Venn both in relationship to the other members of the Clapham Sect[1] and to show how he interpreted their ideas and ideals in his sermons and occasional writings.

[1] This title has usually been attributed to Sidney Smith, who never tired of sneering at "the patent Christians of Clapham". Dr. E. M. Howse in the Appendix to *Saints in Politics*, pp. 187–9, says that he has been unable to discover the phrase "Clapham Sect" in Sidney Smith's writings and concludes that it was coined by Sir James Stephen for the essay that first appeared in the *Edinburgh Review* in 1844, and which was republished in his *Essays in Ecclesiastical Biography*. The title is a misnomer, as Sect suggests a Dissenting Body of Christians. All the members of the Clapham group were Anglicans and those who lived at Clapham were members of John Venn's congregation, apart from William Smith who was a Unitarian. As the name has stuck it seems senseless to attempt to change it, despite its inaccuracy.

The "Clapham Sect" owed its origin to Henry Thornton, third son of John Thornton, and to Henry Thornton's high regard for Wilberforce. "On the whole," he wrote to Grant in 1793, "I am in hopes some good may come out of our Clapham system. Wilberforce is a candle that should not be hid under a bushel."[1] If they had met before the year 1786 we do not know. It was in this year that the newly-converted Wilberforce was advised by his counsellor, John Newton, to spend time with the Thornton family to which he was related by marriage. At this time Wilberforce was twenty-six and Thornton twenty-five. In spite of their youth Wilberforce had already been a Member of Parliament for five years and Thornton for three. Thornton sat for Southwark; his business was that of a banker in the city. It was through Wilberforce that Thornton met the friends who eventually comprised the "Clapham Sect":

> Few men [Thornton writes in his diary] have been blessed with worthier and better friends than it has been my lot to be. Mr. Wilberforce stands at the head of these, for he was the friend of my youth. It is chiefly through him that I have been introduced to a variety of other most valuable associates, to my friends Babington and Gisborne and their worthy families, to Lord Teignmouth and his family, to Mrs. Hannah More and her sisters: to Mr. Stephen and to not a few respectable Members of Parliament. Second only to Mr. Wilberforce in my esteem is now the family of Mr. Grant.[2]

All the people mentioned were members of the "Clapham Sect" though several of them never lived at Clapham. Hannah More, for instance, began her schools at Cheddar at the instigation of Wilberforce after he had visited some of the country cottages in 1787. It was through Wilberforce that she met Henry Thornton, Grant and John Venn, who were in turn taken to Wilberforce's Bath house and introduced to Hannah More, her sisters and her schools. Wilberforce and Thornton financed her schools and her tracts. After Thornton's marriage in 1796 she became an annual visitor to Clapham, always stay-

[1] H. Morris, *Life of Charles Grant* (1904), p. 200.

[2] Diary of Henry Thornton quoted in F. A. v. Hayek's Introduction to his edition of Henry Thornton's *An Enquiry into the Nature and Effects of the Paper Credit of Great Britain* (1939), pp. 19–20.

ing at Battersea Rise. These visits were particularly popular with her friends' children. Thomas Gisborne was a country clergyman and a former college friend of Wilberforce's. Gisborne wrote to him when he heard of his decision to be parliamentary spokesman of the Abolitionists, and in turn he reintroduced Wilberforce to another Cambridge contemporary, Thomas Babington. Though neither lived at Clapham they were both frequent visitors at Clapham and Wilberforce used their homes in Staffordshire and Leicestershire for uninterrupted work on the "slave business" and for holidays. It was of course through Babington that the others met Babington's brother-in-law, Zachary Macaulay, who eventually became a resident Claphamite.

That Clapham became the home of most of the others was in most cases occasioned by Henry Thornton's returning there to live in 1792. His father had inherited two houses at Clapham, next door to one another; when he died his elder sons, Samuel and Robert, occupied these and Henry seems to have made his London house in King's Arms Yard his sole residence, and it was here that Wilberforce and the others gathered to work together. On May 2, 1792, however, he bought a small Queen Anne manor house called Battersea Rise, on the west side of the Common on the Clapham–Wandsworth border,[1] and on May 15th he took Wilberforce and Grant over the house and grounds. Wilberforce accepted Thornton's invitation to live with him and share both the house and the expenses. Within eighteen months Henry Thornton was writing enthusiastically to Grant of the hopes he had of his "Clapham system". "Mr. Wilberforce is a candle that should not be held under a bushel. The influence of his conversation is great and striking. I am surprised to find how much religion everybody seems to have when they get into our house. They seem all to submit and to acknowledge the advantage of a religious life, and we are not at all queer or guilty of carrying things too far."[2]

Charles Hole makes the interesting suggestion that John

[1] See Miss D. Pym, *Battersea Rise* (1934) for a good description of the house and a very unsympathetic description of its occupants, and E. M. Forster, *Marianne Thornton,* chapter I.

[2] Morris, *op. cit.*, p. 200.

Venn's appointment as Rector gave birth to Henry Thornton's idea of a colony of heaven at Clapham.[1] This is not strictly correct, for Henry Thornton bought his house within a fortnight of John Venn being offered the living, and he did not come to a final decision till about the time that Thornton was asking Wilberforce to join him at Battersea Rise. What is far more likely is that when Sir James Stonhouse died on April 14, 1792, Henry Thornton knew that the trustees his father had appointed would fill the vacancy with an Evangelical incumbent, and with this in view he started looking for a house in the parish. If Foster had accepted instead of Venn, Thornton would undoubtedly still have moved to Clapham.

Meanwhile as the grounds were extensive Henry Thornton not only enlarged Battersea Rise but began to build two new houses, Glenelg and Broomfield, to be occupied by Grant and Edward Eliot respectively, thus providing accommodation for, as well as the idea of, a Clapham Sect. Edward Eliot was Pitt's brother-in-law. His wife had died in childbirth a year after their marriage; Eliot was almost inconsolable but through Wilberforce's friendship came to share his faith in Christ. From that day Wilberforce had no more affectionate friend than Eliot. Pitt often came to Clapham to visit his small niece, her father, and the two bachelors at Battersea Rise. On one occasion Thornton said that he was thinking of adding a library to the existing house, which brought from Pitt the rejoinder: "I have always wished to build a library, let me draw you a plan for yours", and at once drew the design of the famous Oval Library which was added in 1797.[2] It was in this room that the Clapham Cabinet usually met.

Eliot's house was a quarter of a mile south-east of Battersea Rise, Grant's about a hundred and fifty yards to the west. All three houses were similar in style. Though the land was divided between the three owners, no attempt was made to separate the gardens, and access from one house to the others through the gardens was easy. Six weeks before the Grants moved in, Charles Grant asked Venn to inspect the house and grounds

[1] C. Hole, *John Venn*, a short MS. life in the archives of the Church Missionary Society.

[2] G. W. E. Russell, *Manchester Guardian*, June 15, 1907.

with him. At Venn's suggestion he ordered the cutting down of several trees near the house which obscured the view.[1] This was in September 1794, by which time he had been fifteen months in Clapham.

From all this it can be seen that when the Venns came into residence in March 1793 they found Thornton and Wilberforce well-established in Battersea Rise and the builders busily erecting Broomfield and Glenelg for the Eliots and Grants respectively. By the end of 1794 both families were in their new homes. They were soon followed by the Stephens. James Stephen was a barrister from St. Christopher's, who, having witnessed an act of injustice done to four negro slaves soon after his arrival in the West Indies, became a Secret Abolitionist. In 1794 he and his family came home for good and shortly moved to Clapham Common to be near Wilberforce. In 1796 Stephen's wife died: like Eliot before him he turned to Wilberforce for consolation, and when Eliot died Stephen took his place in Wilberforce's affections; also like Eliot he came to share Wilberforce's faith. The relationship between the two men became of the same nature as that which existed between Venn and Edwards. In 1800 Stephen married Wilberforce's widowed sister, Sarah Clarke.[2]

In March 1796 Henry Thornton married, and Wilberforce gave up his rooms in Battersea Rise and presumably moved to his London house in Palace Yard. However, he was away from town most of the following year writing his book.[3] In May 1797 he married Barbara Spooner whom he had met at Bath.[4] He

[1] Morris, *op. cit.*, p. 223.

[2] When both families were moving from Clapham, Stephen told Wilberforce what membership of the Clapham Sect meant to him: "I was in a worse world in the West Indies and God brought me to England. I thought my new world here bad and tried, though faintly, alas! to get above it, and God brought me into a better one—into the circle of such people as your B. and my dear S. and Babington, etc." C. E. Stephen, *The First Sir James Stephen* (1906), pp. 136–7.

[3] *A Practical View of the Prevailing Religious System of Professed Christians in the Higher and Middle Classes in this Country, contrasted with Real Christianity* (1797). For John Venn's comments on it see pp. 185–6.

[4] Mrs. Wilberforce seems to have been as unpopular with her husband's Clapham friends as he himself was popular—see Marianne Thornton's remarks in her autobiography (E. M. Forster, *op. cit.*, pp. 42–44). The fact that her name hardly occurs in the Venns' letters suggests that they may have shared the Thornton's aversion.

brought his bride back to Palace Yard, but they were frequently able to stay at Broomfield which Eliot rented to them, presumably in his absence. Broomfield unexpectedly became their permanent home, for Eliot, who had refused the Governor-Generalship of India because of illness, suddenly died in September. "I feel his loss deeply", Wilberforce tells Hannah More, "and shall continue to feel it; except for Henry Thornton there is no one living with whom I was so much in the habit of consulting, and whose death so breaks in on all my plans in all directions. We were engaged in a multitude of pursuits together." Wilberforce and Grant had persuaded Dundas and Pitt that Eliot was the right man to succeed Cornwallis as Governor-General of India. There at least seems some possibility, as we shall see, that his policy with regard to missions would have been less cautious than that of their second choice, John Shore, who on retirement became Lord Teignmouth and in 1802 bought the house Samuel Thornton vacated on his move to Albury Park. He too became a staunch Claphamite with his pew in the front gallery of Holy Trinity Church.

1802 saw the addition not only of Teignmouth but also of Zachary Macaulay to the Clapham circle. Like Stephen, he had first-hand experience of the slavery business, having himself been an overseer in a sugar plantation in Jamaica at the age of seventeen. After four years he returned to England and spent much time at Rothley Temple with his sister Jean, who was now married to Thomas Babington. It was to Babington that he owed his faith in Christ, and the name Thomas Babington Macaulay, which he gave his eldest son, is a testimony of the affection and gratitude with which he always regarded his brother-in-law.[1]

At Rothley Temple he met both Wilberforce and Henry Thornton as early as 1789, who both formed an extremely high opinion of the young man, and appointed him to a place on the Council in Sierra Leone in 1792. After two years he became Governor of the colony. He was only twenty-six but the story

[1] "If you were aware of my obligations to Babington, you would not be surprised that in speaking of him I should express such deep affection. I never think of him but my thoughts are drawn to that Saviour with whom he first brought me acquainted." Quoted in Charles Booth, *Zachary Macaulay* (1934), p. 22.

of his five years in office proves to be an epic of its own, and it is admirably told by Sir George Trevelyan in his *Life and Letters of Lord Macaulay*. Macaulay virtually rebuilt the colony after a French raid during his first year as Governor. In his person he combined the offices of administrator, judge, director of education, and chaplain. The confidence his friends placed in him was not misplaced, for, as Wilberforce told Babington, "he appears to have a manly collected mind".[1] In all his trials and work he was in constant touch with Thornton, who gave him continual encouragement and advice.

In 1799 Macaulay returned to England to marry Selina Mills, one of Hannah More's assistant teachers, whom he had met during his furlough in 1796. He also brought with him twenty-five African children who were settled at Clapham and sent to school there. After two years living over the Sierra Leone Company's offices in Birchin Lane, the Macaulays also moved to Clapham, occupying No. 5, The Pavement, near both the Plough Inn and Holy Trinity Church.

One other name must be mentioned; that of William Smith. He had been living in Clapham since 1773 and had become friendly with the Thornton family. He was a Unitarian by conviction and belonged to the Independent congregation in Clapham.[2] From 1784 he had been successively Member of Parliament for Sudbury, Camelford and Norwich: he was one of the few Dissenters able to obtain a seat in the unreformed Parliament; their interests and the question of political and religious liberty were his chief concerns. Through the Thorntons he met Wilberforce and soon became with James Stephen the most fiery of the Abolitionist team. Wilberforce and Smith seem to have differed on every question save the Slave Trade. In politics Wilberforce was an ardent Pittite, Smith an ardent Foxite and a member of Grey's "Friends of the People".[3] On religion they

[1] "I will by no means forget Macaulay; I think highly of his understanding; he appears to have a manly collected mind." Wilberforce to Babington, Aug. 10, 1792, printed in *Correspondence of Wilberforce*, Vol. I, p. 93.

[2] Many Independent churches had become Unitarian in their doctrine during the course of the eighteenth century.

[3] "Friends of the People" was founded by Grey in 1792 to promote parliamentary reform. Although its aims were moderate the course of the French Revolution caused it to be looked upon with severe suspicion and only the left wing of Fox's party, excluding Fox himself, belonged to it.

talked much but never agreed: "Oh how I wish he were even as we in the most important particulars", Wilberforce remarks in his Journal; but on the Slave Trade they were staunch allies and in private life firm friends. Holding Unitarian views in religion and Radical views in politics was no disqualification from memberhip of the Clapham Sect; in fact this large, healthy Dissenter with his loud laugh and passion for justice seems to have been a general favourite.

Wilberforce, Thornton, Venn, Grant, Eliot, Stephen, Teignmouth, Macaulay, Smith; these, together with their country friends, Gisborne, Babington and Hannah More, formed the core of the Clapham Sect. Yet the house on Clapham Common and the pews in Clapham Church began to see a change of occupants as soon as the latest arrivals had taken up residence. In 1802 the Grants moved back to Bloomsbury and the ministry of Richard Cecil; in 1808 Venn tells Edwards of further changes.

> You have heard no doubt of the losses we have sustained at Clapham. Mr. Wilberforce has left us as he intends to have one house only, and Clapham was too far from the House of Commons. Lord Teignmouth also has sold his house and now lives in town. Stephen is I am afraid going also. Some other of our respectable families have forsaken us—in a short time Clapham will be a very different place to me, and I expect to find myself almost a stranger in it.[1]

Wilberforce moved to Kensington Gore, and Stephen to Ormond Street, with another house at Bledlow in Buckinghamshire. Lord Teignmouth's house at Clapham was taken by Spencer Perceval, who became Prime Minister the following year.

These formed the core—the inner Cabinet of the "Clapham Sect". There were others on the fringe, and there is certain to be difference of opinion as to the membership of the inner group. For instance, Granville Sharp had done as much or more for the negro slave than any of the others; he was responsible for Lord Mansfield's judgment which made illegal the ownership of slaves on English soil, he was Chairman of the Committee for the Abolition of the Slave Trade, the colony at Sierra Leone was his venture, later his friends compelled him to become the first Chairman of the British and Foreign Bible

[1] J. Venn to E. Edwards, Sept. 26, 1808 (MS.).

Society; moreover, he lived at Clapham and worshipped at the parish church. Sir James Stephen says he was "at once the abiding guest and the bosom friend of his more wealthy brothers";[1] this was no doubt true, but it also seems true that he was not a member of the inner Cabinet. His name does not figure in the names Wilberforce mentions when talking of the meetings, nor, as far as the writer can tell, in the diaries and correspondence of the others. In John Venn's papers there is no reference to Granville Sharp which is a great pity as we should have treasured a description of Sharp, trying to convince Venn, as he once tried to convince Fox, of the identity of Napoleon with the Little Horn in the Book of Daniel; unfortunately we have no such report. The fact that he was twenty-five years older than Wilberforce, Thornton, and Venn, may well account for his being rather apart from the rest.

Others whose names have been mentioned in connection with the Clapham Sect include Simeon, John Bowdler and Milner.[2] Simeon together with Venn was chief ecclesiastical adviser of the group; in 1797–8 he is to be found at Battersea Rise urging the necessity of, and making plans for, an Anglican missionary society. Apart from these years, as we have seen, his visits to Clapham were rare; his real circle of influence was Cambridge, not Clapham.

John Bowdler also did not live at Clapham, but he was a much more frequent visitor than Simeon to Battersea Rise where he was greatly respected for his ability and his personal holiness. By profession he was a barrister, but he is chiefly remembered as the prime mover in the agitation for church building which resulted in Government grants being made for the erection of new churches in over-populated and under-churched parishes.[3] Bowdler was a High Churchman and his

[1] Sir J. Stephen, *Essays in Ecclesiastical Biography* (1907 edn.), Vol. II, p. 203.

[2] Dr. Howse would add John Venn's brother-in-law, Charles Elliott, but his claims seem scarcely adequate; he moved to Grove House, Clapham, to be near his brother-in-law. It is true he became a member of the committee of the Church Missionary Society, the Bible Society and the Prayer Book and Homily Society, but his relationship to Venn would be sufficient cause for him to be engaged in this work. His claims to membership of the Clapham Sect are no stronger, say, than those of Samuel Thornton.

[3] Parliament made grants for church building in 1818 and 1824. In 1818 the Church Building Society was formed. See F. Warre-Cornish, *A History of the English Church in the Nineteenth Century* (1910), pp. 77–81.

chief allies were members of the Clapton Sect, Joshua Watson and Archdeacon Daubney, but in the matter of building new churches he could rely on his friends at Clapham as well and he forms an interesting link between the two groups. He died of consumption in 1815 at the age of thirty-two.

Isaac Milner we have already met. He was another of the annual visitors at Broomfield, where his host was quite prepared to leave him the centre of the stage and listen to his loud, dominating conversation.[1]

John Venn's letters and diaries reveal just how close he was to the others and how far their lives intertwined. "Dear Mr. Wilberforce", he tells Mrs. Bewicke at the beginning of 1808, "is better, indeed now pretty recovered. Mr. Henry and Robert Thornton are both in town. Lady Teignmouth not very well. The rest of our friends as usual."[2] Typical entries in the diary are: "Called at Mr. Stephen's and Lord Teignmouth's, supped at Mr. Macaulay's, visited sick, dined at Mr. Wilberforce's with Dean Milner and Lady E. Perceval." "Babington and Macaulay to tea." "Mr. Grant came to spend a day with me." "Took leave of Mr. and Mrs. H. Thornton who set out for Yorkshire." When Venn and his family were staying with the Elliotts at their Brighton house, Wilberforce and his wife came for a night on their way through from Portsmouth to Eastbourne. During the General Election of 1806 Venn sent his children to Southwark to watch Henry Thornton's procession round the Borough. In 1810 John Venn baptized Macaulay's seventh child, who was aptly named Hannah More Macaulay,[3] in the presence of the Macaulays and the Babingtons. When the Macaulays were unable to put Babington up he stayed at the Rectory. In 1795 when Kitty Venn was staying with her father-in-law at Yelling, her husband was so preoccupied with parish business that Charles Grant offered to go to Yelling and accompany her home.

After 1808 Venn's visits to town usually included a visit to Kensington Gore and sometimes he called on either the

[1] J. Stephen, *Essays in Ecclesiastical Biography*, pp. 234 and 236, and E. M. Forster, *op. cit.*, p. 43.

[2] J. Venn to Mrs. Bewicke, Jan. 22, 1808 (MS.).

[3] She married Sir Charles Trevelyan and became the mother of Sir George Otto Trevelyan, the biographer of Lord Macaulay.

Stephens, the Grants or the Teignmouths as well. On one occasion he rode to Kensington Gore to dine with Wilberforce, but his host had forgotten and was out: three days later he met Wilberforce at a dinner party in another house; no doubt Wilberforce apologized very charmingly for forgetting Venn the previous Tuesday.

Evidence of the link that "young" Bowdler formed between the Clapton and Clapham Sects occur in some entries in the diary for August 1809. "Aug. 7, 1809, dined at H. Thornton's with Mr. Knox[1] and Jebb of Ireland, Cunningham, etc." "Aug. 17, dined at Mr. H. Thornton's with Mr. Knox and Jebb of Ireland, Mr. Bowdler, Morgan, Mr. and Mrs. Wilberforce." Aug. 20, "Jebb preached at Clapham Church." Henry Thornton was very impressed by both of them, but perceived doctrinal differences on such matters as the Atonement, which made him write in his diary: "They would not quite coalesce with our evangelical principle."[2]

There is a remarkable passage in Lady Knutsford's *Life and Letters of Zachary Macaulay* which shows that she found in her researches abundant evidence of the same affinity between the members of the Clapham Sect that Venn's diaries reveal. She speaks of them as regarding every member as "forming part of a large united family", behaving towards each other as members of such a family. They treated each other's homes as their own, "taking with them as a matter of course" their wives and children; they kept together for their holidays and while in London arranged to meet for breakfast or dinner to discuss their many common concerns. "The weight of continual business was lightened and cheered by sharing it with congenial companions and the habits of life thus systematically arranged, seemed to ensure considerable economy of time and correspon-

[1] Alexander Knox and John Jebb (see p. 251) were the most distinguished lay and clerical representative of the Church of Ireland. Although Knox owed a great deal to John Wesley, he was a decided High Church Anglican who greatly influenced his school friend John Jebb. Jebb later became Bishop of Limerick. They were country friends rather than members of the Clapton Sect, which was mainly composed of younger men. Another link between Knox and Jebb and the Clapham Sect was Hannah More who maintained a long friendship with both of them, though with Knox in particular. See M. G. Jones, *Hannah More* (1952), pp. 213–15.

[2] Thornton Wigan Book (MS.).

dence when there were no district messengers, and no telegraph or telephone at the service of busy people."[1]

An illustration of their taking their holidays together and their principle of open house is to be found in Wilberforce's purchase of a house near Bath in 1799. This was intended as a retreat from the world but Henry Thornton confided to Hannah More that he was not sanguine about the prospects of its being used for this purpose, for Wilberforce's "heart also is so large that he never will be able to refrain from inviting people to his house . . . and the Bath house will be troubled with exactly the same heap of fellows as the Battersea Rise one."[2] Venn was one of the "heap of fellows" invited there within a few weeks of the Wilberforces moving in. Ten years later Wilberforce showed how accurate Henry Thornton's observations were by writing to Venn from Bath: "We are here in full force and I should be ashamed of pouring into a friend's house thus *en masse*, if I were not really conscious that I should like to receive, as well as to pay, such a visit: for instance it would give me real pleasure to receive under my roof yourself, and sister, and all your descendants."[3]

Although Venn is unlikely to have attended the meetings of the Clapham Cabinet when political questions were being discussed, he was frequently called in, not only as "ecclesiastical adviser" and missionary statesman, but also as an acknowledged authority on education and philanthropy. On these subjects his knowledge fell in no way short of that of his friends.

In an essay in a more recent book, Noel Annan shows how the children of the marriage alliances of the Clapham leaders themselves became prominent as members of the intellectual aristocracy of Victorian England. To take one example from John Venn's own family. His second daughter, Jane, married James Stephen's third son, James Stephen, the famous "Mr. Over-Secretary Stephen" of the Colonial Office, and first biographer of the Clapham Sect. Their children included Sir Leslie Stephen, among whose own children were Vanessa who married Clive Bell, and Virginia who as a writer surpassed her

[1] Lady Knutsford, *Life and Letters of Zachary Macaulay* (1900), pp. 271–2.
[2] *Life of Wilberforce*, Vol. 2, p. 350.
[3] *Correspondence of Wilberforce*, Vol. 2, pp. 189–90.

husband, Leonard Woolf. Here is one of the links between the Clapham and the Bloomsbury Sects; another link is E. M. Forster, who is a great-grandson of Henry Thornton.[1]

Most of the members of the Clapham Sect had some effect on Venn but none more than Wilberforce himself. Venn first met Wilberforce in 1792, within a few months of his appointment as Rector of Clapham.

> I slept on Friday at Paddington [he tells his father] and on Saturday dined at Mr. Thornton's where I found Mr. Wilberforce upon a visit. He regretted much his being obliged to leave Bath, just when he had the hopes of enjoying your acquaintance[2] and I am sorry you had not this opportunity of knowing so extraordinary a man, for extraordinary he is indeed. I am much pleased with his vivacity, he has the most lively mind I ever knew, and never failed as soon as he came to put the company into the best humour. At the same time his liveliness was that of a Christian, innocent and pure, and often interrupted by something which marked the benevolence and purity of his mind.

The effect of Wilberforce's friendship on Venn was revolutionary and decisive. "I hope he will stir him up",[3] was Henry Venn's comment to a friend after describing a brief conversation he himself had with Wilberforce, just before his son and the statesman met for the first time. This hope was quickly fulfilled. It so happened that within a few months of Venn's arrival at Clapham Wilberforce took him as his companion for a summer holiday in July, centred on Bath. It was Wilberforce's custom before his marriage to invite some friend to join him on holiday and get to know that friend really well; in 1790 it was Babington, in 1792 it was Richard Cecil and in 1793 it was Venn.[4] Venn gladly accepted. He told Edwards his health had not been good for the past five or six weeks and he welcomed the oppor-

[1] N. G. Annan, "The Intellectual Aristocracy" in *Studies in Social History. A tribute to G. M. Trevelyan* (1955), ed. J. H. Plumb. See genealogical table p. 285.

[2] H. Venn and Jane Venn were staying in Bath at the same time as Wilberforce and his sister. They arranged to dine together, but Wilberforce was summoned unexpectedly to London the day appointed. H. Venn to J. Venn, July 4, 1792 (MS.).

[3] H. Venn to Lady Mary Fitzgerald, Aug. 1, 1792 (MS.).

[4] Perhaps Wilberforce was following the example of John Thornton, who frequently toured the country with Bull or Foster or some other minister as companion and usually secured a pulpit for them on the Sunday.

tunity of the holiday. They left Clapham in Wilberforce's carriage on July 9th; Venn did not finally return till August 16th. They visited Windsor Castle and saw the King getting into his carriage; at Reading they stayed the night with Cadogan;[1] while Wilberforce took breakfast with Addington,[2] Cadogan looked after Venn and showed him round his parish. From Reading they went to Marlborough and on the next day to Bath; they arrived at Bath in the midst of a heat-wave. The heat was so intense that Wilberforce wrote the next day to Hannah More:

My dear Madam,

After having been detained day after day for above a fortnight in or near London, I at length emerged with Mr. Venn on Tuesday last, and arrived here yesterday afternoon. The heat is such as to render the Bath waters a potation as little suited to health as pleasure, and unless the weather change, we must withdraw from this roasting without and stewing within whilst we have strength to get away, and seek a more genial climate amongst the mountains of Wales. Meanwhile we cannot quit these parts without being gratified, and I hope profited, by a survey of your operations; and therefore we propose, if it be convenient, to be with you to-morrow evening. Both Mr. Venn and I prefer being witnesses of your Sunday lecture before your week-day conventicling. You must not engage a pulpit for him, as all his sermons are in his trunk and he does not extemporize before strangers; but if his trunk arrives in time, he will put one or two sermons in his pocket, and perhaps you could get a pulpit on short notice for the Rector of Clapham, M.A. though not for one of Miss Patty's lank-haired favourites. I am sure you will thank me for making you acquainted with so good and so agreeable a man.

I am always very sincerely yours,

W. WILBERFORCE[3]

[1] Vicar of St. Giles, Reading, and Rector of Chelsea.

[2] Henry Addington, Speaker of the House of Commons, Prime Minister 1801–4. Later created Viscount Sidmouth. As Speaker he was popular and the friend of both Wilberforce and Pitt, as Prime Minister he was entirely inadequate and brought on himself Canning's rhyme:

"Pitt is to Addington
As London is to Paddington."

[3] *Life of Wilberforce*, Vol. 2, pp. 30–1.

Evidently Venn's trunk arrived in time and he preached on Sunday morning at Cheddar and in the evening at Axbridge to large congregations. During the next three days Hannah More whisked the two friends round her schools. What Venn saw made an indelible impression and, as we showed in the previous chapter, Hannah More came to have no more ardent advocate than John Venn. At the time he wrote enthusiastically to Edwards:

> Went to Miss Hannah More's. Here I had a great friend indeed, I preached twice on Sunday and saw her schools. A hundred and fifty children are praising God in loud hallelujahs who but four years ago knew nothing of God but to swear by his holy name. Now many of the children appeared not only to be well instructed in the knowledge of the Bible, and some of them to have 70 or 80 chapters in it by heart, but several seemed to feel very deeply the power of the truth, and others who have gone away have brought their fellow prentices, their masters and mistresses, or their parents, to pray to God night and morning. Indeed I never saw anything which affected me, or which promises more to glorify God, it is indeed the Lord's doing, and it ought to be marvellous in our eyes. Two women (Miss Hannah More and Miss Patty More), remarkably weak in point of health, have thus been enabled to superintend a thousand children who else had been brought up not only without learning but without any knowledge of God.[1]

The heat wave abated, but the idea of visiting Wales persisted. From Cheddar the travellers went on to Bristol, where they met Coulthurst, and on to Wales through the Wye Valley. Ten days later they were back at Wilberforce's house, Perry Mead, near Bath. They stayed three weeks, drinking the waters assiduously. On one Sunday Venn preached at the Abbey church, Wilberforce having asked the incumbent to invite him. On August 16th Venn was summoned home by a letter from his wife that began: "I think now it is time you were at home, the people are not well satisfied with Mr. P. as with yourself. Whether this ought to please you I do not know."[2] The trouble was that John Venn had not heeded Stillingfleet's advice, and

[1] J. Venn to E. Edwards, July 1793 (MS.).
[2] Mrs. J. Venn to J. Venn, Aug. 13, 1793 (MS.).

the preaching of Mr. Puddicombe, who was taking the locum, was causing much offence.[1]

During this tour Venn's character and qualities impressed very favourably both Hannah More and Wilberforce himself. The former wrote to Mrs. Kennicott: "Yesterday Mr. Wilberforce and young Mr. Venn the new rector of Clapham left us, after having spent several quiet and peaceful, though not very cool, days in this little hermitage. . . . As to the latter it is a great compliment to almost any man to say he is agreeable when Wilberforce is in company, because the gaiety of his temper and the vivacity of his understanding make him appear to good advantage more than good men always do; but Mr. Venn is not only extremely pious, but modest, learned and entertaining. I carried him to preach at two of our largest churches, and found him a solid, awakening, and judicious preacher."[2] At about the same time Wilberforce was writing in his diary: "I have had Venn with me near a fortnight; he is heavenly-minded, and bent on his Master's work, affectionate to all around him, and above all to Christ's people, as such. How low are my attainments. . . . Oh let me labour with redoubled diligence, to enter in at the strait gate."[3]

If the influence of Venn's spirituality drove Wilberforce to re-examine his spiritual life on this holiday, the influence of Wilberforce on Venn was even more marked and permanent. Venn tells Edwards: "My dear friend Mr. Wilberforce is extremely devoted to God, we enjoy most pleasant interviews together and he treats me with extreme kindness. May God long protect his valuable life";[4] and to his father he writes: "he makes the lively oracles of God's Word his delight, he has opened his whole heart to me with great familiarity and indeed I have very seldom met with a person who appears to be more devoted to God than he does. He is no common Christian: his knowledge of divine things and his experience of the power of the Gospel are very extraordinary."[5] They talked, they read

[1] Puddicombe had held a curacy at Romford for seven years and lost his post through tactlessness.

[2] A. Roberts, *Mendip Annals* (1859), p. 83.

[3] *Life of Wilberforce*, Vol. 2, p. 32.

[4] J. Venn to E. Edwards, July 1793 (MS.).

[5] J. Venn to H. Venn (MS.).

books together, they read the Bible to each other and they prayed together. The most significant thing about the latter is that it was the layman who took it on himself to comment on the parson's devotional life; three years later Venn told Edwards that Wilberforce remarked on the fact that Venn scarcely ever prayed "to be kept from Satan".

There can be no doubt of the profound impact the layman made on the clergyman of exactly his own age; Venn himself told his father that "he had not received so much benefit from any man as he had done from Mr. Wilberforce".[1] When John Venn visited Yelling the following year, his father rejoiced in the change it was plain to see. Wilberforce had indeed stirred his son up. "John Venn," he tells Riland, "came the second week in February to pay us a visit, we were struck with the great change. All his rustic diffidence is gone. I no sooner proposed his preaching twice than he said he would. Mr. Wilberforce continues his love for him and has been made a great means of his overcoming his natural slothfulness, and the company he is obliged to keep has enabled him to get the better of his great timidity, so troublesome to himself and friends."[2]

On the Somerset holiday acquaintanceship ripened into friendship and close friends Venn and Wilberforce remained till Venn's death. Wilberforce continued to learn from Venn and Venn from Wilberforce. "I got two or three of St. Paul's epistles by heart when otherwise idle," Wilberforce notes in his Journal, "and had resolved to learn Scripture in this way remembering Venn's comfort from it."[3] On the other hand one Sunday evening when Venn called at Battersea Rise to discuss with Thornton and Wilberforce the prospect of a Huntingtonian chapel being built in the parish, his diary reads: "Venn came at night and told us his grief. . . . We discussed, and told Venn his faults."[4] While with Venn at Bath Wilberforce "laid the first timbers" of the tract[5] which grew into his *Practical View of Christianity*. He sought Venn's advice as well as others' but could not accept their suggestions. When, however, the book

[1] H. Venn to Lady Mary Fitzgerald, Jan. 21, 1794 (MS.).
[2] H. Venn to J. Riland, March 28, 1794 (MS.).
[3] Wilberforce, *op. cit.*, Vol. 2, p. 198.
[4] *Ibid.*, p. 136.
[5] *Ibid.*, p. 33.

appeared in 1797 Venn wrote enthusiastically to Edwards: "What a book is Mr. Wilberforce's! I hope it will be the means of doing much good", and adds as a postscript: "I hope it will be the means of converting at least half the aldermen of Lynn."[1]

Later in this chapter we shall consider Venn's preaching. For this Wilberforce had a high regard, which was magnified by his regard for the preacher. In 1829 he wrote to one of his clergyman sons: "If you do not possess a set of Venn's sermons I must send them to you, and recommend them, not for your parishioners' use, but for your own. They contain much good sense and a strain of true piety."[2]

In many ways Wilberforce and Venn were alike in character and it is not surprising that Hannah More should find that Venn did not suffer in comparison with his friend. Both possessed a rich vein of humour which showed itself in wit and an enviable ability to enter into the games and mentality of their own children and other people's. "Every face lighted up with pleasure at his entry", was a contemporary comment on Wilberforce;[3] it might equally well have been said of Venn. Both men were emotional and deeply affectionate, though Wilberforce was not beset by shyness like Venn or given to that occasional melancholia to which Venn was subjected through heredity and bad health. Wilberforce on the other hand had little of Venn's practical efficiency or scientific spirit.[4] Nevertheless there was a sparkle about Wilberforce, Venn and Hannah More which seems to have eluded most of their friends; Thornton and Grant, Macaulay and Babington were by nature more severe but were kept from perpetual solemnity by their gayer friends, and even Henry Thornton could sparkle on occasion.

Though Wilberforce's influence over Venn was probably greater than that of his other Clapham friends, it was Henry Thornton whom he saw most of all, for Thornton was the only one to remain in Clapham during the whole of his incumbency.

[1] J. Venn to E. Edwards, June 27, 1797 (MS.).

[2] *Correspondence of Wilberforce*, pp. 516–17.

[3] R. Coupland, *Wilberforce* (1945 edn.), p. 192.

[4] An example of Wilberforce's weakness here is revealed in a letter to Hannah More from Henry Thornton, who says the Grants and Mr. Venn "shall see your papers to-day. On Monday I will send them to Mr. Wilberforce, but if once in his hands, they are lost for ever." Nov. 22, 1800. Thornton Wigan Book (MS.).

In fact Thornton took Battersea Rise a year before Venn's arrival and died there within eighteen months of Venn's own early death. During this period there was much coming and going between the Rectory and Battersea Rise and the two men's lives interpenetrated at many points. John Venn must have known Henry Thornton at least from the time of his brief stay at Clapham following his ordination and they exchanged letters occasionally. Most of those that are extant belong to the three years preceding the move from Norfolk to Clapham. In 1790 John Venn wrote to Thornton congratulating him on his re-election to Parliament;[1] later he asked Thornton whether anything could be done to safeguard a shipwreck from being pillaged by a mob who considered it theirs by right; he had a specific case in mind. On his side Thornton sent Venn a copy of the report of the Sierra Leone Company, asking him to pass it on to his father. Later he requested Venn to subscribe for him for two numbers of Milner's *Church History*, which was appearing in serial form. Just before the Venn family moved into the Rectory Thornton made himself responsible for the cellar being well-stocked with wine.

The two days Venn spent at Battersea Rise in September 1792 gave him his first real opportunity of assessing Thornton's character. He writes to his father:

> I spent Monday and yesterday with Mr. H. Thornton and was more pleased with my visit than I have been with any for a long time. He was very open and friendly and we had a great deal of conversation upon a variety of subjects both of a religious and a civil kind. I am extremely pleased with his sterling sense, his just remarks, his attentive observation of men and manners, his tenderness of conscience and his earnest desire to be always employed in doing good. I was much struck with his resemblance to his father, the same mode of living, the same separation from the world, the same liberality were very visible; nay, his voice and person often put me in mind of that venerable man. . . . My mind is much more at ease since this visit; with such friends as I shall enjoy at

[1] The letter reveals that young John Venn, like his father, was an ardent Tory. "We have a contested election for the county. The design is to throw out Mr. Coke who has been one of Mr. Fox's partisans and elect in his stead Sir John Woodhouse whose ancestors have generally been the representatives of this county." J. Venn to H. Thornton, June 1790 (MS.).

Clapham, such advice to have recourse to, and such persons to watch over me, I shall not be so much afraid.[1]

Closer contact with Henry Thornton no doubt revealed to Venn that the resemblance to old John Thornton which he thought he had detected was in fact very superficial. E. M. Forster maintains that Henry Thornton reacted strongly against his father and was critical of his coarseness and indifference to education. Mr. Forster underlines the contrast by these two sentences on their respective portraits. "Slumped and pot-bellied, John sits,"[2] whereas Henry stands, "cold, intellectual, public-spirited, fastidious and full of integrity."[3]

Of course they had much in common, not least the liberality Venn mentions, but even here there was a deep difference. John Thornton was warm-hearted and impulsive in his generosity; Henry thought wise and well-planned investment was as essential in philanthropy as in banking. This was the same difference which Macaulay noticed between Henry Thornton and Wilberforce. Macaulay wrote to his future wife: "Wilberforce's active love flies immediately to the relief of an object in distress and gives almost instinctively. Thornton's consideration leads him to weigh the best mode of imparting relief so as to raise no false hopes, and to produce no future unhappiness and to join, if possible, the interests of eternity to those of time."[4]

Before his marriage Henry Thornton gave away sums up to £7,500 a year, after, from £2,000 to £3,000.[5] Among the many causes he assisted with his purse were Hannah More's schools and tracts and the Elland Society, which probably received the biggest grant of all.[6]

[1] J. Venn to H. Venn, Sept. 26, 1792 (MS.).

[2] E. M. Forster, *op. cit.*, p. 22. John's portrait was by Gainsborough, his son's by Hoppner.

[3] *Ibid.*, p. 23.

[4] Knutsford, *op. cit.*, p. 202. The whole letter presents an interesting contrast between the two friends and shows for what reasons Macaulay thought Wilberforce Thornton's superior.

[5] The proportion he gave away varied from year to year. See F. A. v. Hayek's introduction to Henry Thornton's *Enquiry into the Nature and Effects of the Paper Credit of Great Britain* (1802), p. 25. Inglis says he had been told by a friend that Thornton gave £1,400 per annum "for the education of pious men for the Church".

[6] Canon Hulbert says that between 1778–98 Thornton had contributed £3,880 to the Elland Society. Claudius Buchanan was trained at Queens' College, Cambridge, entirely at Thornton's expense.

The "tenderness of conscience" which John Venn mentions in his letter to his father is illustrated by a jotting in Henry Thornton's diary which reads: "I am asked to a ball in the Borough.[1] It is difficult to exercise a right spirit in the manner of my refusal."[2] Though wealthy and comfortable in many ways there was something of an ascetic about Henry Thornton. He thoroughly disapproved of his eldest brother Sam, who moved up from merchant to country gentleman, taking Albury Park as his residence, becoming Lord Lieutenant for Surrey and boasting of a sister who had married into the aristocracy.[3] (John Venn on the other hand had no such qualms; both he and his son Henry paid frequent visits to Albury Park and Sam Thornton junior became Venn's pupil.) Henry Thornton's motives for keeping a diary are revealing in this connection:

> I think I have discovered that my religion consists too much in active duties and in efforts to edify and convert others, and too little in serious self-examination, attentive reading of the Scriptures, prayer and secret self-denial. In particular I wish to begin in some measure a new life in respect to the last head of self-denial. I have been drawing up a sermon on that subject, being the substance of one preached at my house on that subject by Mr. Venn, to which I have made much addition.[4]

Some of the strictures that he makes of himself through this continual self-examination seem a little out of character. "I was too eager and talkative as usual," he writes after breakfast with the Venns, and again after another conversation with Venn, "I talked too much and heard too little, though I profited much by what I heard."[5] It seems that in Venn's company at least the cold and silent manner disappeared and in Venn he found a ready listener and a wise counsellor.

Others like Wilberforce relied on Thornton's judgment; Thornton in many things relied on Venn's. He discussed with Venn moral problems connected with his business as a financier and with Venn too he discussed his own progress in the Chris-

[1] i.e. his constituency, Southwark.
[2] Journal, Feb. 27, 1795. Thornton Wigan Book (MS.).
[3] E. M. Forster, *op. cit.*, pp. 35–6.
[4] Journal, Jan. 7, 1794. Thornton Wigan Book (MS.).
[5] April 10, 1795. Thornton Wigan Book (MS.).

tian life. One entry in the diary reads: "Venn thought my religious character more established than I suspect it is",[1] and another, "I went the day before yesterday to Battersea Rise wishing chiefly to visit Mr. Venn."[2] At Battersea Rise on Sundays, and perhaps at other times, Venn came in to preach a sermon at family prayers, after which the two friends got down to discussing it. They were also drawn together in the work of assisting Macaulay in every way possible with the *Christian Observer*, and as collaborators with Hannah More in her tracts.

The story of the founding and purpose of the *Christian Observer* has been told by Lady Knutsford in her *Life and Letters of Zachary Macaulay*[3] and retold by Dr. E. M. Howse in *Saints in Politics*.[4] However, as their account can be amplified and as in some particulars it requires modification, it seems essential to say more about the *Christian Observer* than would otherwise have been necessary. In particular Venn seems to receive more credit than the facts warrant.

Lady Knutsford says that during the summer of 1798 Wilberforce was discussing with Babington and Henry Thornton the possibility of starting a religious periodical with some reference to current affairs. He also discussed this with John Pearson,[5] surgeon at the Lock Hospital, who suggested that an editor should be appointed responsible to a committee composed half of town, half of country clergy. We learn from the minutes of the Elland Society that as early as August that year Josiah Pratt, then curate to Cecil at St. John's Chapel, Bedford Row, had agreed to "take the editorship of a magazine under the title of the *Church of England Magazine*, if he could be assured of proper support".[6] An approach had also been made to William Hey, the Leeds surgeon, either by Pearson, who had trained

[1] Feb. 22, 1795 (MS.).
[2] March 14, 1795 (MS.).
[3] pp. 250–7.
[4] pp. 105–8.
[5] Lady Knutsford confuses John Pearson (1758–1826) with the Rev. Hugh Pearson, Venn's future curate, who was still an undergraduate in 1798. John Pearson was possibly a convert of William Hey, himself a convert of Henry Venn. His name occurs in J. Venn's diaries; he was on the original C M.S. Committee. He was responsible for the appointment of Thomas Scott as Chaplain to the Lock Hospital. His daughter married one of Babington's sons. He wrote Hey's biography.
[6] Elland Society Minutes, Aug. 23, 1798 (MS).

under him, or Pratt, who was related to him by marriage, or by Wilberforce himself, for they were great personal friends. Hey in his turn corresponded with others and secured the interest of the Elland Society, who were presumably asked to form the country section of the committee. The minutes for the Elland Society's meeting on August 24, 1798, includes this resolution:

> Resolved that Mr. Pratt be desired, by means of Mr. Hey, to acquaint the Society at the next meeting, who his two coadjutors, as editors, are, and that the Elland Society hope that the revisal of any papers they may send will be subject only to a Committee of their own appointment, the London Committee, nevertheless, having still the power of rejecting *in toto*.[1]

This is the first time assistant editors are mentioned and it would be interesting to know whom the promoters had in mind.

In February 1799 Pratt proposed the question to the Eclectic Society: "How far might a periodical publication be rendered subservient to the interests of religion?" Venn was in the chair; he has left this summary of Pratt's proposals:

> The objects proposed by Mr. Pratt were "To correct the false sentiments of the religious world, and to explain the principles of the Church"; in addition to which "Religious Communications", there were to be articles Miscellaneous; Literary; Reviews; a Review of Reviews; and historical events of the month, with a particular reference to Providence.[2]

In spite of the fact that Venn and Pratt were actively engaged in the founding and establishing of the new missionary society, whose life officially began on April 12, 1799, it seems that towards the end of the year they were both embroiled in incessant discussion about the proposed periodical with Pearson, Thornton and Zachary Macaulay who had returned from Sierra Leone in May. Henry Thornton has left some account of their aims and plans. He says that uppermost in their minds was the idea of a review of English political and religious works "that have done most mischief", and he mentions those of Paine, Goodwin, Mary Wollstonecraft, Hume, Gibbon and parts of

[1] Elland Society Minutes (MS.).
[2] J. H. Pratt, *Eclectic Notes* (1856), p. 92.

Adam Smith: of foreign writers he mentions Voltaire and Rousseau.[1] On October 30th he reports to Hannah More:

> I had on Thursday a long talk with Macaulay, Venn and Pearson, about the new magazine, and it was agreed that Venn should draw up a paper proper to be circulated in order to announce it, that Bean[2] should be asked to be the Editor, and that friend Hatchard should be sounded as to printing. It appeared to me that the main object should be to get the work into the hands of the Church of England common clergy. As to the Eclectic sort of clergy, they are few comparatively speaking, and it is not so much worth while to write for them. Venn, Pearson and Macaulay to be the secret committee, and Bean to be overlooker of the press, being paid for it. You and I shall be asked for opinions on the things sent, and your aid as a scribbler is most humbly sought. The Committee names not to be known—some persons must supply or engage for about £100.[3]

All very secretive—so secretive that it is difficult to say what happened next. The prospectus appeared before the end of the year, but it was not till 1802 that "friend Hatchard" released the first number in print, and then the editor was not Bean but Pratt who, as we have seen, was the original choice. Within three months Macaulay took over from Pratt and remained the very successful editor till 1830.

He says that for the first year he was assisted by a nominal committee which included Thornton, Wilberforce and Charles Grant as well as Pratt, Pearson and Venn. "But after the first year, there was little or rather no interference, except in the way of criticism and suggestion after papers appeared".[4] It is doubtful in fact whether Venn wrote the prospectus, which had been his assignment. Though Lady Knutsford says that it "was composed chiefly by Mr. Venn", Macaulay told his successor, "For the original prospectus of the *Christian Observer*, a paper of hints was provided by Mr. Hey of Leeds. It was drawn up by Josiah Pratt, in connection with Mr. Pearson of Golden Square

[1] Thornton Wigan Book (MS.).

[2] The Rev. James Bean, author of *Zeal without Innovation*, which was published anonymously in 1808 and caused a stir.

[3] Thornton Wigan Book (MS.).

[4] Pratt, *op. cit.*, p. 93.

and myself."[1] Venn himself claims no part in its writing and in a memorandum-book refers to what "the projectors say in the prospectus".[2] Venn left his children a complete list of his writings, including all his contributions to the *Christian Observer*, in which this prospectus does not figure. However, it does, of course, include the Account of the newly formed missionary society, which is a prospectus; it is quite possible that Lady Knutsford mistook a reference to this for that of the prospectus for the *Christian Observer*.

However, if Venn was not the author of the prospectus he did take a considerable share both in writing for the new publication and in getting it known. Macaulay found Venn a contributor he could rely on and an adviser whose judgment he valued. By the end of January 1802, Venn is writing to Edwards: "With respect to the *Christian Observer*. I hope you will do something, though I can really do very little myself on account of my numerous engagements. You must recommend and sell it in your neighbourhood."[3] In September he tells Kitty that during his tour of Yorkshire he had discussed the *Christian Observer* with Richardson of York, who was highly critical of it. "He is truly a High Churchman and an undaunted champion for it, fearing no one." The following July Macaulay reports considerable success from Scotland where "The *Christian Observer* is much read and greatly liked by the Scottish Ministers". John Venn was convalescing at Cheltenham after Kitty's death and his own illness; Macaulay asks him to review Eli Bates' *Rural Philosophy* but only if his health permits. His health did permit and the review appeared in the August number. In December 1804, Venn writes to Edwards: "I am very glad to find how successful the *Christian Observer* is. Last week I heard of no less than four clergymen who owe their serious impressions entirely to it. Two of these, a father and son in Staffordshire, men of some fortune." (The new periodical was obviously reaching the public for whom it was chiefly intended.) Venn continues:

But while the work is doing so much good it only wants support, I mean the support of the purse. For though it does now clear

[1] Pratt, *op. cit.*, p. 93.
[2] *Ibid.* The author derived the note from H. Venn of C.M.S.
[3] J. Venn to E. Edwards, Jan. 27, 1802 (MS.).

itself, yet it allows little for the payment of that assistance which is absolutely necessary; and the editor is giving up occupations in which he might make a considerable profit, in order to devote his time to this work, which he does most assiduously, rising early and sitting up late. Could not you get a few more subscriptions, or could you and Hankinson take a copy or two which might be usefully given away to your children or to some needy clergyman. If all the friends of the work who are able, were to do this, the work might be continued to advantage.

Venn's testimony to Macaulay's energetic editorship was well deserved. Lady Knutsford says he not only fulfilled meticulously his editorial duties, he also wrote a large number of the articles himself, and even many of the sermons he published came from his pen. His chief contributor was his great friend, Henry Thornton, who also provided the necessary funds for launching the periodical. Thornton contributed 83 articles in the first twelve years of the *Christian Observer's* life, Venn 36 in the first nine.

Although the majority of Venn's contributions were sermons or book reviews, his writing was on subjects almost as wide and varied as we know his interests to have been. In 1802 he contributes three reviews of the *Philosophical Transactions of the Royal Society* in which he discusses and summarizes these articles on scientific subjects with the scholarship of one who is himself a scientist and moves easily in that field. In one issue he gives a paraphrase of his favourite Psalm, Psalm 50; in another he writes a letter on Dry Rot, outlining the means he had taken to secure his Rectory from "the intrusion of so unwelcome a guest". We have already quoted from his long articles on Lenten Observance, Charity Schools, and from one of his three Letters to a Young Clergyman. He also published in the *Christian Observer* his address to his parishioners on keeping the Sabbath. There are several articles on Christian ethics, an article "On the Moderation necessary with respect to the Calvinistic and Arminian systems", "A Preface to the Account of the Execution of Lord Strafford", and "Remarks on the late Establishment of Religion in France".

This latter article was published in April 1802, almost as soon as the Concordat had been finally signed. Venn gives a full summary of its provisions; he rejoices that the re-establishment of religion in France proves that religion is a political necessity. Nevertheless he is suspicious of the Concordat because he is suspicious of its promoters and of the scheme for the state to pay clergy salaries. He also rejoices in the toleration granted to non-Roman churches and "the humiliation of popery" itself, but he deplores the ban on proselytism.[1] In his account of Strafford's death he reveals his own attitude on the effect of public hangings on the bystanders. "In our own country the scaffold has frequently been the scene of Christian edification. The crowds surrounding it have felt the force of religious impressions; their faith has been fortified; and their piety kindled by the tranquillity and resignation of the sufferer, by his affecting prayers, his penitent confessions, and his well-founded hopes of pardon with God."[2]

Another person who tried to persuade John Venn to write was Hannah More. Venn, we know, had made a deep impression on her when he visited Cheddar with Wilberforce in the summer of 1793. In the following December she wrote to Grant asking him to coax Venn into writing stories for children. Here is Venn's reply to Grant on the subject:

> Though I hope I should not only be willing, but even desirous, to do anything which would promote the glory of God and the good of my fellow-creatures, yet I cannot think that I should have much probability of doing it with success in the way which Miss More mentions. I feel continually how much I want that simplicity and perspicuity of language which are so essential to the instruction of children. This alone appears to me an insurmount-

[1] *Christian Observer*, April 1802.

[2] *Christian Observer*, April 1802, p. 199. Cf. a letter which Venn had received from Simeon some twenty years earlier giving an example of this. "On Saturday last a man hang'd at Cambridge for stealing a watch. He had been visited by Brown of Magdalen: such an end! Never did truth triumph more at the stake than then: The Lord had taught him in about a fortnight as clear views of the Gospel as you or I have, and had given him so strong a faith that death had entirely lost its sting; not a fear disturbed his breast. He addressed the people for near half an hour, humbling himself, exalting Christ, exhorting them to faith and repentance; and declaring the full assurance he had of being received into glory. After which I harangued them on the same scaffold for a few minutes on the nature of that religion which could give such serenity and joy in death. He then commended his soul into the hands of Jesus and launched into eternity without a doubt, without a sigh." C. Simeon to J. Venn, 1784 (MS.).

able objection. Add to this I have really no stock of anecdote or religious knowledge suitable for children. The stories I mentioned at Cowslip Green such as they were, were of older people and calculated only for those who were arrived at years of maturity. I really have not a single instance of children's experience. Besides all this, I should think it presumption in me if I were better qualified to take the work out of her hands whom experience and Nature have pointed out to be the preceptor of children. Ask all who best understand the instruction of children, who has been peculiarly called of God to it. You will no doubt join with me in pressing it upon her with all the force which the importance of the case demands.[1]

In 1795 Hannah More started her *Cheap Repository Tracts* but these were intended for adults even more than children, though she was prepared to distribute them as consolation prizes among the children at her schools.[2] The *Cheap Repository Tracts* were intended to supply the newly literate, who had learnt to read in Charity Schools and dames' schools, with a supply of "safe" literature, anti-Jacobin in politics and Evangelical in religion. For three years three tracts appeared each month. These consisted of stories, ballads, Sunday readings and Sunday prayers. In all 114 tracts were published, about half of which came from Hannah More's pen. They achieved an enormous circulation, being far more widely read than either books or newspapers. In one year more than two million tracts were sold in this country when the total population was less than nine million. They were the perfect antidote to the writings of Tom Paine and had the same aims for the working classes as the *Christian Observer* had for the middle classes; as anti-Jacobin they were supported by several bishops. The secret of their success lay in the simple crude English in which they were written, in their exciting plots with plenty of action, in their popular format and their very efficient distribution through hawkers and pedlars as well as through the normal channels of the book trade.

In this task both of educating the poor and providing them with suitable reading matter, Hannah More enlisted the support of her Clapham friends. Henry Thornton was her treasurer,

[1] Quoted by Grant in letter to Hannah More, Dec. 26, 1793. H. Morris, *Life of Charles Grant*, pp. 201–2.

[2] M. G. Jones, *Hannah More*, p. 160.

Zachary Macaulay her agent, though it seems it was the treasurer and not the agent who sought out the hawkers and learnt from them the mysteries of their trade. Both of these wrote for her on occasion; so did John Venn. In 1795 when Venn was on tour in Norfolk he received the following directive from Henry Thornton:

> I hope you will note whatever you may meet with in your travels of the Huntingtonians and will inform us Cheap Repository People of the state of the country both in this and other respects —I send you a paper you will like to see respecting the measures likely to be taken at York. Can you not forward the sale of the tracts by calling now and then at shops or by other means while you are on your travels?[1]

Thornton also mentions having heard from Hannah More who obviously believes Thornton and Venn are travelling together and suggests that they might write one or more "pennyworth of prayers".[2] On another occasion she renewed the request to Venn, again via Henry Thornton:

> If Mr. Venn will write a pennyworth of prayers it will be very useful. They should consist of a family prayer for Sunday morning, ditto for Sunday evening. A morning and evening prayer for a family on weekdays, or two if they can be crammed in. A morning and evening prayer for a person in private, ditto for a child—ditto for a young person—a morning and evening prayer for a Sunday school, to be read by a master, a grace or two. I do not send the enclosed for any reason but as a kind of pattern to follow for the children's prayer; nor do I think the family prayers should exceed two prayers—I shou'd think a few lines recommending the use of prayer might be prefixed; and also a hint to such families as have time to read a Psalm or a few verses before they pray . . . the whole should be done with an eye to the very little time poor people have, and we must allure them by our moderation.

She says she only mentions these details because, though she has no fears as to the suitability of the content of what Venn will write, as he "knows the common people so well", she is afraid he may exceed a pennyworth in length. John Venn's list of his

[1] H. Thornton to J. Venn, Sept. 25, 1795 (MS.).
[2] H. Thornton to J. Venn, undated (MS.).

published writings makes no mention of prayers but in 1795 three of his sermons were published as *Cheap Repository Tracts*. The titles were, *Daniel in the Den of Lions*, *Character of Onesimus* and *Reflexions on Harvest*. None of these seems to have been preserved.

John Venn's lucid preaching was appreciated by his friends more than his writing, which is only to be expected. The prospect of preaching before the Thorntons, Wilberforce and Grant had made him hesitate to "accept Clapham". He need not have worried, for his sermons were a continual source of enlightenment, spiritual strength and occasional debate amongst these friends. In April 1795 Henry Thornton wrote in his diary: "Heard an excellent sermon by Venn on 'Thy Kingdom come' —I was rather too severe with Wilberforce for his severity of criticism."[1] But Wilberforce was not always critical, for the following autumn Venn was preaching a course of sermons on Friday evenings and Wilberforce borrowed the manuscript of one, whilst Grant had a long talk with the preacher after another and Henry Thornton continued to be appreciative.[2] The three volumes of sermons that were published after Venn's death were edited by Thornton, Macaulay and young Henry Venn. The other Clapham friends bought them and recommended them to others. The sale was sufficiently large for some of Henry Venn's college fees to be paid out of the profits.[3]

The clearest exposition of the achievements of the Clapham Sect is to be found in the Anniversary Sermon which Venn preached for the C.M.S. at St. Anne's, Blackfriars, on June 5, 1805. He introduced his subject by saying that lawgivers and philosophers have always tried to reform depraved human nature and have always failed. He criticizes the Greek philosophers for failure in philanthropy and social reform:

> Little regard was paid by them to the poor, the illiterate or the distressed part of the community. Affecting chiefly the company of the wealthy, and of men of science and reputation, what did they attempt to do for the benefit of the lower classes of mankind?

[1] Thornton Wigan Book (MS.). There are many notes on Venn's "excellent sermons".

[2] J. Venn to Mrs. J. Venn, Nov. 25, 1795 (MS.).

[3] *Annals*, p. 135.

Was a single hospital founded through their persuasion? Were schools provided through their suggestion for instruction of the inferior orders? Did they bear a testimony against slavery? Or was the civil state of the poor at all meliorated by their labours?[1]

This is a little hard on the Greek philosophers but it is a very accurate description of the achievements of the Clapham Sect, by whose standard the Greeks were being judged by the preacher. They paid great regard to the poor, the illiterate and the distressed part of the community, on which fell the most severe hardship engendered by the Napoleonic wars and the earliest phases of the Industrial Revolution; they made the social, as well as the spiritual, welfare of the lower classes their concern. It was they who by the turn of the century were extending the great philanthropic movement which in the first half of the eighteenth century had built or rebuilt our great London hospitals; it was they who promoted and financed the Sunday School Movement and the day schools of Hannah More in Somerset; it was they who gave practical encouragement to the educational schemes of Bell and Lancaster; above all it was they who were bearing testimony against slavery.

For this remarkable record the Clapham Sect has seldom received from social historians, either in the last century or this, the credit they deserve. Writer after writer has traduced them as reactionaries who, whilst concerned with the miseries of black slaves in West Indian cotton and sugar plantations, were insensitive to the sufferings of white slaves in English factories. Dr. Howse in his recent book has pointed out that to reproach those who abolished one evil for not also exterminating another, "is like reproaching Columbus for not also discovering Australia".[2] His book goes on to show that Clapham philanthropy was not confined to the West Indies but that its effects were to be seen among those very people they have been accused of neglecting. (Dr. Howse's revelations are not new; the evidence, with references to where further clues can be found, are all in Elie Halévy's *History of the English People in 1815* which was translated into English as long ago as 1913.)

[1] *Proceedings of the C.M.S.*, Vol. 1, p. 402.
[2] Howse, *op. cit.*, p. 134.

In the Anniversary Sermon Venn refers to some of the things the Clapham Sect did for the poor. In the last chapter we saw how John Venn provided Clapham with an early effective experiment in social service. An account of Venn's organization is to be found in the reports of a body to which it was related, which bore the somewhat cumbrous title of "The Society for Bettering the Condition and Increasing the Comforts of the Poor". This society was founded in 1796 by Thomas Bernard, Wilberforce, and Shute Barrington, Bishop of Durham, and attempted to check the worst evils of the Industrial Revolution and to care for some of its casualties. The reports include one from Thomas Bernard which gives an account of the treatment and schooling of the children at Dale's factories at New Lanark, suggesting that other employers might follow his example.

> Our national and individual increase of wealth from the manufacture of cotton, has been attended with so much injury to the health and morals of the poor, and is so utterly destructive of that which constitutes the essential and fundamental virtue of the female character, that if I am not permitted to suggest a doubt, whether it would not have been better for us *that cotton mills had never been erected in this island*, I may at least express an anxious wish that such regulations may be adopted and enforced, as shall diminish, if not entirely remove, the injurious and pernicious effects which must otherwise attend them.[1]

The regulations Bernard wanted included the limiting of hours for child apprentices, some provision for education, the exclusion of night work, regulation of age and conditions of apprenticeship, a total separation of boys and girls, periodical inspection by the magistrates, who should "have power to order the regular whitewashing and cleaning and the warming and the ventilating of the workrooms; and who should receive quarterly or monthly reports from each manufactory of the number, the health, and the respective ages of all the apprentices and other persons employed there".[2] When Sir Robert Peel, senior, was collecting evidence for his Factory Bill for the

[1] *Reports of the Society for Bettering the Condition and Increasing the Comforts of the Poor*, Vol. II (1800), p. 255.
[2] *Ibid.*, p. 256.

protection of children in the textile industries, he called at the Society's offices to increase his information and was so impressed by its work that he made a gift of £1,000. A reading of the provisions of Peel's Act of 1802 will show how similar were his regulations to Bernard's suggestions.

The chief credit goes to Sir Thomas Bernard, but Wilberforce was associated with him in the work; he spoke for Peel's Bill and asked that its benefits might be extended to other industries. Most of the reports that were published were the work of Bernard himself; written contributions came from members of the Sect, for example Wilberforce himself, Lord Teignmouth, Gisborne and, indirectly, John Venn himself. The Committee included Wilberforce, Grant, Stephen, Teignmouth and John Venn's old patron from Little Dunham, Edward Parry, and among the subscribers were the three Thornton brothers, Josiah Pratt, then Secretary of C.M.S., and a young Oxford don, Daniel Wilson, who later became Bishop of Calcutta.

Gisborne devoted himself to a useful study on the earning and spending habits of miners in various parts of the country and gives an account of the paternalism of the Duke of Bridgewater, who had devised ways and means for seeing that some of the miner's earnings went to his home rather than to the pot-house. The reports also include descriptions of Rumford's schemes for heating and feeding institutions, of societies to protect "the climbing boys" who hand-swept the chimneys of the stately homes of England, of schemes for providing the unemployed with small-holdings, and accounts of numerous soup-kitchens and poor societies started to relieve want.

This was all done by a group of men and their friends who are supposed to have been insensitive to the evils on their doorstep. It may be said with more justice that their methods were mainly those of a haphazard philanthropy, and that as we saw in the previous chapter they worked for the poor rather than with them. While we have to realize that in their attitude to class and rank these men were children of their time, we have to realize too that in their willingness to allow state interference and regulation they were ahead of their time. Although there is some relation between the Society for Bettering the Condition of the Poor at Clapham and the social services of a modern borough, many of the underlying assumptions have changed, and so on a wider scale do the assumptions of Bernard and Wilberforce differ from those of Beveridge and Rowntree.

In his Anniversary Sermon Venn makes special mention of the founding of hospitals. Thomas Bernard was for eleven years Treasurer of the Foundling Hospital, started at the beginning of the century by the kindly sailor Thomas Coram. During Bernard's time it was so well run both as a hospital and a school that London shopkeepers were constantly requiring Foundling boys as assistants and clerks. Between 1800 and 1815 there were established in London alone a cancer hospital, a fever hospital, two eye clinics, two societies for the treatment of hernia, and a large number of dispensaries. Besides this there was a hospital for the blind at Liverpool and a Samaritan Society for convalescents from the London Hospital, which also made provision for patients not provided for in public hospitals. There were also "lying-in" charities all over the country and directions were made available for the prevention of infectious diseases and the care of the dying. It was the object of the Society for Bettering the Condition of the Poor to make the system of special hospitals for infectious diseases universal.[1] In this work Evangelical clergy played a prominent part; one of the societies for the treatment of hernia was started by Richard Cecil, one of the founders of C.M.S. and minister of St. John's, Bedford Row.[2] By 1811 more than two thousand patients had been treated by this society.

Thomas Scott, the Commentator, who became the first Secretary of C.M.S., was for a time chaplain to the Lock Hospital near Hyde Park Corner. The hospital treated about five hundred girls annually for venereal disease, but provided no after-care, so that most of the girls returned to prostitution. Scott raised the money, no doubt mainly from Clapham pockets, to build a hostel for the girls to stay till he had found them a job. While this was being built he had several erstwhile prostitutes lodging in his own house. He received no salary for this work but had the satisfaction of seeing similar hostels estab-

[1] E. Halévy, *History of the English People in the 19th century*, Vol. 1, *England in 1815* (1949 edn.), pp. 554–5.

[2] J. Pratt, *Cecil's Remains* (1854). Introduction by Mrs. Cecil, p. 22.

lished in another part of London, and in Dublin, Bristol, and Hull.

As we have seen, Venn himself was an ardent advocate of vaccination and in 1800 made arrangements for the whole parish to be vaccinated. The propaganda for vaccination was so successful in London that in 1806 for the first time a whole week passed without a single death from smallpox in the city.[1]

In his sermon Venn mentions provision of schools as well as hospitals. He was doubtless thinking chiefly of Hannah More's Schools at Cheddar. In addition to the Cheddar Schools Wilberforce had a scheme for elementary education in England which he abandoned when he heard of Lancaster's British and Foreign School Society, of which he became a Vice-President. He and the others subscribed also to Bell's National Society whose methods they preferred to Lancaster's. Bernard placed his own school at Durham (named, after the bishop, the Barrington School) under Bell's personal supervision, and Bernard tried to act as mediator in the dispute between the two reformers. In 1816 Wilberforce served on Brougham's "Committee of Enquiry into the education of the Lower Orders" with Burdett and Romilly, but he would not give his full support to Brougham's non-sectarian University of London, on whose council Macaulay sat with James Mill, Grote and Hume.

Of the testimony of the Clapham Sect against slavery it is unnecessary to speak here, but even when that campaign has been included there were many other Clapham enterprises not mentioned in Venn's sermon. The Clapham Sect did a great deal for the poor; they did even more for the upper and middle classes. One has only to contrast the familiar picture of eighteenth-century society, with its tendency to widespread corruption, with the sobriety and high moral standards of early Victorian England to realize that a great transformation had taken place within an even shorter period than is generally recognized.

In 1829 Francis Place, who was no friend of Evangelical religion, wrote: "I am certain I risk nothing when I assert that more good has been done to the people in the last thirty years than in the three preceding centuries; that during this period

[1] Halévy, *op. cit.*, p. 555.

they have become wiser, better, more frugal, more honest, more respectable, more virtuous than they ever were before."[1] For this transformation Wesley was partly responsible, and the Clapham Sect built on Wesley's foundations, bringing their influence to bear in circles which the Methodists could never hope to reach.

Wilberforce's *Practical View*,[2] published in 1797 and addressed to "The Higher and Middle Classes", soon became a best-seller. Burke, Arthur Young, Thomas Chalmers, Legh Richmond, all claimed to have been influenced by it. Among those Wilberforce had in mind were those who were making their fortune in the new factories. In Parliament by their example "the Saints", as they were called, restored integrity to our public life. Forming an alliance with Quakers and free-thinking Radicals of the Benthamite school, they attacked, as well as slavery, many of the other evils of the day. They called for reform of the corrupt Parliamentary system and advocated Roman Catholic Emancipation. They denounced the barbarous criminal code which regarded the rights of property as more sacred than the rights of human beings, and they called for an inquiry into the state of the prisons. They made duelling illegal in the Services and though the House would not pass Bills against cock-fighting and bull-baiting, they forced these evils out of our public life by vigorous propaganda. It may be added that the tracts that Hannah More and Legh Richmond wrote and Thornton financed were so effective that they drove pornographic literature from the market. It must have been the experience of belonging to such a group of activists that made John Venn say in another of his sermons that the one drawback of entering Heaven might be the irretrievable loss of opportunities of doing good: "There will be no sick to visit, no naked to clothe, no afflicted to relieve, no weak to succour, no faint to encourage, no corrupt to rebuke or profligate to reclaim."[3]

In his address to departing missionaries in 1806 Venn tells them that they are to show not only the difference between

[1] Quoted in M. Quinlan, *Victorian Prelude* (1941), p. 173.
[2] Its full title is *A Practical View of the Prevailing Religious System of Professed Christians in the Higher and Middle Classes in this Country contrasted with Real Christianity.*
[3] Venn, *Sermons*, Vol. 1, pp. 272–3.

their religion and that of Africans, but between their religion and "that of nominal Christians". This distinction between "real" and "nominal" Christians which Wilberforce pressed so persistently and successfully in his *Practical View* is to be found again and again in Venn's sermons. This is not surprising, as Wilberforce was a regular member of Venn's congregation and Venn was with Wilberforce at Bath when he first thought of writing his book.[1]

Venn knew that this Clapham congregation contained many nominal Christians; thus it was his constant endeavour to bring those whose religion was a formality to a religion of faith, and those whose personal faith was real to a deeper commitment of themselves which would result in their religion permeating every corner of their lives. On the first he says: "Nothing but a lively faith in Christ, influencing the heart and producing the fruits of righteousness, can render us Christians in the sight of God."[2] On the latter he says: "Godliness is not a cold assent to the truths of religion: it is not a natural softness and benevolence of temper: it is not the abstaining from gross sins, or the giving to God a part of our hearts and some vacant portions of our time, while the bulk of both is alienated from him. . . . No, godliness is the entire subjection and devotedness of the soul to God himself."[2] Elsewhere he speaks on the same subject even more forcibly:

> Religion is not merely an act of homage paid upon our bended knees to God; it is not confined to the closet and the church, nor is it restrained to the hours of the sabbath; it is a general principle extending to a man's whole conduct in every transaction and in every place. I know no mistake which is more dangerous than that which lays down devotional feelings alone as the test of true religion. . . . Let us be convinced that all prayer, all preaching, all knowledge, are but means to attain a superior end; and that end the sanctification of the heart and of all the principles on which we are daily acting. Till our Christianity appears in our conversation, in our business, in our pleasures, in the aims and objects of our life, we have not attained a conformity to the image of our Saviour, nor have we learned His Gospel aright.[3]

[1] "Saturday, Aug. 3rd. I laid the first timbers of my tract." Wilberforce's Diary, *Life of Wilberforce*, Vol. II, p. 33.

[2] *Sermons*, Vol. 1, p. 266.

[3] *Sermons*, Vol. 2, 238–9.

In another place he asks: "How many imperious masters, idle servants, unkind husbands, undutiful children, and unfaithful friends are zealous in their prayers, in attendance upon preaching, in reading the Scriptures, and in religious discourse, without, perhaps, a doubt of the genuine nature of the religion in which they confide?"[1] Work itself, Venn believed, should be done to glorify God. "How cheerfully would a good man go forth to his labour, could he regard his daily occupations as the service of his God."[2]

Venn would have found the modern conception of salvation as "wholeness" entirely congenial. His sermons continually stress that Christianity affects the totality of existence, not just a part of it, that it is a seven-day-a-week religion and not just a Sunday one, that is concerned not only with religious observances but with every-day living. God must be glorified in the whole of life. Venn saw that wholeness and holiness are inseparable. "Such a principle" (i.e. glorifying God) "will sanctify our whole conduct. It will set a sacred stamp of sanctity and honour even on little things. In the bold imagery of the prophet Zechariah, 'there shall be upon the bells of the horses, Holiness to the Lord'."[3] It was Venn's constant endeavour to lead his people into an experience of holiness which affected both their relationship with God and their relationship with their fellowmen. Because, as he once told his hearers, "we all have to appear for our future audit at the bar of God",[4] what will be sought will not be men's approval but God's. In another sermon he says:

> The man who is guided by this motive sets God ever before him as his Supreme Lord, whom he is bound by every obligation readily, constantly, universally, implicitly, supremely, to obey. Whether the commands of God, therefore, be easy or difficult; whether they be agreeable to the maxims and practice of the world or not; whether he shall be despised and ridiculed, hated and persecuted, or esteemed and applauded, for his obedience to them, makes no difference to his conduct. He intensely feels the

[1] *Sermons*, Vol. 3, p. 137.
[2] *Sermons*, Vol. 2, p. 330.
[3] *Ibid.*, p. 327.
[4] *Ibid.*, p. 225.

value of God's approbation and its sufficiency to compensate the loss of every earthly good.[1]

It was this sense of accountableness to God which gave the Clapham Sect that entire integrity which acted as salt and leaven in the House of Commons; it was this sense of accountableness to God that enabled the Anti-Slave Trade team to persevere with their campaign during a major European war and in the face of twenty years of defeat, disappointment and disillusionment. Pitt once asked Henry Thornton why he voted against him on one occasion. Thornton replied: "I voted to-day so that if my Master had come again at that moment I might have been able to give an account of my stewardship."[2] These men reckoned themselves accountable to God for their words and actions and also for their time and money. Most of them kept time-tables and diaries to keep a check on their time, and their money they treated as belonging to God. Yet the Puritan idea that integrity might pay dividends in this world as well as in the next was not lost on Venn or his wealthy friends. In an article in the *Christian Observer* he writes:

> The man who truly fears God will preserve his integrity inviolable cost him what it will. But even in this life he will seldom eventually be a loser by such conduct. For so much value is necessarily affixed in commercial transactions to the principles of the parties: and so much confidence must necessarily be reposed in them, that it will not often be found that the truly upright will ultimately sustain any even worldly disadvantage from a rigid adherence to the rules of integrity.

Venn's preaching and writing did on a smaller scale what Wilberforce's *Practical View* achieved on a larger one: through them a steadily increasing section of the upper and middle classes embraced Evangelical religion. The times with their fear

[1] *Sermons*, Vol. I, p. 238.

[2] Quoted by Peter Green, *The Profession of a Christian* (1933), p. 58. Cf. "Integrity is the thing we want, both for safety of character and promotion of Evangelical truth", and "Have you heard that Babington stands for Leicester and they bid us hope that he will carry it against a treating, bribing, extravagant sort of antagonist?" Both are quotations from letters from H. Thornton to Miss H. More, quoted in Thornton Wigan Book.

of foreign invasion and internal revolution were favourable to doctrines which demanded a stricter morality than had been practised for some time, and by the middle of the nineteenth century Evangelical influence had become predominant. R. C. K. Ensor has said that no one will understand Victorian England who does not understand its Evangelical religiousness,[1] and he adds a sentence which echoes Venn's remarks about commercial integrity: "If one asks how nineteenth-century English merchants earned the reputation of being the most honest in the world (a very real factor in the nineteenth-century primacy of English trade), the answer is: because hell and heaven seemed as certain to them as to-morrow's sunrise, and the Last Judgement as real as the week's balance sheet."[2] It is possible that Clapham started a tradition of communicating the Gospel in commercial terms, so that Evangelical preachers were known to urge their hearers to "close with the offer of salvation",[3] and a well-known evangelist to-day, belonging to the same tradition, speaks of people "doing their own business with God".[4]

Ensor says that the corollary of this moral accountancy was the belief that this life is only important as a preparation for the next, for Evangelicalism made other-worldliness an everyday conviction and induced a highly civilized people to put duty before pleasure to a quite amazing degree. Nowhere is this other-worldliness, this living "as seeing Him who is invisible",[5] more clearly discernible than at Clapham. All the Clapham friends rose early to meet their Lord through Bible study and prayer, all of them viewed the things of this world *sub specie aeternitatis*—all of them were enabled by God to bring to bear on this age "the powers of the age to come". Perhaps here is the final secret of their achievement. In the sustaining of this ideal and outlook John Venn's preaching undoubtedly played a major part. The themes of Easter, Ascension and All Saints'-tide moved him to great imaginative eloquence, so much so that in the funeral oration Hugh Pearson spoke of "that spirituality

[1] R. C. K. Ensor, *England (1870–1914)*, 1936, p. 137.
[2] *Ibid.*, p. 138.
[3] I owe this point to Mr. N. G. Annan.
[4] Bryan Green, *The Practice of Evangelism* (1951), p. 143.
[5] Ensor, *op. cit.*, p. 138.

and heavenly-mindedness which made him occasionally speak of heaven as if he had been there".[1]

What was the content of this preaching? What did Venn say of the nature of heaven itself? In what relation did he view heaven and earth? What importance did he attach to this world and what is done in this world? How did he lead his congregation to desire to be heavenly-minded and give the things of eternity their proper preference over the things of time? When speaking of heaven itself he refuses to press the details of Scripture literally; he says "Of the nature of heaven . . . we do not know much." All that the Bible gives are "general descriptions, suited to convince us that it is a happy and glorious place, rather than to inform us in what particulars the happiness and glory of it consist".[2] Yet by use of powerful contrasts and exploration of the Scriptural imagery, he is able to suggest something of that glory and that happiness.

In one sermon he contrasts the "external grandeur" which kings accumulate to distinguish themselves from their subjects with the glory that God delights to share with His people "grace for grace, glory for glory, bliss for bliss. Because he lives they shall live also. Because he reigns they shall reign also. . . . He rejoices to impart his own resemblance to them. . . . The splendour of his kingdom consists in the splendour of his subjects, and in the profusion of that bounty from which their splendour is derived."[3]

Again by careful contrasts he is able to speak of the happiness of heaven. Like his friend, John Newton, in *Glorious things of thee are spoken*,[4] and like C. S. Lewis in *The Great Divorce*,[5] it is the solidity of heavenly joys that he praises. In a sermon on "The State of the Saints Above", he speaks of heaven, "where all things are as substantial as here they are vain: where all things are as momentous as here they are frivolous; where all

[1] J. Venn, *Sermons*, Vol. 1, preface, p. XVI. Cunningham makes the same point; see *The Velvet Cushion*, pp. 174–5, and the brief obituary in the *Christian Observer* says "Heaven itself seems to have taken full possession of his mind" (1815, p. 37).

[2] *Sermons*, Vol. 2, p. 247.

[3] *Sermons*, Vol. 3, pp. 171–2.

[4] "Solid joys and lasting treasure,
None but Zion's children know."

[5] C. S. Lewis, *The Great Divorce* (1945), pp. 27–29.

things are as great as here they are little; where all things are as durable as here they are transitory; where all things are as fixed as here they are mutable."[1] Elsewhere he says, in heaven opportunity is subject neither to frustration nor limitation. "There we have not to dread a termination to good and great designs—a sudden extinction of knowledge acquired and digested with anxiety and labour."[2] "In heaven there is scope for infinite enlargement and perfection; for boundless good and immeasurable glory."[3] This removal of restraint is what makes for heaven without end on the one hand and hell without end on the other.

Solidity, reliability, genuineness, freedom; these are the marks of heaven. In heaven there is no cheating, no false values. In heaven all the pettiness of this world will be dissolved and all its exclusiveness done away. One All Saints' Day he gave this commentary on the multitude of "all nations and kindreds and tongues":

> There, it will be no cause of jealousy, or rivalry, or hatred, that one man received his birth on this, and another on that side of a river or sea. A man will not despise his brother on account of the different shade of his complexion: he will not seek his destruction because he spoke in another language, nor renounce communion with him because he praised the same God with the same spirit of piety in a house of a different form. All these petty distinctions will either have ceased to exist or will be completely annihilated in the general spirit of love which will then animate every mind. One pursuit will occupy every heart; each will strive only to glorify God. There will either be no distinctions, or the distinctions will be like the variety we see in the works of God—like flowers enriched with different colours to delight the eye, or with various perfumes to gratify the smell. . . . In heaven . . . no odious denominations will parcel out the regenerated church, no frivolous distinctions be suffered to break the unity of the members of Christ: but people of every nation and kindred and tribe and tongue, will unite in one worship, will be animated with one spirit, will be actuated by one principle—and that, the principle of pure and universal love.[4]

[1] *Sermons*, Vol. 1, p. 85. [2] *Ibid.*, Vol. 3, p. 177. [3] *Ibid.*, Vol. 2, p. 256.

[4] *Ibid.*, Vol. 1, pp. 88–9. There is a striking parallel between what Venn says here about unity in distinction and L. Hodgson, *The Doctrine of the Trinity* (1943), pp. 186–7.

These words speak home to us with our ardent desire for the reunion of the Church and the abolition of racial discrimination; they originally gave heart to the men who abolished the Slave Trade, founded the Church Missionary Society and served as the first officers of the interdenominational British and Foreign Bible Society. It is because the Clapham Sect lived and acted as citizens of heaven that they overcame so many of the petty distinctions that divide men on earth: it is for this reason that we are eternally their debtors.

What has just been said shows that Venn's stress on otherworldliness produced rich fruits in this world. This he tried to explain to his congregation. He tells them a just hope of heaven does not tend to produce "a listless indolence" towards the business of this life.

> The happiness of heaven [he says] consists in submission to God's appointments, and active obedience to His Will. It is not a paradise of sensual enjoyment and dishonourable sloth; but it is the exertion of the best energies of the soul, directed to the highest and noblest objects. He, therefore, who entertains a just idea of heaven, and desires its happiness, will be disposed by that very desire to be active in doing whatever is pure, and just, and honourable, and holy; and his activity will flow from the noblest and the most powerful motives by which men or angels can be influenced.[1]

Contemplation of the after-life for Venn did not lead away from the world but into it.

Nor was he world-renouncing in his attitude to the things of earth. In a sermon on 1 Corinthians 3: 21–23, "All things are yours", etc., he says:

> Yours is the world, who use it for those ends for which its gracious Creator formed it; who survey its delightful scenery, its mountains, its valleys, its rivers, and feel that they are yours because they were made by Him who is your Father. The world is yours, who receive the bounty of heaven with a thankful heart, and employ it, as God intended, to your own lawful advantage and the good of others. The world is yours to enjoy it with moderation, thankful for the convenience it affords you while a

[1] *Sermons*, Vol. 2, p. 210.

pilgrim and a stranger in it, in your way to a better and heavenly country.[1]

The poet and scientist in Venn refused to allow any false emphasis of the doctrine of total depravity to spoil his delight in natural creation. Other-worldliness, he believed, begets the right attitude to nature and suffering in this world.

> A worldly frame of mind is fitted to feel trouble and affliction keenly and bitterly; heavenly-mindedness teaches us to use the world without overvaluing it; to enjoy its lawful pleasures, yet not unduly to grieve for their loss. And if ever religion fails ultimately to produce cheerfulness, it is because it has not had its proper and full influence; it is because it has not yet produced a lively and cheering hope of immortality.[2]

A man with such an outlook was naturally unsparing towards thorough-going materialism. In his article in the *Christian Observer* "On the Observance of Lent", he writes:

> Excess is the great evil of the present day. Excess in business, in pleasure, in every pursuit. It is a serious evil attendant upon our extensive commerce and increasing wealth: the whole soul is engrossed in it. Men live, in the metropolis especially, in a continual hurry of business which leaves them neither a moment for leisure nor a disposition to employ it profitably. By a natural effect, excess in business disposes the mind to excess in amusement, and this worldly-mindedness prevails to such a degree as to be utterly subversive to the Christian life.[3]

In fact, other-worldliness produces true detachment and enables a rich man to enter the kingdom of heaven.

Venn returns to this theme in his exposition of the Epistle for Easter Day: "Set your affection on things above, not on

[1] *Sermons*, Vol. 3, p. 193. He made the same point in an article entitled "Reflections on the Nature and happiness of the Heavenly World." "Upon this earth... we see on every side proofs of infinite wisdom, power and goodness; the endless variety of natural productions; the wonderful structure of the human mind; all these proclaim the presence and hand of a master whose wisdom must be infinite and power uncontrollable. But yet these no otherwise give us an idea of the skill of the great Architect than the broken columns, the disjointed arches and the mouldering capitals of some ruined edifice convey to us an adequate idea of the beauty and grandeur of the original building." *Christian Observer*, June 1803.

[2] *Ibid.*, Vol. 2, pp. 209–10.

[3] *Christian Observer*, March 1805, p. 146.

things on the earth." The text, he says, "forbids us to set our affection upon the things on the earth. We are not to make these our chief pursuit; to be inordinately elated when we are successful in obtaining them, and exceedingly depressed when we lose them."[1] On the contrary, as he says elsewhere, "We are to act as those who look beyond this world."[2] John Venn continually suggests that the key to this heavenly-mindedness lies in a disciplining of the desires and affections. He is concerned for those of his people who "enjoy no more the pleasures of piety than the pleasures of profaneness".[3] He states, "Everything is tedious in which the heart is not engaged; everything delightful in which it is interested."[4]

> When the heart has truly become engaged in devotion and love to God the objects which used to hold its affections will be found in their own nature vain and unsatisfactory, perpetually exciting and perpetually disappointing expectation, difficult to be possessed, and when possessed, failing and transitory in their enjoyment. Hence by degrees the affections will be weaned from worldly things and fixed upon higher and better objects. Love to God will now begin to direct and sweeten every religious service. What was before done from a sense of duty will now be performed with the full and free choice of the heart.[5]

The expulsive power of a new affection will make victory over temptation easier, "for where the mind is much occupied about divine things the tempter will meet with little encouragement".[6] In his commentary on the sixth chapter of the Epistle to the Romans, Professor C. H. Dodd, employing the terms of modern psychology, seems to be saying much the same thing when he talks about good sentiments focused on Christ driving out less worthy ones.[7]

To maintain such "a lively impression of eternal things" and a desire for them, Venn says "daily retirement, meditation and prayer" are essential.

[1] *Sermons*, Vol. 3, p. 286.
[2] *Ibid.*, Vol. 2, p. 403.
[3] *Ibid.*, Vol. 2, p. 259.
[4] *Ibid.*, Vol. 3, p. 216.
[5] *Ibid.*, Vol. 3, pp. 215–16.
[6] *Ibid.*, Vol. 2, pp. 275–6.
[7] C. H. Dodd, *The Epistle to the Romans* (Moffatt Commentary, 1932), pp. 90–1.

> By secret prayer, an intercourse is maintained with Heaven, and the idea of the nearness and the importance of the eternal world become familiar to our souls. But let secret prayer be neglected, and we shall soon lose the impression of divine things; the eternal world will appear to recede from us; we shall have only an imperfect and confused idea of it as of an object almost vanishing from the sight, and in the same proportion the things of time and sense will occupy our attention and engross our thoughts.[1]

In these extracts on this subject of heavenly-mindedness stands revealed the discovery of a man who has made both the Pauline Epistles and the Collects of the Book of Common Prayer very much his own. It was this man who made it easier for his friends, "the Saints", to breathe the air of heaven while they grappled with the powers of hell on earth. Perhaps here is the secret of their great achievement, and here the deepest reason for the high regard they had for John Venn and his Ministry of the Word to them. If, as P. T. Forsyth once said, "Preaching is the organized Hallelujah of an ordered community",[2] then John Venn's preaching was the organized Hallelujah not only of the Clapham congregation but of the Clapham Sect. In a sense Venn was a junior member of this influential circle of men, in another he was their prophet, instructor and spiritual guide. That other-worldliness was the outstanding characteristic of the group is no doubt partly due to their own piety, and partly to the piety of Wilberforce, but it was sustained and continually renewed by the preaching of John Venn.

[1] *Sermons*, Vol. 2, p. 401.

[2] P. T. Forsyth, *Positive Preaching and the Modern Mind* (1949 edn.), p. 84.

5

JOHN VENN AND THE CHURCH MISSIONARY SOCIETY

THE year 1799 can hardly have seemed propitious for the founding of a missionary society. For six years England had been at war with revolutionary France and was getting the worst of it. The name Napoleon Bonaparte was already in use as a bogey to frighten disobedient children and only a year earlier the threat of invasion had been so strong that Volunteer Associations were being formed on Home Guard lines to fight invaders. John Venn had written to his friend Edward Edwards on April 11, 1798, "The French will, it is expected, make their attacks on all points at once, on Holland, on Rochefort, for the army of England extends so far. As it is impossible that all these bodies can be intercepted by our ships some must reach us and land upon our coasts."[1]

It was true that Napoleon was now in Egypt dreaming of an Eastern empire that would rival that of Alexander the Great, but there was still the possibility that he might suddenly return to Western Europe and put earlier plans into operation. At home Pitt's repressive domestic policy had clamped down on all political clubs, Habeas Corpus had been suspended and the Trade Unions were being made illegal by the Combination Acts; harvests were poor and the price of bread higher than ever before. Added to this the clergy who were gathered together on April 12, 1799, at the Castle and Falcon, Aldersgate Street, were men of no standing in the Church; only three of them were beneficed; they were supported by no bishop, and it took them over a year to obtain any recognition from Archbishop

[1] J. Venn to E. Edwards, April 11, 1798 (MS.). He must have meant "from" Holland and "from" Rochefort, as these places were both in French hands.

Moore of Canterbury and his episcopal colleagues. They were scorned in the Church and in society as "Enthusiasts", as men who, like the Jacobins and Methodists, carried things a good deal too far. It is for this reason that they were unable at first to reinvigorate the missionary enthusiasm of the earlier Anglican societies, the S.P.C.K. and the S.P.G.

The original ideas that led to the formation of C.M.S. go well back before 1799. They lie in the thoughts and efforts of Charles Grant in India and later in England, and in the discussions of Evangelical clerical societies in this country, especially in those of the Eclectic Society in London; in all these discussions one figure stands out—Charles Simeon.

The story of Grant's conversion in 1776 has already been told. Soon, the chief preoccupation of his mind became the promotion of a large-scale Protestant mission to India. Although the East India Company sent out their own chaplains, these had no responsibility for evangelization of Indians; however, something was being done in this direction in the south. In 1706 the S.P.G. gave generous support to a Danish mission in Tranquebar, but was unable, because of its Charter, to send missionaries to a country which was not at the time a colonial dependency of Great Britain. From 1726 the S.P.C.K. took over some responsibility and employed German and Danish missionaries in Lutheran orders, of whom the most famous were Schwartz and Kiernander.

In 1758 Kiernander arrived in Calcutta, having been expelled by the French from the Madras Presidency. In Calcutta he married a wealthy English widow and with her money built a church, a school and a cemetery. After her death he squandered her money and by 1787 his property was for sale. Grant bought the church, the school and the cemetery for ten thousand rupees, enrolled his friends William Chambers and David Brown as fellow-trustees, and made the property over to the S.P.C.K., who were asked to supply a missionary at once. This, strange to say, the S.P.C.K. were able to do and the Rev. A. T. Clarke arrived in 1789; thus the first Anglican ordained missionary arrived three years before the Baptists, Carey and Thomas. Unfortunately Clarke proved unsatisfactory and stayed only a few months. When he left, David Brown became minister at the "Old Church" as it was now called, and with a brief interlude remained there till his death in 1812. This church became the centre of Evangelical influence in India.

David Brown was a Yorkshireman and a former pupil of Joseph Milner's; in 1782 he went up to Magdalene College, Cambridge, and soon became a friend of Simeon.[1] In his second year he was introduced to a major on leave from India who was looking for a married chaplain for the Military Orphan School in Calcutta.[2] Brown was neither married nor ordained but thought that both requirements could be met and accepted the job. To find a bishop who would accept him for ordination for work overseas proved more difficult than finding a wife to go with him. The Bishop of London declined his overtures, and it was only after considerable delay that the unjustly notorious Bishop Watson of Llandaff ordained him in 1785. Meanwhile he had made friends with Cecil and Newton, both of whom were willing to offer him curacies if his plans failed. With these men and with Simeon he maintained a considerable correspondence, thus forming the original link between Grant's circle in India and the Eclectic Society in England.

The other trustee of the "Old Church", William Chambers, was related to Grant by marriage and was a friend of Schwartz; he was a distinguished orientalist whose translation of parts of St. Matthew's Gospel into Persian was discussed at early C.M.S. Committees. George Udny, Grant's assistant, and later his successor at Malda, also shared this concern for missions.

Just over a year after Brown's arrival in Calcutta his name appeared, together with those of Grant, Chambers, and Udny, as a signatory to a document entitled "A proposal for establishing a Protestant Mission in Bengal and Behar". In this it was asserted that the only hope of good government in India lay in a reformation of Indian moral standards, and to bring this about missionaries were required. The authors proposed that British Bengal and Behar should be divided into eight parts with an ordained missionary in each, who was to be given a

[1] Brown was four years John Venn's junior so would have missed him both at school and at Cambridge.

[2] This was a Charity School in Calcutta, built by Kiernander to provide for the children of soldiers who died in India, whether born of European or native mothers. Officers had pay deducted at source to finance this establishment.

small plot of land for his house, school and church. The scheme envisaged a mission sponsored by the State and aimed at securing the support of the Government and of the East India Company.

Copies of the Proposal were sent to the Archbishop of Canterbury, the Bishop of Llandaff, the Secretary of the S.P.C.K., three members of the Eclectic (namely Newton, Cecil and Foster), Simeon, Wilberforce, and about six others. The Archbishop did not reply but Bishop Watson was enthusiastic, seeing in Christianity a rational religion which the Indians might do well to exchange for an irrational paganism, and seeing in a Christian India a bulwark against Russian imperialism.

Watson's support was valuable, but it was on Wilberforce and Simeon that the authors' hopes were pinned; Wilberforce to commend the scheme to the politicians, and Simeon to commend it to the Evangelical clergy; further, it was to Simeon that they looked for recruits and he became their agent. This marks the beginning of his long connection with the Church in India of which he was so justly proud. In 1830 he wrote on the front of Brown's covering letter: "Almost all the good men who have gone thither have been recommended by me." (These included David Brown, Claudius Buchanan, Henry Martyn, Thomas Thomason and Daniel Corrie.) "I used jocosely to call India my *Diocese*. Since there has been a bishop I modestly call it my Province!" In 1789 Brown wrote to Simeon somewhat impatient of the delay, saying that, if a Government-sponsored scheme came to nothing, something should be attempted on "a private footing".[1] Though Brown was possibly thinking of the S.P.C.K. doing a little more, it was from ideas like these that C.M.S. came into being.

In July 1790 Grant returned to this country partly with the object of canvassing for his mission scheme. He called on the Archbishop of Canterbury and the Bishop of London, and even succeeded in persuading the former to seek an audience with George III on his behalf;[2] he made friends with Wilberforce and used the opportunities of the discussions he had on India

[1] *Memorials of D. Brown*, p. 250.

[2] C. Padwick in *Henry Martyn* (1922), p. 35, describes this interview, taking her material from Thackeray's *Four Georges*.

with Pitt and Dundas, the President of the Board of Control, to put forward his views on missions. He visited the offices of the S.P.C.K., then in Bartlett's Buildings, Holborn, and he travelled to Yorkshire to consult George Burnett and to see whether there were any possible missionaries among the pensioners of the Elland Society. Burnett was away unfortunately but he wrote hopefully. Through Simeon, Grant met Claudius Buchanan in Cambridge; five years later Buchanan was in India.

Meanwhile Wilberforce was making himself master of the facts that Grant placed before him concerning moral conditions in India. In May 1793, when Parliament was discussing the renewal of the East India Charter, Wilberforce made proposals for increasing the number of the Company's chaplains, and also for sending out "fit and proper persons" acting as schoolmasters, missionaries or otherwise. These were to be approved by the Archbishop of Canterbury and the Bishop of London. The East India Directors feared the consequences of proselytizing Hindus and the Lords threw out the Bill. This meant that all hope of State-sponsored missions to India had to be abandoned.[1] Whatever was to be done would have to be done on "a private footing", and with regard to India, Grant and Simeon had to be content with a working partnership that sent out chaplains instead of missionaries.[2] With regard to a wider strategy, their thoughts increasingly turned from India to Africa and from a state missionary society to a church missionary society.

These developments were assisted by discussions that were taking place in the Eclectic and other Evangelical societies. In an earlier chapter something was said of the nature and proceedings of these societies and the close family relationship that existed between them. The Eclectic Society, however, was rather different from the rest, mainly because it was a London Society.

[1] This was the Dutch method of missions.

It is usually reckoned that Simeon was responsible for five chaplains in India: Brown, Buchanan, Martyn, Corrie and Thomason. In 1813 the joint efforts of Wilberforce, Grant and Buchanan persuaded Parliament to reverse their decision with regard to missionaries, and the Church Establishment "in the British territories in the East Indies" was placed "under the superintendence of a Bishop and three Archdeacons". Stock, *History of the Church Missionary Society* (1899), Vol. 1, p. 103.

It was founded in 1783 by John Newton, three years after he had come from Olney to be Rector of St. Mary Woolnoth, Lombard Street. The other founder members were Richard Cecil, minister of St. John's Chapel, Bedford Row;[1] Henry Foster, who was Romaine's curate at St. Andrew Wardrobe, and a layman, Eli Bates. In 1786 they were joined by Thomas Scott, who after succeeding Newton at Olney had become chaplain to the Lock Hospital. His contribution to the Society was as great as that of Newton or Cecil.

They first met at the Castle and Falcon, Aldersgate Street,[2] which lay opposite the Moravian meeting hall where the Wesleys were converted. The proprietor, Dupont by name, was a regular attender at Spa Fields Chapel and hence welcomed religious meetings on his premises, which probably accounts not only for Newton's choice but also for the fact that the London Missionary Society and the Church Missionary Society also chose to be founded here. When the Eclectic Society was six weeks old Newton wrote to William Bull, "Our new institution at the Castle and Falcon promises well. We are now six members and voted a seventh last night. We begin with tea; then a short prayer introduces a conversation for about three hours upon a proposed subject, and we seldom flag." He concluded by saying that he thought they deserved the title of the Royal Society rather than that which met at Somerset House, "as with us, I trust, the members are all of the royal family and the King himself condescends to meet with us".[3] To a new member he wrote: "Next meeting Monday 14 August. The hour four. No admission after six. Penalty for absence (except the plea is approved by the Society) two shillings and sixpence. The Society has no name and espouses no party."[4] It soon, however, adopted the name of "The Eclectic" chosen probably from a sentence in Isaac Watts.[5]

[1] This was a proprietary chapel in the parish of St. Andrew's, Holborn.

[2] The "Castle and Falcon" was demolished in 1905–6 to make way for offices and buildings mainly connected with the General Post Office. The site was not actually built upon till 1924 when it was taken by the City of London Electric Company. The old cellars still remain and with them the smell of beer and spirits.

[3] Josiah Bull, *John Newton* (1868), p. 262.

[4] Bernard Martin, *John Newton, A Biography* (1950), p. 322.

[5] *Ibid.*, p. 322.

After three years the Society moved to the Vestry of St. John's, Bedford Row, but the rules and procedure remained substantially the same as has been revealed by some notebooks of John Newton's which have recently come to light.[1] These contain brief jottings on meetings between 1787 and 1795 and "thus afford a valuable supplement to Josiah Pratt's 'Eclectic Notes' ".[2] In the cover of one of Newton's books are the Rules as they stood in 1791. From these we learn that they met every second Monday, absentees were still fined two shillings and sixpence, but those who attended contributed one shilling each time. Tea was moved back to 4.15 p.m. and was served from a silver teapot[3] presented to the Society by a member, John Bacon, who was a prominent sculptor. Procedure was then much the same as before; a member, probably the chairman for the session, introduced a question for discussion and the others spoke in order.

Most of the questions concerned Biblical exposition, the personal life of the clergy, preaching and pastoral care: "How may we suppose St. Paul would preach if he were now in London?[4] How far public protest against sin from the pulpit will excuse silence in the parlour?"[5] "A brother going to settle where smuggling abounds, proposed, How he should direct his preaching against this enormity?"[6] In fact many of their sessions were concerned with social, moral, and political questions of the day, the French Revolution, the attitude of members to the war and the question whether a minister should bear arms, Roman Catholic Emancipation, the Slave Trade and the Lottery; others were given to discussing the Christian family and the bringing up of children both in the home and in the Church.

Apart from these discussions the main business concerned

[1] Those from April 30, 1787–June 1789 are in the possession of Mr. F. W. Bull of Newport Pagnell, who is a descendant of William Bull; those from July 6 1789–Feb. 9, 1795 are in the Cowper Museum at Olney.

[2] J. H. Pratt (ed.), *Eclectic Notes* (1856).

[3] The teapot can be seen in a glass case outside the General Secretary's Office in Church Missionary House.

[4] May 21, 1792, Cowper Museum MS.

[5] July 7, 1788, Bull MS.

[6] Aug. 31, 1789, Cowper Museum MS.

election of new members and visitors. Because membership was limited to those residing within "five mile stones round London", meetings could be much more frequent and of shorter duration than those of their sister societies in the provinces. Though nothing is said about it in the rules, membership was open to laymen and Dissenting ministers; it was restricted in number to thirteen, but thirteen others living outside the five-mile limit were elected annually as Rural Deans and were allowed to attend six times during the year. Simeon frequently availed himself of this privilege. Others elected as Rural Deans in 1792 included Coulthurst and Henry Jowett, Isaac Crouch from Oxford and Robinson of Leicester.[1] Other visitors were allowed to attend single meetings "if balloted for the preceding meeting and there being no negative", an exception allowed for missionaries and "what may be deemed by this Society, extraordinary cases". On seeing a later addition of this significant clause Henry Venn the younger commented "so early had the thoughts of these excellent men been turned to missionary work".[2] The clause goes back to 1791 for certain, possibly to 1786 when the subject was "What is the best method of planting and propagating the Gospel in Botany Bay?" and Richard Johnson was invited to attend.

The question was prompted by the appointment of Johnson, a graduate of Magdalene College, Cambridge, to accompany the first consignment of convicts to New South Wales. Wilberforce had persuaded Pitt to make the appointment and the salary was £180 per annum. The suggestion seems to have been made either by Newton or John Thornton to Johnson. Henry Venn regarded Johnson's appointment as "a means of sending the Gospel to the other side of the globe"[3] while Newton himself broke forth into verse at the same prospect:

Go, bear the Saviour's name to lands unknown,
Tell to the Southern world His wondrous grace;
An energy Divine thy words shall own,
And draw their untaught hearts to seek His face.

[1] Coulthurst by then had left Cambridge for Halifax.
[2] H. Venn, *Founders* (1848).
[3] *Life of H. Venn*, p. 446.

Many in quest of gold and empty fame
Would compass earth, or venture near the poles;
But how much nobler thy reward and aim
To spread His praise, and win immortal souls.[1]

The Eclectic Society followed Johnson's fortunes closely; their meeting for April 27, 1789, was given to "reading Johnson's Journal". He was joined in 1793 on Simeon's recommendation by Samuel Marsden, who later became the father of the C.M.S. Mission in New Zealand.[2] He also attended the Eclectic as a missionary.

During the course of the year 1788 Newton, Cecil and Foster received their copies of Grant's Proposal and on February 16, 1789, Cecil introduced the subject: "What is the best way of propagating the Gospel in the East Indies?" Newton has left us quite a full account of what was said, though the failure, which the notes reveal, to grapple with the problem on this occasion is most disappointing. The discussion was side-tracked by Cecil into considering the character of a missionary, and Foster accurately said: "It requires much grace to be a Christian, more for a minister, most for a missionary";[3] but the only contribution on method came from John Venn's cousin, James Gambier,[4] who said that they must labour for the Gospel and not for a particular Church—which, of course, is the exact opposite of the "Church principle" on which John Venn laid such stress at the C.M.S. foundation in 1799. The Eclectic discussion can have been of little use to Grant. It provided neither ideas nor recruits, it merely stimulated concern; what was lacking was practical initiative and missionary statesmanship. This Simeon and John Venn were later to provide.

On April 9, 1792, discussion at the Eclectic was on the Slave Trade. What was said is not recorded, but it was the Slave Trade which was to provide an opening for missionaries in Africa denied to them in India; twelve years later there were

[1] Bull, *op. cit.*, p. 287.

[2] Hole in his *Early History of the Church Missionary Society*, p. 7, suggests that Johnson came home having proved unequal to the task, and that Marsden was his successor. Actually they were working together in July 1796, as a letter from Newton to Wilberforce proves. *Correspondence of Wilberforce*, Vol. 1, p. 132.

[3] Bull MS.

[4] James Gambier, Rector of Langley in Kent, was one of the Rural Deans.

two full-time missionaries in West Africa. In 1787 a colony for freed slaves had been started by Granville Sharpe[1] as a private venture. By 1791 it was in danger of extinction but was preserved by the formation of the Sierra Leone Company.

This was a typical Clapham enterprise with Henry Thornton as Chairman and Wilberforce, Eliot and Grant as his co-directors. Friends were invited to invest their money in the cause of Abolition and humanity and soon there were a hundred members, at least seventeen of whose names we find either among the names of the first C.M.S. Committee or among those of the earliest country members, so closely allied were the movements for Abolition and missionary enterprise. John Venn at Dunham received this personal appeal from Thornton in November: "I send a printed Report of the Sierra Leone Company which occupies me so much that I have hardly leisure to enlarge in my letter so much as my inclination would lead me to do. . . . If you have an opportunity without his paying the postage I will beg you to send the report to your father. . . . It is on a subject that is likely to interest him."[2]

Owing mainly to the energy of Thornton at home and of Zachary Macaulay, whom the Directors eventually sent out to Africa, the colony survived further misfortunes and became, as Newton put it: "the first instance we can find in the annals of mankind in which the civilization and salvation of the inhabitants were the primary objects in settling a colony".[3] This claim is supported by colonial historians who see here the germ of the concept of trusteeship.[4]

The salvation of the inhabitants was undertaken in all earnestness early in 1792 when Thomas Clarkson's brother set sail for Sierra Leone with over a thousand new colonists, a pre-

[1] The Government gave Sharpe considerable assistance; they provided a naval officer, free transport with a grant of £12 per head and a promise of six months' maintenance of the settlement. (See Prince Hoare, *Memoirs of Granville Sharpe*, 1820, p. 280.) Few of the original settlers survived as the colony first suffered an epidemic of fever, and later was subjected to a ferocious raid by a neighbouring chief whose own village had been destroyed by an English slave-trader.

[2] H. Thornton to J. Venn, Nov. 1791 (MS.).

[3] Martin, *op. cit.*, p. 324.

[4] R. Coupland, *Wilberforce* (2nd edn.), pp, 228, 314–15, 323, and C. P. Lucas, *A Historical Geography of the British Colonies*, Vol. III, *West Africa* (1900), pp. 111, 116–17.

fabricated chapel and two chaplains, Nathaniel Gilbert and Melville Horne. On October 26th, the previous year, Horne had attended a meeting of the Eclectic as a "missionary" and the society devoted their next meeting on November 7th to the subject: "What may be suggested to the missionaries who are going to Sierra Leone?"[1] Although Newton has left us with no notes of this meeting, the use of the word "missionaries" with regard to these chaplains is highly significant. The Sierra Leone Company was not, as Hole claims,[2] "virtually a missionary society", but it did provide facilities for missionaries in its territory and encouraged them.

Both Gilbert and Horne, unfortunately, were quickly forced, because of ill health, to return home. Wilberforce was summoned to London from Bath by Thornton to meet Gilbert in the Christmas recess of 1792,[3] and in the following August Macaulay wrote, "Horne has already put pen to paper on the subject of Missions in general; and he means on going home to excite if possible the sleeping activity of his brethren in the ministry".[4] On his return he published his *Letters on Missions* which appeared in 1794, advocating that "a general union of all denominations" was the only sufficient basis for a mission. "As a minister of the establishment", he wrote in the Preface, "I did not dare hope to find ministers to act with me. If in this I have wronged the Church to which I belong, I am ready to ask pardon; and I shall rejoice to find facts to disprove my judgement and to shame my temerity."[5]

This means he saw little prospect of a missionary society emerging from the Eclectic Society, whose meeting he had attended before sailing; nevertheless when C.M.S. was formed he gave regular support and became a country member.[6] However, his book was partly responsible for the birth of a missionary

[1] Hole *op. cit.*, p. 18, and Stock, *op. cit.*, Vol. 1, p. 61, follow Pratt, *Memoir*, p. 468 in saying the question was "What is the best method of propagating the Gospel in Africa?" Newton's version is likely to be the correct one.

[2] Hole, *op. cit.*, p. 18.

[3] *Life of Wilberforce*, Vol. 1, p. 353.

[4] Knutsford, *op. cit.*, p. 47.

[5] Horne, *Letters on Missions* (1794). Preface, pp. V, VI.

[6] Horne went first to Newton's old parish at Olney, 1796–9 and then became Vicar of Christ Church, Macclesfield, where he was when C.M.S. was founded.

society, namely, the London Missionary Society, which was founded at the Castle and Falcon on September 21, 1795 by some Dissenting ministers and Thomas Haweis who had reviewed Horne's book in the Evangelical Magazine. Moreover, another stimulus was undoubtedly the reading by a number of people of the *Journals* of William Carey, who with John Thomas had been working in Danish possessions in Bengal, having been sent there by the Baptist Missionary Society founded in 1792.

The missionary revival, which had its outcrop in the last decade of the eighteenth century in the formation of three societies in England, and two in Scotland,[1] originated itself from the Evangelical Revival and from the new emphasis of world evangelism which is to be found, for instance, in many of Charles Wesley's hymns, with their reference to

> the Lamb who died for all
> The general Saviour of mankind.[2]

The example of the Moravians, who themselves sent out missionaries from 1752 onwards, was a great inspiration to the Wesleys. Others looked back to English missionaries working in the American colonies, especially to David Brainerd, whose life exercised a deep influence over Carey, Marsden, John Venn and Henry Martyn. Other factors were the interest in Australia and the South Seas which the publication of Captain Cook's *Voyages* engendered, and a similar interest in India aroused by the publicity given to Warren Hastings' impeachment. The Slave Trade itself provided another contact with non-European peoples, and the Abolitionist campaign made people ask what could be done for those subjected to the horrors of the Trade. Added to this the great Roman Catholic seafaring powers, Spain and Portugal, were in decline and their place after two centuries of exploration and empire was being taken by a Great Britain made rich by the Industrial Revolution, and made to care by the Evangelical Revival for "the salvation as well as the civilization" of the people whom it colonized and with whom it traded.

[1] The Baptist Missionary Society (1792), The London Missionary Society (1795), The Church Missionary Society (1799), The Scottish Missionary Society, The Glasgow Missionary Society (both 1796).

[2] The stress on universal Atonement was emphasized in contrast to the limited Atonement theories of Whitefield and the Calvinists.

The connection between the three English societies was extremely close. One of the chief promoters of the Baptist Missionary Society was John Sutcliffe, the Baptist minister at Olney, and a close friend of both John Newton and his successor Thomas Scott. Carey once said that he owed much of his faith to the preaching of Thomas Scott,[1] and it was Scott who asked Grant to try to obtain a passage to India for the Baptist cobbler.[2] Grant, Wilberforce and the Thornton brothers[3] were all subscribers to the Baptist Missionary Society, and avid readers of the *Periodical Account* which the Society published; Simeon made the contents of this periodical known among undergraduates, which may eventually have borne fruit in offers for India.

Obviously Anglicans could do no more than support the Baptist Missionary Society in these ways. With the London Missionary Society it was different, for here was an interdenominational society and some of its leading members, like Haweis, were in Anglican orders. The clergy of the Eclectic and the laymen of the Clapham Sect were inclined to regard Haweis and his associates as "irregular churchmen".[4] Scott for instance wrote to a friend saying that it was inexpedient to unite fully with the London Missionary Society because it was not altogether approved of by "our staunch churchmen, especially our rulers",[5] and Henry Thornton wrote to John Venn, "I have heard to-day from Mr. Rippon that £10,000 is said by Mr. Haweis to be already collected for the Missionary Society.[6] . . . What a striking thing it is that a Bishop of London is hardly

[1] "If there be anything of the work of God in my soul, I owe much of it to his preaching, when I first set out in the ways of the Lord." *Life of T. Scott* by J. Scott (1822), p. 173. Cf. a similar tribute by J. H. Newman "to whom (humanly speaking) I almost owe my soul—Thomas Scott". *Apologia pro Vita Sua* (Everyman Edn.), p. 32.

[2] Grant at first refused to do anything, as Carey wanted to take John Thomas with him, and Grant knew from experience of Thomas in India that his character was unsatisfactory for a missionary.

[3] Basil Woodd, Minister of Bentinck Chapel and a member of the Eclectic, was another subscriber.

[4] Thomas Haweis was really now the leader of the Huntingdonians who had been forced since 1780 to work outside the Church of England, when obliged to take out a licence for their chapel. A. S. Wood, *Thomas Haweis, 1734–1820* (1957)

[5] *Letters of T. Scott*, edited by J. Scott (1822), pp. 174–6.

[6] This was its original title; it was called the London Missionary Society to distinguish it from those founded in Edinburgh and Glasgow the following year. See Stock, *op. cit.*, Vol. 1, p. 60.

able (as I suspect) to scrape a few hundred pounds together for the Missionary plans in his hands among all the people of the Church Establishment,[1] and that £10,000 should be raised in such a few days by the *Irregulars*, who are also so much poorer a class of people than the others."[2]

Perhaps it was this contrast that made Thornton and his friends realize that a missionary society was required which would enable the enthusiasm of "the irregulars" to flow also within the regular channels of the Anglican Church. The formation of the London Missionary Society was welcomed by the Eclectic Society and their Clapham colleagues,[3] but they never really countenanced the possibility of throwing in their lot with an interdenominational society; its foundation had the effect of making them work more intently for the formation of a Church of England missionary society.

From 1795 to 1799 there is evidence of purposeful activity in the library at Battersea Rise, the vestry of St. John's, Bedford Row, and the meeting places of at least four other clerical societies. The first of these was at Rauceby in Lincolnshire on May 6 and 7, 1795, where the Vicar, the Rev. John Pugh, drew attention to the fact that he was an executor of a legacy of £4,000 left by the Rev. Joseph Jane to be used in the service of true religion. Pugh asked the meeting whether they thought the money might be given to any scheme already in progress or to any new enterprise at home or abroad; if abroad, "the thing desirable seems to be to send out missionaries".[4]

Amongst the visitors present was Simeon, who no doubt pressed the Society to take the matter of missionaries seriously and came himself to the next meeting the following autumn, when the question put was: "Is it practicable to send out a missionary?—and when?—and how can it be done to the best

[1] In 1793 Dr. Beilby Porteous, Bishop of London, opened a fund, disbursing about £1,500 per annum in aid of Anglican work among the natives of the West Indies. See Hole, *op. cit.*, Introduction, p. XXIII.

[2] H. Thornton to J. Venn, Sept 25, 1795 (MS.).

[3] It is worth noting that in the L.M.S. Report of 1801 the writers say that they regret that the founders of C.M.S. could not come in with them, but that they wish the new society abundant success. (R. Lovett, *History of the London Missionary Society* (1899), pp. 98–9.) This spirit of generous co-operation was patent on both ides.

[4] Carus, *op. cit.*, p. 107.

advantage?"[1] The question after discussion was framed to read: "Is it practicable and expedient to form an Institution for educating young men professedly with a view to their becoming missionaries under the sanction of the Established Church?" This meant, of course, that the meeting as a whole was prepared to contemplate a missionary college, not a new missionary society. No decision was reached, but it was decided before the next meeting to consult three other clerical societies, namely, those at Elland, Hotham, and London; that is, the Eclectic. However, before any of the other societies could meet, Pugh lost heart and Jane's legacy went to help the formation of the Bristol Education Aid Society for Evangelical ordinands.

Nevertheless Simeon was not deterred by this. On February 6, 1796, at his own suggestion he proposed the question at the Eclectic: "With what propriety, and in what mode, can a mission be attempted to the heathen from the Established Church?" Of the seventeen men present most were not prepared to go beyond the final Rauceby suggestion that men should be trained for the mission-field, but that they should give no grounds for accusations that they were poaching on the preserves of the S.P.G. and the S.P.C.K. Two or three supported Simeon's suggestion of a new society; these included Thomas Scott and Basil Woodd. The latter added to his own notes at a later date: "This conversation proved the foundation of the Church Missionary Society."[2]

Simeon made his proposal again by letter to the Elland Society which met on May 17th and also enclosed several resolutions made at the Rauceby meeting, suggesting that in this matter of encouraging the training of missionaries the two societies should act jointly. Elland agreed, and the Rev. S. Knight, who had been Chairman of the second Rauceby meeting, wrote to the Bishop of London asking him what his attitude would be to the formation of a society "formed for the purpose of educating young men, with a view to their being missionaries upon the plan and under the sanction of the established

[1] Carus, *op. cit.*, p. 108.
[2] *Ibid.*, p. 111.

Church", and went on to ask whether he would ordain men trained for such work. The bishop replied that he would probably be prepared to ordain candidates for the West Indies, which was his special concern, but not for other parts of the world.[1]

The Elland Society considered this reply sufficiently favourable to instruct Miles Atkinson to "signify to the Rauceby Society that we are in earnest, and will most heartily co-operate with them".[2] Knight, who had written the letter to the Bishop of London, was actually present as a visitor. He was there again a year later representing Rauceby and so was Henry Foster, representing the Eclectic. The stage seemed set for the appearance of a missionary society of the Established Church, but in October the following year another representative of the Rauceby Society reported that they "had determined to suspend consideration of the missionary business, until there should be some probable hope of a termination of the war."[3]

But this was not the end of Simeon's plans. In December 1796 there are entries in Wilberforce's diary which show that he, Grant and Eliot were still discussing the possibility of missions to India, in spite of their parliamentary defeat in 1793. The following year they were discussing a definite mission plan, doubtless put before them by Simeon. The entry for July 20th reads: "To town and back to dine at Henry Thornton's, where Simeon and Grant to talk over Mission Scheme"; July 22nd "Simeon with us, his heart glowing with love for Christ"[4] and November 9th "dined and slept at Battersea Rise for missionary meeting—Simeon-Charles-Grant-Venn. Something, but not much, done—Simeon in earnest."[5] "That dinner at Clapham on November 9th," comments Eugene Stock, "was more important in the world's history than the Lord Mayor's banquet at the Guildhall the same evening!"[6] But even this meeting seems to have had no immediate result.

It is at this late stage that John Venn comes to the fore. He had

[1] Both letters are published in full in the Elland Society Journal (MS.)

[2] *Ibid.*

[3] *Ibid.*

[4] *Life of Wilberforce*, Vol. 2, p. 225.

[5] *Ibid.*, Vol. 2, p. 251.

[6] Stock, *op. cit.*, Vol. 1, p. 63.

been elected as a member of the Eclectic on his arrival at Clapham; as early as December 1793 Newton signed a letter to him, "Your Eclectic brother John Newton", and during the same month John Venn had a letter from his father saying: "I shall be glad to know this Eclectic Monday that I may be particularly engaged in prayer."[1] Venn was not present when Simeon made his revolutionary proposal in 1796, possibly because of the imminent arrival of another child; in fact Henry Venn, the future Secretary of C.M.S., was born four days after the meeting. In all probability Simeon privately put to Venn the urgency of the missionary question and enlisted his support. Simeon arranged to meet Venn at the Eclectic on the first Monday in August, which would have been ten days after his discussions with Wilberforce and Grant. At the November meeting Venn was present.

Between the end of 1797 and the spring of 1798 Venn had become the virtual leader of the Eclectic Society. There is some evidence of this in the notes that young Josiah Pratt, Cecil's curate, began to take from the beginning of 1798. These notes show that the main contributions come from Cecil, Newton, Scott, Foster, John Bacon, the sculptor, Pratt himself, and Venn, whose attendance record was better than most of the others. By 1799 Newton was seventy-four, Cecil was thought to be dying of a tumour of the bowel (from which in fact he recovered), Pratt was only thirty and Scott and Foster seemed content to follow where Venn led.

It was the rather ambiguous situation created by the London Missionary Society (which was already sending out missionaries to the South Seas and which had Anglican "irregulars" on its committee), that made the Eclectic take the final step and form a new society. What happened is described by John Venn in a letter to Simeon dated February 23, 1799; he writes: "Mr. Burn of Birmingham has been applied to by the (London) Missionary Society to preach their Anniversary Sermon. Demurring on account of the little countenance given to them by their evangelical brethren in the Establishment, he wished to know the reason why the Eclectic Society in particular did not unite with them. This wish was stated to the Society and

[1] H. Venn to J. Venn, Dec. 21, 1793 (MS.).

brought on a long conversation at our last meeting respecting the nature of missions."[1] Edward Burn was curate to John Riland, who as we have seen was a close family friend of the Venns; it was probably to Venn that Burn had written. The discussion took place on February 18th.

There was general agreement on two points; firstly they could not unite with the London Missionary Society because they could not accept their fundamental principles; secondly they ought to do something themselves. With regard to the latter, the question was could they do this "without being irregular" and "without infringing upon the order of the Establishment in any material point"? It was also agreed that on March 18th Venn should open discussion on the question: "By what methods may we most effectually contribute to the propagation of the Gospel amongst the heathen?" Venn's letter ends: "It is not proposed that the Eclectic Society should do more than be the father of such a plan. . . . Recollecting that we once before, at your desire, discussed a similar question, the Society felt the propriety of inviting you to assist at our next meeting, and I undertook to write to you upon that head."[2]

Simeon needed no second bidding and at the meeting held on March 18th he made certain that the outcome was something more than resolutions: something ostensible—something held up to the public. He said that during the four years following his own resolution "we have been dreaming while all England, all Europe has been awake". He also gave it as his opinion that it was hopeless to wait for missionaries; catechists should be sent out: this was part of the plan he and Wilberforce had drawn up two years previously.

Simeon was probably speaking to an audience already convinced, for Venn had introduced his subject with consummate skill and suggested certain principles which the Society has followed ever since. After giving his reasons for not favouring uniting with L.M.S., he enunciated three simple principles: "Follow, do not anticipate God's leading"; "Success will depend upon the kind of men employed"; "Proceed from small beginnings."

[1] Carus, *op. cit.*, p. 167.
[2] *Ibid.*, p. 168.

As Stock says, these look a little trite, yet on closer examination they will be seen to be profound and wise. John Venn did not suggest looking on a map for a likely mission-field, but waiting to ascertain to what part of the earth the Holy Spirit was pointing; as we have seen, India seemed at first the obvious territory, but that door closed and it was in West Africa that the Society was in fact to begin its work. A scrupulously careful selection of men was obviously right; as Venn put it: "They must be men of the Apostolic spirit such as Brainerd——men not careful about the things of this world."[1] One of the first two missionaries turned out badly, but on the whole the high standard required of candidates, with proof of real vocation, has been a policy which has been as wise as it has been rewarding. Its corollary is also important—men must come before money. As Venn put it: "To raise funds in the first instance" would be beginning at the wrong end. Beginning on a small scale was in marked contrast to the L.M.S. which had bought a ship and sent out in 1796 thirty missionaries, six wives and three children.

To these three fundamentals Venn added a fourth: the new Society, he thought, should be "founded upon the Church principle, not the High Church principle". Whereas on the one hand he rejected the L.M.S. fundamental principle of evolving on the field "such form of Church Government as to the converts shall appear most agreeable to the Word of God";[2] on the other hand he realized that, although the support of the bishops must be sought, they were neither going to be asked nor if asked were likely to accept the position they were given in the S.P.G. The new society was to be controlled by its own committee, not by the bishops.

To these principles five points were added which were really a revision of suggestions made during the discussion of February 18th. Each member of the Eclectic Society was to instruct his people on the necessity of missions; it should be a matter of prayer both at the Society's meetings and in private that all the members might feel a deep concern on this matter. Practical details should be made a matter of thought and prayer. The idea of "each one bring three" goes right back to this meeting,

[1] From W. Goode's account, *Eclectic Notes*, p. 96.

[2] N. Goodall, *A History of the London Missionary Society (1895–1945)*, p. 3.

when it was resolved that each member should strive to influence "at least three of his Christian friends, endeavouring to excite the same spirit in them . . . and to look out for men endued with the true missionary spirit".[1] When two or three had been found, to discover the best methods of using them. As a final suggestion, following the precedent of the S.P.C.K., he suggested sending out laymen as catechists. "I would sacrifice a great deal to preserve Church order," Venn said, "but not the salvation of souls."[2] As we saw, this proposal had Simeon's strong support. Of the other speakers, Scott agreed with Venn on the Church-principle, but he said that he wished the L.M.S. well; Grant thought that now was the time for founding a missionary seminary. Goode and Pratt gave unqualified support, but the latter thought that the choosing of a committee should be left to a larger meeting.

On April 1st the Eclectic Society had "a general conversation on the establishment of a mission". Pratt tells us no more than that, but William Goode,[3] who was present, has given us a full record. Venn was in the chair. All the leading members of the Eclectic were there apart from Newton: there were four visitors, Simeon, Charles Grant, Nathaniel Gilbert, the former Sierra Leone chaplain, and Thomas Haweis of the London Missionary Society.

Haweis questioned the "episcopal nature" of the proposed society; he thought it would be a pity to stamp it in its infancy with the indelible marks and liturgy of the Church of England. Further, although he thought that ultimately episcopal government would be an advantage, he feared that the formation of this new Anglican society might dispose the bishops to regard his own missionary society less favourably. Other contributors to the discussion, including Henry Foster and Basil Woodd, still, at this late hour, said that they thought that the work should be done through the S.P.C.K., not through a new society, and others pressed the overwhelming needs of the Church at home.

Both these arguments were successfully combated by Scott and Cecil. Scott said that the new society would "set things stirring, set up a spirit of prayer" which would affect the Church

[1] *Eclectic Notes*, p. 97.
[2] H. Venn, *Founders*, p. 4.
[3] This MS. account is in Church Missionary House.

at home as well as overseas. Cecil agreed with those who feared that the bishops might be alarmed at the multiplication of societies, but the first priority of the Eclectic was to consider the state of the heathen; "for them if anything can be done, let it be done". He went on to answer Haweis by saying: "In an established church the missionaries are in less danger of being wired up into a little sect by private opinion." He insisted that it was useless to go forward without "episcopal forces"; they could not put their shoulder to any other wheel. He also added whimsically that bishops might be prepared to ordain men "to go and preach abroad" whom they would not commission to work under their noses. To this discussion Simeon's contribution was limited to a question concerning the training of missionaries: Venn appears to have held his peace. What need was there for either to say more when Scott and Cecil put forward so forcibly views all four held in common?

On April 12, 1799, the larger meeting envisaged by Pratt took place at the Castle and Falcon Inn, Aldersgate Street. Venn was in the chair; there were present sixteen clergy, nine of whom were members of the Eclectic, and nine laymen. However, the decisive meetings were those of March 18th and April 1st; on this occasion the two chief architects of C.M.S., Charles Grant and Charles Simeon, evidently regarded the issue as certain, for neither of them was present.

The resolutions passed at the foundation meeting were:

(1) That it is a duty highly incumbent upon every Christian to endeavour to propagate the knowledge of the Gospel among the Heathen.

(2) That as it appears from the printed Reports of the Societies for Propagating the Gospel and for Promoting Christian Knowledge that those respectable societies confine their labours to the British Plantations in America and to the West Indies, there seems still to be wanting in the Established Church a society for sending missionaries to the Continent of Africa, or the other parts of the heathen world.

(3) That the persons present at this meeting do form themselves into a Society for that purpose, and that the following rules be adopted. [The rules are then printed.]

(4) That a deputation be sent from this Society to the Archbishop of Canterbury as Metropolitan, the Bishop of London as

Diocesan, and the Bishop of Durham as Chairman of the Mission Committee of the Society for Promoting Christian Knowledge, with a copy of the Rules of the Society and a respectful letter.

Wilberforce was asked to be President of the new society. He refused, but allowed himself to become a Vice-President alongside Grant, Parry, Samuel Thornton, Henry Hoare, Vice-Admiral Gambier and Sir Richard Hill. Henry Thornton was appointed Treasurer; the Committee consisted of thirteen clergy and eleven laity. Of the inner circle of the Eclectic there were Newton, Cecil,[1] Venn, Scott, Pratt, Foster and Basil Woodd. Thomas Scott was later appointed the first Secretary by the Committee. Of the laymen, three were relations of John Venn and at least three members of his congregation. A fourth with practical experience of the field in which the first work was to be done was soon added in the person of Zachary Macaulay.

The Rules[2] laid down that the General Committee was to appoint two sub-committees, the Committee of Correspondence and the Committee of Accounts. The office of the Committee of Accounts is self-evident. "The office of the Committee of Correspondence is to seek for proper missionaries to superintend their instruction, and to correspond with them when sent out" (Rule VIII). This Committee was also responsible for suggesting the names of, and keeping contact with, country members of the Committee who were recruited from the universities, and from outside a ten-mile radius of London. The Committee of Correspondence formed an inner executive in these early days; it consisted of Venn, Scott, Pratt and four other members of the Eclectic, together with Henry Thornton, who as Chairman of the Sierra Leone Company was considered knowledgeable on African affairs, and Charles Grant who was known to be an authority on the East.

Most of the other rules concern the appointment and terms of employment of missionaries. Rule XVII reads: "Each Missionary elect shall consider himself as engaged to go to any part of the world, and at any time which the Committee shall choose, respect however being had to his personal circumstances, or to

[1] Cecil refused owing to his ill-health.

[2] The Rules are printed in full in Hole's *Early History*, Appendix B, pp. 646–8.

any previous stipulation made by him with the Society. As soon as he quits England, he shall keep a regular Journal of his studies and proceedings, a copy of which he shall send, as often as opportunity shall serve, to the Committee of Correspondence." Rule XIX provided for an Anniversary Sermon in London and Rule XX reads: "A friendly intercourse shall be maintained with other Protestant Societies engaged in the same benevolent design of propagating the Gospel of Jesus Christ."

The Rules must have been drawn up with considerable haste, probably between March 18th and April 12th; they were revised and amended at the second General Meeting, which was held on May 27th. It is nowhere stated who was responsible for drafting this document, but there is much in the wording, style and practical wisdom to suggest John Venn, especially as the new Society came to rely on him for writing all their public documents. It was he who drafted and signed the letter to the Archbishop, and it was he who was asked at the second General Meeting to draw up the Account of the Society; further, most of the early Annual Reports came from his pen. During the first three years of the new Society's life, John Venn was its real leader. Scott managed the correspondence but the policy, publicity and direction seem to have been in Venn's hands. At nearly every committee meeting at which he was present from April 1799 to June 1802 he took the chair, though it became less usual for him to do so towards the end of this period. In the summer of 1802 he was seriously ill, his wife died as a result of nursing him and it was not till June 4, 1805, the day he preached the Anniversary Sermon, that he attended again. Meanwhile at the end of 1802 Josiah Pratt had taken over the Secretaryship from Scott, and together with it, in Venn's absence, the policy and direction of the Society: in reality it has remained in the Secretary's hands ever since.

The story of these first six years is the story of the winning through in the persistent struggle to keep going in the face of delay, frustration and disappointment. They could do nothing as a Church of England missionary society without some official recognition from the authorities of the Church. On July 1st the Committee approved of the following letter:

To His Grace the Archbishop of Canterbury,

London, July 1, 1799.

MAY IT PLEASE YOUR GRACE—

The Committee of a Society now forming for Missions to Africa and the East have sent a deputation of their members to present, in the most respectful manner, to your Grace, as Metropolitan, a copy of the Rules which they have framed, together with the Account of the nature of their Institution, which is designed for publication. They humbly trust that your Grace will be pleased favourably to regard this attempt to extend the benefits of Christianity, an attempt peculiarly necessary at a period in which the most zealous and systematic efforts have been made to eradicate the Christian faith.

With the utmost submission and reverence they beg leave to subscribe themselves

Your Grace's most obedient humble servants,

Signed on behalf of the Committee,

JOHN VENN,

Chairman.[1]

The deputation appointed to carry the letter to the Archbishop, the Bishop of London and the Bishop of Durham, consisted of Grant, Wilberforce, and Venn. Wilberforce had an informal conversation with the Archbishop in August, and found him friendly disposed and willing to receive a deputation. Grant called on Bishop Porteous of London; his attitude was identical with that of the Archbishop. In October Grant reported to the Committee that both bishops thought the subject of the new missionary society important, so important that the whole bench would have to be consulted. The official deputation, however, although it made several efforts to secure an audience both at Lambeth and Fulham, always seemed to choose to call when their lordships were either away or out. Perhaps it was contrary to the ecclesiastical etiquette of those days to make an appointment.

This further delay might have been fatal to the infant society, and the first half of 1800 was an anxious time for the Committee. On March 3rd Wilberforce was reported as using every endeavour to obtain an answer from the Archbishop; on April 7th the original deputation was asked by some means to obtain

[1] Quoted in Hole, *op. cit.*, pp. 45–6.

an answer as numbers attending committee meetings were falling off. On May 7th as there was still no news John Newton and John Pearson, the surgeon, were the only members to present themselves; in June there was no meeting, in July insufficient for a quorum. Scott wrote to his son: "The Missionary Society lies off the 'Bishop and His Clerks', where, if not wrecked, it may rot for what I can see. They return no answer and, as I foresaw, we are all nonplussed."[1] It was during this month that Venn wrote to Wilberforce to ask him to try to see the Archbishop again and extort an answer from him. Here is Wilberforce's reply, dated July 24, 1800:

> I had promised myself a quiet morning at Chelsea, charming from its novelty as well as its intrinsic comfort, but your letter determined me to sally forth. I have had an interview with the Archbishop who has spoken in very obliging terms, and expressed himself concerning your Society in as favourable a way as could be expected. I will tell you more at large when we meet what passed between us. Meanwhile I will just state that His Grace regretted that he could not with propriety at once express his full concurrence or approbation on an endeavour in behalf of an object he had deeply at heart. He acquiesced in the hope I expressed that the Society might go forward, being assured he would look on the proceedings with candour,[2] and that it would give him pleasure to find them such as he could approve.

The Archbishop had expressed himself in such guarded and cautious terms that some members of the Committee felt it unwise to proceed further. Possibly they were not aware of the facts that Josiah Pratt made public eventually, that all three bishops who had been approached directly, privately encouraged the Society to go forward and promised to look kindly on their work till it had reached such obvious maturity for them to give their open approval.[3] (This, in fact, is what the Archbishop meant to convey by his message.) Obviously they had found that not all of their colleagues approved and they realized that general Church opinion was against the new society and its founders. Both Archbishop Moore and Bishop Porteous died before the Society was really established, but Shute Barrington,

[1] Hole, *op. cit.*, p. 51.
[2] At the time "candour" meant "kindliness, freedom from malice".
[3] Stock, *op. cit.*, Vol. 1, p. 73.

the Bishop of Durham, made liberal donations and left £500 to the Society on his death in 1824.[1]

However, approval, even apparently lukewarm, was all that the Committee required. Until this was obtained they were not able to do much. A few country members were enlisted and the search for recruits was begun, but not much support was forthcoming till the attitude of the bishops was known. Simeon at Cambridge and Isaac Crouch at St. Edmund Hall, Oxford, were asked to be particularly vigilant. Simeon confessed in the summer of 1800: "I feel a little discouraged at my want of success." So discouraged that he sent no subscription. Till the Archbishop's attitude was known, even such sympathetic friends as the members of the Elland Society were not prepared to commit themselves, but when the decision was communicated to them they resolved unanimously: "That this Society will be happy to encourage the undertaking of the said Society for Missions in every way that we can, and that the Society in London be requested to favour their friends in the country with a short advertisement concerning their plan for circulation—in order to invite subscriptions."[2] Thus began a very happy and fruitful partnership, for many Elland Society candidates have served with the C.M.S. overseas.

During the long period of waiting some things were done. On August 5, 1799, news came that the ship *Duff* belonging to the London Missionary Society had been captured by the French; those of the Committee who were present subscribed £50 and in faith made the sum up to 100 guineas, sending it the same evening as an expression of their sympathy and goodwill. This oecumenical act[3] brought from Joseph Hardcastle, the Treasurer of L.M.S., a letter in which he said that this "competition of kindness and goodwill" might well result in their rejoicing together "in the progress of our Saviour's kingdom among the nations which are now surrounded with darkness and the shadow of death."

[1] The decision marks the turning-point. After it was taken Scott wrote: "What will be the final issue, what the success of these missions we know not now. I shall know hereafter. It is glorious and shall prevail. God hath said it and cannot lie."

[2] Elland Society Journal (MS.).

[3] The gift was prophetic of the mutual help given to-day through the World Council of Churches.

The Committee met once a fortnight in William Goode's study at St. Anne's Rectory, Blackfriars. From the time of the second general meeting in May the title "The Society for Missions to Africa and the East"[1] had been adopted, but it was not till the committee meeting of November 4th that a definite field was chosen. On that day John Venn read a memorandum on educating African children with a view to their becoming missionaries to their own country. His argument was so persuasive that though the Committee asked for time to consider the suggestion they decided there and then that Sierra Leone was the area where the Society should begin its work.

Venn's suggestion really arose from an idea that Zachary Macaulay had conceived whilst still Governor-General of Sierra Leone, for Henry Thornton tells Hannah More a few months before Macaulay was expected back in this country: "I expect that when Macaulay arrives he will make his triumphal entry into this island with a train of 20 or 30 little black boys at his heels, the trophies which he brings from Africa. They have been living chiefly at his house and are somewhat instructed already."[2] In May 1799 Macaulay arrived and with him twenty-five African children, four of them girls. The girls were found a home with a generous woman in Battersea who looked after them for nothing. For the boys Venn and Thornton assisted Macaulay to found a school, but their first master was not a success, for we find Thornton again writing to Hannah More: "We have withdrawn the present blacks from the grasp of Mr. Haldane, and it now stands in our minutes that 'Mr. H. Thornton, Messrs. Wilberforce, Grant, Parker and the Rector of Clapham, have superintendence of the school.' They come to Clapham Church and we have chosen a master, who is, as I conceive, Church of England."[3] This master was William Greaves, an able Yorkshireman, who had been influenced by both Grimshaw and Henry Venn. He proved an excellent master. He taught them printing, carpentry and the elements of mechanics.

[1] The name was changed to "The Church Missionary Society for Africa and the East" in 1812 in order to distinguish it from the other missionary societies.

[2] H. Thornton to Miss H. More, Oct. 26, 1798. Thornton Wigan Book (MS.).

[3] H. Thornton to Miss H. More, 1800. Thornton Wigan Book (MS.).

Meanwhile Henry Thornton had suggested a parliamentary grant, augmented by private subscriptions, "for the education of Africans". Whether it was intended to extend the Clapham experiment and bring more Africans to this country or to open new schools in Sierra Leone is not clear, but he tells Hannah More "I think of giving £200, Wilberforce £100, Robert Thornton £50. I hope there are a good many rich Mr. Peels and Mr. Arkwrights who will step forward in the cause."[1]

The children seemed happy at Clapham, receiving much attention from the members of the Sect and from others living on the Common who had them brought into their houses, wishing to see for the first time what black children looked like. Newton paid a visit to Clapham and "saw the twenty African blackbirds". He was delighted to find that some of them spoke the language he had learnt as a slave in Sierra Leone. On February 10, 1805, John Venn baptized two of them. On May 12th a further twelve were baptized in the presence of a large congregation which included Macaulay, Thornton, Wilberforce, Grant, Thomas Thomason, Admiral Gambier and Lord Muncaster. Venn preached on Colossians 3:11: "Where there is neither Greek nor Jew, circumcision nor uncircumcision, Barbarian, Scythian, bond nor free: but Christ is all and in all." He reminded them of the noble work awaiting Africans taking the Gospel to their fellow-countrymen. "This nation was once a heathen nation, and the time may come, will come, when Africa shall embrace the Truth in Christ."[2]

The boys he baptized were all in their teens. Unfortunately the experiment had to be abandoned, as the majority of the Africans failed to accustom themselves to the rigours of the English climate and died at Clapham; the six survivors were shipped back to Sierra Leone where a new school had been opened. Even if these Africans did not become missionaries to their own countrymen they did focus attention on their part of Africa; moreover, the idea of training missionaries among the people of the receiving country was an idea fully and successfully worked out by John Venn's son, Henry, when he was Secretary of the Society.

[1] H. Thornton to Miss H. More, 1800. Thornton Wigan Book (MS.).
[2] *Christian Observer*, November 1872, p. 808.

One direct result of the Archbishop's recognition of the Society was that widespread distribution of the *Account* could now be undertaken. John Venn had written the first draft shortly after the foundation of the Society; he had submitted it to the Committee of Correspondence at Pratt's house in Doughty Street on June 10, 1799. With their approval it had been printed together with the Rules, but the first printing was limited to five hundred copies; because of the delay in obtaining official recognition, these were circulated privately. After the bishops' attitude was known, a second printing of five thousand copies was commissioned and through the *Account* the Society presented itself to the Church as a new missionary society with a definite policy. The text of the *Account* is printed as an Appendix,[1] but it was the central section of this brief document which was not acceptable in some quarters and had to be withdrawn when another printing was called for to accompany the first Annual Report.

The offending paragraphs concerned the employment of catechists as missionaries, should ordained men not be forthcoming; this was a principle that both Simeon and Venn had put forward on March 18th, and Venn proceeds here to explain why the Committee favour it. The proposal was evidently made to keep out social climbers—the Committee were afraid of men offering to go abroad as ordained missionaries who were not really qualified, intellectually and in other ways, for ordination in this country. They feared that these might use a short period of service overseas as a stepping-stone to clerical preferment and social advancement in this country. Venn justifies this recommendation by appealing to the practice of the primitive Church. Rule XVIII puts the suggestion in succinct form and adds that a catechist "shall not administer the Sacraments except that of Baptism in cases of necessity."[2]

It was this clause that caused most difficulty. John Newton was so unhappy about it he refused to preach the First Anniversary Sermon; several, including the Bishop of Durham, were critical; Dr. Hawker of Plymouth disapproved of the whole idea of lay missionaries. "No one", he said, "ought to be

[1] p. 280. [2] Hole, *op. cit.*, p. 647. Haweis said he could not imagine any catechist preaching to heathen 20,000 miles away being unworthy of ordination,

requested to go as a missionary from the Church of England without ordination." As a result of this agitation alterations were made both to the Rules and the *Account*. Although Venn never abandoned the hope of using catechists, Pratt was against it; in 1804 the Germans, Renner and Hartwig, were sent abroad as "missionaries" in Lutheran orders, and when the first lay missionaries sailed for New Zealand in 1809 the Committee were careful not to call them missionaries or give them the office of catechists; they were simply designated "lay settlers". However, other of John Venn's missionary ideas and principles had a longer life.

In the *Account*, in his Anniversary Sermon and in his charge to the second group of German missionaries on their departure for Africa in 1806, Venn's missionary ideas and policy are clearly seen. The faith that sustained him and the Committee is transparent in this last address in which he says:

> Though we have not met with immediate success, are we not laying a foundation on which much may be successfully built hereafter? But what have we to do with success? Success belongs to God—duty is our part. Shall we sit still and make no effort for the conversion of our fellow-creatures? Can we acquit ourselves of guilt by waiting longer till we see a more favourable prospect? Our duty, our indispensable duty, is to endeavour; nor are our endeavours at all less acceptable to God, even though they may be unsuccessful.[1]

Both in this address and in the *Account* he refers to the need of reparation being made to Africa for the Slave Trade. Here is what he said in 1806, the year before Abolition:

> The Church of God in every country will turn their eyes from the desolations and vices which now deform the earth, to the rising hope of better times, when the true knowledge of God will more generally prevail. They will look to the infant Church of Africa, and will watch with anxious desire its progress. Africa expects from you some reparation for her wrongs.[2]

In the *Account* the work of the S.P.G. and the S.P.C.K. is gratefully acknowledged and that generous spirit which, as we

[1] *Proceedings*, Vol. 1, pp. 427–8.
[2] *Ibid.*, Vol. 2, p. 90.

saw in a previous chapter, rejoiced in unity in diversity is again seen in this passage: "Wide is the field which lies before this Society; great is the importance of their object." They do not need financial assistance from those already supporting other societies. . . . "What they ask of them is their counsel, their good wishes, their prayers. . . . The world is an extensive field, and in the Church of Christ there is no competition of interests. . . . Let there be cordial union amongst all Christians in promoting the common salvation of their Lord and Saviour."[1]

Two things he said over and over again were, firstly: "If Asia and Africa ever receive the faith of Christ, they must owe it to the successful labour of missionaries"; history showed God did not act otherwise; secondly he repeated his fundamental principle that everything depended on the quality of the men chosen. "We must fix our hope of success", he said in his Anniversary Sermon, "chiefly under God, on the nature of divine truth and on the spirit and temper of the men who preach it."[2] In the same sermon he gave this picture of his idea of a Christian missionary, so reminiscent of his own heavenly-mindedness. A Missionary

> is one who like Enoch walks with God, and derives from constant communion with Him a portion of the divine likeness. With the world under his feet, with Heaven in his eye, with the Gospel in his hand and Christ in his heart, he pleads as an ambassador for God, knowing nothing but Jesus Christ, enjoying nothing but the conversion of sinners, hoping for nothing, but the promotion of the Kingdom of Christ, and glorying in nothing but in the cross of Christ Jesus by which he is crucified to the world and the world to him. Daily studying the word of life, and transformed more and more into the image which it sets before him, he holds it forth to others as a light to illuminate the darkness of the world around him, as an exhibition of the light and glory of a power and higher world above.[3]

The spirit which was the mainspring of the anti-slavery crusade and of all Clapham philanthropy and missionary en-

[1] *Ibid.*, Vol. 1, p. 11.
[2] *Ibid.*, Vol. 1, p. 424.
[3] *Ibid.*, Vol. 1, p. 424.

deavour is seen in the closing words of Venn's Anniversary Sermon:

> Deny them not the crumbs that fall from your table. As you have received mercy impart mercy. As Christ has been full of compassion to you, be ye compassionate to these your destitute and perishing brethren.[1]

This reference to "destitute and perishing brethren" is not isolated; in another place he refers to "poor benighted pagans".[2] Part of his motive for missions was undoubtedly the desire to save the heathen from hell, yet there is something of a universalist ring in the final words of the *Account*. "They" (the Committee) "expect that the prayers daily offered up that the Kingdom of God may come" will at length be answered; and they hail the rising day when the glad tidings of salvation, being conveyed to the lands lying in darkness and the shadow of death, "the wilderness and the solitary place shall be glad of them, and the desert shall rejoice and blossom as the rose".[3] The same note is to be found in the sermon he preached at Clapham on 1 Timothy 4: 8, "Godliness is profitable unto all things", in which having spoken of the effect of godliness on a Christian family, he speaks of its possible effect on a world that has become Christian.

> Enlarge this view and suppose (what is alas! but too unlikely soon to happen) the whole world partaking of the same spirit, and how profitable would godliness appear for all things, even in the present life! There would be no jealousy between subjects and their governors, no party spirit of animosity, no more war and bloodshed. The sword would be beat into the plough-share and the spear into the pruning-hook. Every man you met would be a brother. No scenes of cruelty would shock the eye; no cry of oppression would wound the ear. Tyranny and slavery would be only remembered with a sigh that human nature should once have suffered them. The voice of joy and praise would be heard in every cottage, and the sufferings which still remained in the earth would be alleviated by the affectionate tenderness of every

[1] *Ibid.*, Vol. 1, pp. 428–9.
[2] *Ibid.*, Vol. 2, p. 99.
[3] *Ibid.*, Vol. 1, p. 428.

neighbour and every stranger; for every stranger would be a friend. The wolf would indeed dwell with the lamb, and the leopard lie down with the kid.[1]

The First Annual Report was presented by Venn at the General Meeting held at the New London Tavern, Cheapside, on May 26, 1801, following the Anniversary Service at St. Anne's Blackfriars, at which Scott had been the preacher. Although the Society had been in existence for more than two years,[2] Venn had to admit there was little to show apart from an encouraging abundance of zeal. The search for "men endued with an apostolic spirit" had so far proved unavailing, but there was one person, "highly recommended", whose offer was being considered. This was an undergraduate of St. Edmund Hall, Oxford, who had the appropriate name of John Bull; he was recommended both by Isaac Crouch and Daniel Wilson, and expressed his willingness to go to any part of the world the Committee might choose. Although unfortunately he had to withdraw his offer through ill health, his sermons and newspaper articles on missions led a schoolmaster, Henry Baker, to offer himself to the Society in 1814—he became a successful missionary in Travancore.

Apart from the search for missionaries progress had been confined to preparatory work of commissioning translations of the Bible into Arabic and Chinese, the compilation of a Susoo grammar, and the printing of tracts. The Society had already purchased a printing press. Venn also mentioned the decision to teach Susoo boys to read and write with a view to employing them in their own country as schoolmasters and catechists. The capture of Ceylon from the Dutch at the time the Report was going to press was the cause of a postscript which reported that

[1] *Sermons*, Vol. 2, pp. 236–7. His letter to John Owen, the first Secretary of the Bible Society. "I have no doubt the time is near at hand when the knowledge of the Lord shall cover the land as the waters do the channel of the sea, when in every house the book of life will be found, and men shall everywhere draw waters with joy from the wells of salvation." J. Venn to J. Owen (MS.).

[2] The reason for the First Anniversary being held when the Society was two years old was that in April 1800 the Society was still awaiting the Archbishop's reply, and was unwilling to have anything as official as an Anniversary Service without it. For the first twenty years the Anniversary Service was held on Whit Tuesday.

Grant had been asked to make inquiries about the possibility of opening a mission there; this came to nothing.

The following year Venn had still little to report. Progress was being made with the various translations. Although no missionaries had yet been engaged, the Committee, following the example of the S.P.C.K., was making inquiries in Germany; the Committee had knowledge of a missionary seminary at Berlin which prepared men for the mission field "without knowing where and by whom they were to be employed".

The year 1802, as we have seen, marked the end of the leadership of the Society by Venn and Scott—in July Venn was taken ill and in December Scott, having accepted the living of Aston Sandford, handed over to Pratt who in effect became the successor of them both. To keep a missionary society in existence without missionaries and to increase both support and enthusiasm for it was no mean achievement; this is what Venn and Scott did. When it became apparent to Scott that Newton, who had been asked to read the first Anniversary Sermon, was going to withdraw, Scott wrote to his son: "The first sermon of the Mission Society will, I suppose, fall to my share. I feel it one of the most important services I was ever called to."[1] Bishop Handley Moule tells a story of how a young clergyman asked Scott just before an annual meeting how they were getting on with men and money. "We have collected about £1,200," was the answer, "and we have hopes of an offer of service from two German students." A smile came into the questioner's face and Scott turned solemnly upon him: "Young man, you don't believe in this work. But if you live to be as old as I am, you will see our missionaries enter China and Japan."[2] It was vision of this quality which made perseverance possible and ultimate success inevitable.

After prolonged negotiations two students from the Berlin Missionary Seminary, Melchior Renner and Peter Hartwig, came to England for training; they sailed for Sierra Leone in February 1804. They were given lodgings at Clapham a year previously in order to be near both Venn and Macaulay; they

[1] T. Scott to J. Scott (MS. in C.M.S. House).

[2] H. C. G. Moule, *Charles Simeon*, p. 120. China and Japan were then "hermetically sealed".

learnt English from Greaves, and Susoo from Greaves' African pupils. Although Venn was unable to attend committee meetings he saw more of the missionary recruits than the rest of the Committee. At the end of 1803 Renner and Hartwig went back to Germany to receive Lutheran Orders and on their return Hartwig married Sarah Winsor, governess to the Venn family. The wedding was taken by John Venn in Clapham Church on January 25, 1804. The Committee, although offended that their permission had not been asked, accepted Hartwig and his wife as married missionaries.

How far Venn himself really approved of the marriage it is hard to say, for in 1805 he wrote saying that there would be no collection for the Society at Clapham at present. "Both the missionaries and Mrs. Hartwig having resided in this place so long, the attention of the people has been a good deal directed to them, and tho' nothing has been said, as far as I can find, against Renner, yet the two others have afforded but too much matter for observation and censure. Mrs. Hartwig had, you know, the entire care of my children during the three months I and my sister were at Bath and Cheltenham, and the remarks made upon her conduct were extremely general and not very favourable."[1]

The Clapham congregation had further occasion to gossip when they learnt that in Africa Hartwig had turned from missionary to slave-trader. Before this happened there had been reports of his idleness and unsatisfactory conduct, and Mrs. Hartwig became so seriously ill that the Committee brought her home. She arrived in May 1806 and went straight to Clapham Rectory; Venn, who had returned home ill instead of going to the Anniversary Service, found her waiting for him. Within a few days he felt well enough to go up to London and see Pratt about making arrangements for her. Till the end of 1807 she lived at York and was maintained at the Society's expense; after this she obtained a post and was able to look after herself. Venn seems to have seen her quite frequently.

When Hartwig was dismissed by the Society in September 1807, Venn was given the task of writing to Mrs. Hartwig. He also wrote to Hartwig on his own account. Hartwig eventually

[1] J. Venn to J. Pratt, April 1805 (MS. in C.M.S. Archives).

repented and in 1814 the Society consented to engage him as interpreter and translator, but not as a missionary, although he was given full missionary pay. His wife was courageous enough to return to Africa to join her husband. A year later both were dead.

In spite of his illness Venn managed to attend the Anniversary Services in 1803 and 1804, but he neither attended committee meetings nor wrote Reports during these years. In November 1804 he was invited to preach the Fifth Anniversary Sermon—he refused at first but later said he would prepare a sermon and hoped to be well enough to deliver it. On June 4, 1805, he not only preached the sermon but took the chair at the meeting that followed.

Next year when a farewell charge was to be given to four more German missionaries, destined for Sierra Leone, Venn was invited to give it. Pratt, however, failed to give him sufficient notice of the date. Venn's diary for January 6th reads: "Employed in considering and preparing a Charge—being much hurried by the neglect of the Secretary in informing me of the day";[1] and for January 13th it reads: "Rose at five, went with Mr. Elliott and Pearson to town and delivered a Charge at the London Tavern to four missionaries going to Africa—dined at Mr. H. Thornton's with Miss Broderick and Miss Grant—home at evening by stage."[2] When Venn replied to Pratt's request that the Charge should be published, he concluded: "With my best respects and wishes to the Committee whose meetings I lament I am so little able to attend."[3] It was not surprising that two years later, on April 23, 1808, he wrote resigning from the Committee: "The state of my health is indeed such as to preclude any engagements which expose me to the night air—and I do not think it right to continue my name where I cannot give my attendance."[4]

The Committee requested him "to continue his name", but he refused and on June 6, 1808, his official connection with the Society over whose foundation he had presided came to an end.

[1] J. Venn, MS. Diary, Jan. 6, 1806.
[2] *Ibid.*, Jan. 13, 1806.
[3] J. Venn to J. Pratt, Feb. 4, 1806 (MS. C.M.S. Archives).
[4] J. Venn to J. Pratt, April 23, 1808 (MS. C.M.S. Archives).

Just before his resignation he dined with Samuel Marsden, who had come home from Botany Bay with a scheme for a mission to New Zealand. On March 21, 1808, John Venn opened a discussion at the Eclectic on missionary methods to which Marsden, who was present, made a small contribution.[1] In the same month Venn and Elliott dined with Marsden. Also in March Venn was named as a member of the Committee of Correspondence to consider Marsden's plan. He probably never attended, but he was enthusiastic. He concludes his letter of resignation to Pratt, "I congratulate you on the promising appearance of the prospects in New Zealand."

During the following year both Marsden and Buchanan were staying at Clapham; Marsden at the Rectory. In April there was quite a missionary gathering at the Rectory. "Visit from Dr. Buchanan from India, Jas. Farish going to India, Mrs. Marsden, Botany Bay, Mrs. Hartwig, Sierra Leone." When it was possible he still attended the Anniversary Services and from 1805 to 1812, the year before his death, he wrote the Annual Report.

John Venn's influence over the Church Missionary Society is out of all proportion to the time he gave to its affairs. He only became involved at a late stage in the plans for the formation of an Anglican missionary society; three and a half years after the Society's formation ill health made him cease to be a regular committee member, and before the Society was ten years old the same reason led to his resignation. Within this brief period he laid down a policy, which in the main the Society has continued to follow to this day, and together with Thomas Scott he saved the Society from dissolution, first when the possibility of episcopal sanction seemed doubtful, and later when the Committee had to tell its supporters that during the first three years of its life the Society for Missions to Africa and the East had been unable to engage a single missionary. His patience was rewarded and his policy was executed and developed for thirty years by his son, Henry Venn, the ablest of the C.M.S. secretaries of the nineteenth century.

[1] J. H. Pratt, *Eclectic Notes* (1856), pp. 426–7.

EPILOGUE

EARLY in 1813 John Venn wrote to his youngest sister, Kitty Harvey: "My sister [Jane] will inform you that I have been and am very unwell. Dr. Baillie says it is only a very slight species of jaundice, but I do not think so favourably of my own case."[1] In fact from November 1812 it was known that Venn was suffering from dropsy as well as jaundice for which he was receiving some relief by tapping. It is possible that the nature of the second complaint was kept from him as long as possible. However, at the beginning of March 1813, he went to Cambridge to visit Henry and introduced him to all his old friends still living there. Later in the month he rode to Chelsea to call on the Bishop of Winchester in order to discuss the Act of Parliament necessary for the erection of the chapel of ease. The next day he gave one of his Lent lectures for young people and rode off to Harrow the same evening; he returned the following day, calling on Wilberforce on the way home. The diary entry for both days has the note "much fatigued". The following Friday, however, he gave his next Lent lecture but by the end of the month he was conscious that he was seriously ill. However, he struggled on through April; but from the first week of May he was forced to confine himself either to bed or a sofa in his study till July 1st, when he died.

From May onwards John Venn and his family were well aware that he was a dying man. As was mentioned earlier, three of his daughters wrote full accounts of the last weeks of their father's life, giving exact details of what he said to them and to the many friends who came to say "Good-bye". Those who came a distance included Simeon and Farish, but not Edwards, who had been staying at the Rectory as recently as

[1] J. Venn to Mrs. K. Harvey (MS.). The date of this letter is not given but can be guessed approximately.

January. To Edwards and to many others he wrote farewell letters; these were written while handicapped by ebbing strength and excruciating pain. He told Hannah More in his letter to her that he could not write more than a few lines for days together. In spite of this he managed to write to Stillingfleet ("my dearest, oldest, best friend, and my father's friend, my master and my guide"),[1] and also to Stephen, Pearson, Cunningham, Parry, and at least three others. He also wrote a Pastoral Farewell "to his respected and beloved flock", which he was unable to complete. Though prevented from writing much he was able to dictate to his daughters and it was on his death-bed that he embarked on the memoir of his father he had always intended to write, for which Emelia took notes in shorthand. This too he had to leave unfinished, although the break occurs only when he had almost completed the account of his father's ministry at Yelling.[2]

However, his chief concern was with his family, two boys and four girls,[3] and in particular with Henry his eldest son, who was now seventeen. To Henry he committed the rest of his family: "Your dear brother will be your protector. Henry, look after your sisters, they must be your charge."[4] It is significant that though his second wife received a fair share of attention she was not given the care of her stepchildren. Of Henry his father had the highest opinion and thought him well able to undertake his heavy responsibility: "It relieves me much," he tells his daughters, "to think you have such a prudent and cautious and kind and affectionate brother—I do not doubt that he will do well at the university, and that he will be everything to you, my dear children, that you could wish."[5] Henry himself he committed to the care of his cousin, Henry Venn

[1] J. Venn to J. Stillingfleet, June 22, 1813 (MS.).

[2] See p. 97. Simeon promised to complete it but found the task too great. Henry Venn himself published *The Life and Letters* of his grandfather in 1834.

[3] The youngest girl, Maria, died in 1809.

[4] June 18, 1813 (MS.). Henry Venn justified his father's trust in him and in particular made himself responsible for his brother John's education. Mrs. Venn returned to her family after her husband's death; the children, after a round of staying with their very many friends and relatives, settled down with Aunt Jane as mother again in 1814. The second daughter, Jane, married James Stephen at the end of that year.

[5] June 12, 1813 (MS.).

Elliott, who was already training for the ministry at Trinity College, Cambridge.[1] John Venn asked his nephew to try to maintain the bond of friendship that had always existed between his family and that of his favourite sister. To Henry himself he gave a final charge on the importance of the office to which he was called: "Give yourself wholly to it. . . . You have a holy work before you, Christ to help you, the Holy Spirit to enlighten you, heaven for your home, the Bible for your guide. Travel with these companions through this world as a pilgrim and a stranger seeking one above, and may you bring many sons to glory."[2]

John Venn did not joy in death as his father had done, rather he resigned himself to it. His illness had been so protracted and painful, his death so long in view, his temperament so unlike his father's, that his attitude was certain to be different. Pearson in his funeral address says that John Venn had quoted Hooker: "Since I owe thee a death, Lord, let it not be terrible, and then take thy own time; I submit to it. Let not mine, O Lord, but let thy will be done."[3] During this last illness there seems to have been no complaining, no return of the melancholia that had dogged him all his life, only a wistful looking at how things might have been had his health been better. "Few people have been happier than I am with such friends, such a living and such a dear family—if I had but health to enjoy them."[4]

The Clapham Parish Register has this entry for July 1, 1813: "Mr. Venn died between 11 and 12 at night, aged 54, having been Rector 20 years." Three days later Hugh Pearson preached his funeral sermon to a large congregation which included many of his friends, clerical and lay. The Vestry thanked Pearson "for the excellent sermon" and requested that it might be printed and distributed to each householder for a small sum, the profits going to the poor of the parish.[5] Meanwhile his

[1] John Venn told H. V. Elliott that he had intended offering him a title at Clapham in order that he might train him himself. H. V. Elliott became a Fellow of Trinity and later was renowned as a preacher at Brighton. Charlotte Elliott the hymn-writer was his sister.

[2] June 22, 1813 (MS.).

[3] *Sermons*, preface, p. XXII.

[4] June 2, 1813 (MS.).

[5] Vestry Minutes, July 18, 1813 (MS.).

friends unanimously agreed to erect a memorial tablet to John Venn's memory in the church,[1] the wording of the inscription being left to Zachary Macaulay, Henry Thornton and the Rector-designate, William Dealtry.[2] The inscription reads:

> To the memory of the Reverend John Venn, M.A., for twenty years Rector of this parish. He was son of the Reverend Henry Venn, Vicar of Yelling; and his progenitors for several generations were ministers of the Church of England. He was endowed by Providence with a sound and powerful understanding: and he added to an ample fund of classical knowledge, a familiar acquaintance with all the more useful parts of philosophy and science. His taste was simple. His disposition was humble and benevolent. His manners were mild and conciliatory. As a divine he was comprehensive and elevated in his views, and peculiarly conversant with theological subjects; but he derived his chief knowledge from the Scriptures themselves, which he diligently studied and faithfully interpreted. As a preacher he was affectionate and persuasive, intellectual and discriminating, serious, solemn and devout; anxious to impress on others those evangelical truths which he himself so deeply felt. By his family, among whom he was singularly beloved, his remembrance will be cherished with peculiar tenderness. Having been sustained during a long and trying illness by a steadfast faith in that Saviour whom in all his preaching he laboured to exalt, he died 1 July, 1813, aged 54 years, leaving to his surviving family and flock an encouraging example of the blessedness of those who embrace with their whole hearts the religion of Jesus Christ.
>
> Remember them which have the rule over you, who have spoken unto you the Word of God; whose faith follow, considering the end of their conversation; Jesus Christ, the same yesterday and to-day, and for ever. *Heb. XIII.7,8.*
>
> This monument was erected, as a testimony of respect and affection, by friends of the deceased.

It was fitting that two of those responsible for the epitaph should be Thornton and Macaulay, for they were the only two members of the Sect still residing at Clapham. Henry Thornton felt Venn's loss keenly. He noted in his journal: "We have lost Mr. Venn—a sound, affectionate, very pious and discerning

[1] Vestry Minutes, Aug. 2, 1813 (MS.).

[2] The memorial is to be found on the north aisle wall.

minister—a man who had much of the best kind of experience in religion—a warm friend to the whole Thornton family—a very superior being and one who I doubt not, will shine bright in the Kingdom of Heaven."[1] The brief obituary in the *Christian Observer* is doubtless from Macaulay's pen and adds nothing to the epitaph, the writer having been explicitly charged by Venn himself to avoid "the language of panegyric". Neither Pearson's sermon nor that preached by Cunningham at Harrow adds much that is not in the epitaph.

The fullest estimate of John Venn's character is that left by Henry Venn in the notes he made for the life of his father.[2] He too draws attention to the qualities of his mind, the width of his interests, the soundness of his judgment. He goes on to elaborate a point made also by Pearson; his father's complete integrity.

> He was eminently disinterested; intimate with powerful friends, he never seemed to have thought of procuring any personal advantage from their patronage, though never backward to apply on behalf of others. When a friend became a Cabinet Minister he rather dropped his acquaintance than cultivated it. When the Prime Minister, William Perceval, resided in his parish he courted no attention.[3]

He was utterly devoid of ambition—of a retiring and somewhat indolent constitutional temperament. Hence he never pushed himself forward—he required to be known and drawn out before the real strength of his mind was discovered: and those who knew him best, and for the longest time, esteemed him most highly. Henry Thornton on more than one occasion exclaimed: "I shall never know the extent of Venn's power." Another of Venn's closest friends gives a similar testimony: in recommending one of his sons to accept a gift of Venn's sermons Wilberforce wrote:

> He was a man for whose writings, it will, I doubt not, be a strong recommendation to you, that I entertained for the man

[1] Thornton Wigan Book (MS.).

[2] Sketch of the Character of the late John Venn of Clapham (MS.).

[3] William Spencer Perceval was Prime Minister from 1808 to 1812, when he was assassinated in the lobby of the House of Commons by a fanatic; he died in the arms of James Stephen who was his great Clapham friend.

> himself the highest esteem and affection. There was in him a singular compound of the pathetic and the humorous. He was very shy, as is commonly the case with those who most deserve that we should take pains to obtain their friendship; but when you did succeed, you obtained a prize well worth the price you had paid, how great so ever, of pains and perseverance, for it.[1]

Wilberforce had done more than any other man to draw Venn out and to some extent he had succeeded; however, it is significant that to the end he considered him a shy man.

Both Venn's curates also came to know him on a deep level. Pearson in his funeral sermon speaks of "the character of him whom for myself I revered as a father and loved as a brother and a friend".[2] The portrait of Berkely in Cunningham's *Velvet Cushion* is drawn by one inspired with the same depth of affection.

The source of Venn's inner power was that "heavenly-mindness" of which he so often and so effectively spoke from the pulpit. Linked with this, and unmentioned by his son, is Venn's extraordinary generosity of view and character which is to be seen in his teaching on the Fatherhood of God and is well exemplified in the letter he sent to John Owen, the first Secretary of the British and Foreign Bible Society, in which he says: "What an honour you enjoy that you have been the first secretary of the finest institution in the world"[3]—and this from the first Chairman of the Church Missionary Society!

On his father as a preacher, Henry Venn's judgment may seem to us illuminating but a little severe. He says that his father's reserve made him a better parson out of the pulpit than in it. "He had no address as a public speaker—as a preacher his delivery wanted animation and relief." Although he had "a profound knowledge of the hidden springs of feeling and action" which made him occasionally, on certain themes, preach with great effect, "yet [he] scarcely ever did justice to his own powers as a preacher, because he wrote his sermons on Saturday evening, and often the greater part of Sunday morn-

[1] *Correspondence of Wilberforce*, Vol. II, pp. 516–17.

[2] H. Pearson, Sermon at the funeral of the Rev. J. Venn (MS.). This section is not reproduced in the Preface to Venn's Sermons.

[3] J. Venn to J. Owen, undated (MS.).

ing." Doubtless Henry Venn's own practice was different, but there have been, and are, effective preachers who find it difficult to write down a sermon in full until the occasion of its delivery is imminent. A sermon prepared on Saturday night and finished on Sunday morning is not necessarily a bad sermon. John Venn may have procrastinated till the last possible minute, but he was well aware of his great responsibility as a preacher. He once said in a sermon: "A minister should study his subject in his closet, and then bring the result of his investigations before his hearers. But as many of them must necessarily receive much upon his authority, let him remember that he is strictly answerable to God for the diligence, the impartiality, and the sacred reverence for truth, with which he has pursued his inquiries."[1]

However Venn's sermons sounded to his congregation, they read well to-day: they may be somewhat verbose by modern standards, but they are not excessive in length[2] by the standards of his day. Examples enough have been given during the course of this book to demonstrate their power. John Venn's teaching sermons are more remarkable than his evangelistic ones. Sermons on the Work of Christ or Justification by Faith are too heavily theological; they say much the same things in much the same way that many other preachers have said them before and after his time. In his teaching sermons Venn enters a territory all his own. Here there is a freshness of approach, an illuminating power of Scriptural exposition, a wealth of homely illustration that come direct from one who enjoys a rich experience of life with God and with the people of God. It is these sermons which ignore the barriers of time and speak home to us to-day, even though their construction may seem to us that of an essay rather than of a sermon, and their phrases, in places, quaint. As for his own day, the fact that the three published volumes reached their fourth edition within ten years of his death shows how highly they were valued.[3]

Henry Venn attributes his father's real influence to his writ-

[1] *Sermons*, Vol. I, p. 102.

[2] The average length is about 7,000 words; it would take about forty-five minutes to deliver.

[3] The set now in the writer's possession was originally the property of the Hon. G. Agar Ellis, later Lord Dover, who read them on Sundays to his wife; most of them on two separate occasions.

ing, his counsel of his parishioners in private, and his known character.

> The solidity of his judgement—the weight of his character—the amiableness of his disposition, procured for him a very great influence—and that not merely over a large congregation, and a very extensive circle of friends—but over a select band of more intimate associates, who themselves occupied posts of great influence and importance: Mr. Wilberforce, the three Mr. Thorntons, Mr. Grant, Lord Teignmouth, Mr. Macaulay, Mr. Stephen. Such men valued his opinions very highly, and the indirect effect of his labours through their instrumentality upon the interests of religion in this country was considerable.[1]

We have tried to make this point in Chapter 4, but there we have attributed more importance to the sermons themselves—possibly the truth lies somewhere between the two opinions.

In the third chapter, when talking of the strategy of Venn's preaching at Clapham, we saw how without weakening the challenge of his message John Venn managed to retain and increase his congregation, and gradually persuade his hearers that the doctrines of Scripture were not the ravings of an "enthusiast". John Venn was a child of the "age of reason and benevolence" as well as of the Evangelical Revival. He knew how to use the fruits of the former, which were acceptable to his congregation, in the service of the latter, which at first was not. Though he was highly critical of the style of Tillotson adopted by his contemporaries outside the Evangelical movement,[2] there is more in common between the style of John Venn and John Tillotson than there is between John Venn and John Wesley. What Venn did here had a significance far beyond Clapham Church: his son claims:

> It is not too much to say that the name and labours of Mr. Venn of Clapham more than of any other individual were effectual in allaying the prejudices of the world against Evangelical religion, and of evincing its reasonableness and excellence to men of candour and understanding. And thus he very materially, but

[1] Sketch (MS.).

[2] He criticized them for their failure to appeal to the feelings of their congregations.

unobtrusively, strengthened the hands of the more sturdy champions of the truth, such as Scott and Simeon.

Here lies Venn's great importance in English Church History: if his lay friends were responsible for showing that Evangelical religion was not incompatible with middle-class respectability and good taste, he was responsible for demonstrating that it was not incompatible with what he himself would call "soundness of mind in religion". We shall return to this point when considering his relationship to Dissenters; meanwhile it may be worth suggesting that this effective approach was learnt when he was leader of a group of "serious" undergraduates at Cambridge and was successful in maintaining the good offices of university authority. The lesson he learnt from his father then, he never forgot—to the lasting benefit of the Church.

Also speaking of his father's wide influence Henry Venn says: "With leading Evangelical clergy in London and Simeon at Cambridge he exercised also a very important office."[1] This is, of course, a reference to his work with the Eclectic Society, but Henry Venn makes no direct reference to the Church Missionary Society which emerged from the coalition Simeon made between Clapham and the Eclectic Society; which is strange, as he himself served C.M.S. as Honorary Secretary for thirty years. This omission is made good by Zachary Macaulay, who finding himself precluded from using "the language of panegyric" in Venn's obituary in the *Christian Observer* found it possible to add a footnote to his review of Cunningham's booklet *Church of England Missions*. Cunningham had written: "The only effort which has been made to excite a missionary spirit has been confined to a small, but we trust, a growing number of clergy, who for about fourteen years have laboured with zeal and assiduity in kindling and fanning the missionary flame", to which Macaulay added: "It is with no slight emotions that we are reminded by this allusion to the Church Missionary Society, that the person who projected and formed that society was our dear friend and fellow labourer, the Reverend John Venn. We doubt not it is one of these works which have followed

[1] Sketch (MS.).

him into the realms of light: and the recollection of which, as he marks its growing importance, will heighten the fullness of his joy."[1]

The Society for Bettering the Condition of the Poor at Clapham is noted by Henry Venn. "His parochial arrangements and the management of the poor by a society of ladies, were far in advance of his age, and anticipated much which has since been adopted in the organization of various benevolent and district visiting societies." This is very much in line with what was said in Chapter 4. John Venn was the first of the nineteenth-century "town parsons".

Henry Venn's final paragraphs about his father read:

> As a theologian he was pre-eminently scriptural. He had thought and read carefully upon all the great and essential articles of our faith, and his attention was given to each in proportion to its practical importance. He had no system, not even a favourite writer; the liturgy, articles and homilies of the Church were never appealed to as authority and very sparingly as illustrations of Christian truth, he never spoke of the doctrines as exhibited in the formalities of the Church, but he spoke of them in their just and native simplicity.
>
> He was cordially attached to the Church of England, he was scrupulously regular in all his ministrations, notwithstanding his hereditary associations, but he regarded the Church as the mere creature of Scripture.[2]

These words require some elucidation. In saying that his father "had no system", Henry Venn means that he was neither a Calvinist nor an Arminian. In asserting that "he was scrupulously regular in all his ministrations", he means that John Venn was a loyal Anglican who kept to his parish boundaries and in no way regarded the world as his parish. Finally the stress on the Church "as the mere creature of Scripture" is Henry Venn's attempt to show that his father's attitude to the problem of authority differed from that of the Tractarians, who at the time of writing had come to the forefront of the theological scene. Let us consider these three points in order.

Henry Venn of Huddersfield reacted first against the teaching

[1] *Christian Observer*, 1814, p. 309 footnote.
[2] Sketch (MS.).

of Wesley and later more violently against that of his former patroness, the Countess of Huntingdon, who had continued the tradition of Whitefield.[1] Having become strongly Calvinist as a result of his first wife's influence, his views altered after her death, and in his later years at Yelling he tried to keep free from either label. John Venn himself started his ministry as a high Calvinist, but he came gradually, partly through his father's influence, even more through his own study of Scripture, to a position considerably more liberal in its general attitude than that either of his father or of some of his friends in the Eclectic Society.

In a letter to the Editor of the *Christian Observer* in 1803[2] he makes his attitude clear. In this he congratulates the Editor on being equally censured by both parties. There was a time when he would have condemned the position taken by the *Christian Observer* as unsound, but age and experience have modified his views. He once thought every Arminian deficient in understanding, if not destitute of grace,[3] till "a very venerable Calvinistic clergyman" (i.e. his father) spoke highly of Fletcher of Madeley. Since then, John Venn says he has met Arminians who were Christians of a high order, and sound Calvinists who were bad Christians though good Calvinists. Further, on reading the Fathers he has found much that could not be fitted into the Calvinistic system and much in the New Testament itself of which the same is true.

> It was a wise precept delivered by our blessed Lord to call no man master. Would to God that the names of Calvin and Arminius, as leaders of a party, had, like the body of Moses, been buried in oblivion. It should be the peculiar glory of the Church of Christ that it has but one master, the best, the wisest and the highest. By ranging under the banners of a party, we in effect desert those of Christ, and imbibe a spirit which is far more opposite to Christianity than any deviation in non-essential points

[1] See pp. 23–24.

[2] *Christian Observer*, December 1803.

[3] In a letter to Frances Turton, before she became his wife, he says much the same: "Twenty-six years ago when I was first ordained I was a high Calvinist, and thought every Arminian either extremely weak in judgement or blind in religion. More knowledge of myself, the world and of the Scriptures have very much altered my views on these points." J. Venn to Miss F. Turton, 1809 (MS.).

from the Christian faith. Love to the brethren was laid down by our great Master, as the characteristic of His disciples, but, wherever a party spirit is embraced, there the love, which like that of Christ should be universal, is narrowed and confined to a set; and Christian character degenerates into a mode of selfishness.[1]

He concludes:

> I really do not know what to call myself at present except a Church of England man; for indeed I think the Church of England in her liturgy, articles and homilies, speaks more in unison with the Scriptures than any systematic writers I know.

Like the Anglican Reformers whom he greatly admired, he was not prepared to go beyond Scripture on any doctrine and for this reason came to reject the conclusions the Calvinists drew on the doctrines of Predestination and a limited Atonement. On the former, he tells Frances Turton, he seldom talks and never preaches; on the latter he meets the arguments of a Calvinist friend of hers thus:

> You speak (or rather Miss . . .), of Christ not having died for those who do not believe. I do not think the Scripture speaks of Christ having offered Himself a sacrifice for only a particular number, but as having given Himself for an expiation for the sins of the whole world in general, so that everyone who repents and believes in Him may have the benefit of His death. What does the Apostle say? "and not for our sins but of the whole world". And what does our Church say? "He made there by His oblation of Himself once offered, a full perfect and sufficient sacrifice for the sins of the whole world." None indeed will receive the benefit of His death but those who are partakers of the grace of God, and sealed by His Spirit, but it does not therefore follow that His death was not offered up equally for all mankind; that is, that anyone should be at liberty to partake of its benefits.[2]

This outlook is clean contrary to all the opinions put forward

[1] Cf. *Sermons*, Vol. 3, p. 192: "How has the Christian world been divided and its peace destroyed by the adoption of the names and tenets of particular ministers as the badges of different parties in the Church: I am of Calvin, and I of Arminius, and I of Luther. Would to God that it had been always remembered that Christians are of Christ alone."

[2] J. Venn to Miss F. Turton, undated (MS.).

by members of the Eclectic who were present on April 14, 1800, when Basil Woodd proposed the question "Is redemption general or particular?" and answered it: "Redemption is both general and particular; but in different senses. It is not general, so as to be available to all. But it is so far general, that the ransom-price is sufficient to save the whole world."[1] Foster, Pratt and Scott all acquiesced in this. John Venn's difference of view from his friends, who presumably would describe themselves as "mild Calvinists", is significant; it also explains a sentence in Henry Venn's character sketch in which he says "there was no one except Cecil with whom he entirely coalesced",[2] and Cecil too was known to be tired of this particular controversy. Henry Thornton was also pleased to discover Venn's liberalism in this matter. In his diary Thornton notes: "an interesting conversation [with Venn] in which I found myself very nearly agreed with him. He differs from many of the Calvinists nearly as much as myself; takes an encouraging view of religion and has mild principles towards those who differ from him."[3]

It is not altogether surprising to find that a man who turned his back on Calvinism and thought of God's attitude to sinners in terms of "parental love" should have expressed himself in terms verging at times on Universalism, and at others in words that showed that he preferred to use the language of love rather than that of fear in commending the Gospel. "However useful, in its proper place, and to a limited extent, the fear of Divine punishment may be, it is not that motive which has the greatest efficacy in subduing sin."[4]

In his writings and sermons John Venn is almost as critical of "enthusiasm" as other Anglican clergy. This attitude the other members of the Eclectic shared. In a sermon "On Soundness of Mind in Religion" Venn attacked the idea of special providence, so beloved by Evangelicals of an earlier generation and so distorted by Calvinistic enthusiasts:

> A man of sound mind will cherish no extravagant notions of

[1] J. Pratt, *Eclectic Notes*, p. 165.
[2] Sketch (MS.).
[3] Journal, Jan 14, 1795. Thornton Wigan Book (MS.).
[4] *Sermons*, Vol. 3, p. 321.

divine communications. He will consider his own nothingness, and will form the most lofty conceptions of God, as chiefly manifesting his wisdom by the general rules according to which he directs his administration. An enthusiast, on the contrary, entertains lofty notions of himself, and degrading conceptions of the Deity: he conceives that the course of nature is to be regulated with a view to his own interest. The sun shines, or the rain descends, according to his occasions. Is he in want? God, at once, and in some remarkable manner, sends him a supply. Is he opposed? The judgements of God fall upon his enemies. Is he doubtful on any question? The spirit of God reveals it to him. Is he disposed to act in any extraordinary manner? The ordinary rules, even of morality, must yield to his convenience. He and his connections have a peculiar dispensation: they are the particular favourites of God; and all things are to minister to their exclusive good.[1]

It might be thought from all this that as Venn shook off his Calvinism he would become more favourable to the work of the Methodists. This was not so; although he was prepared to defend the work of Wesley and Whitefield alike from the stigma of "enthusiasm" in its worst sense, and drew attention to their great positive achievements in a review of G. F. Nott's Bampton Lectures,[2] he had little sympathy with the Methodists of his own generation. In one of his *Letters to a Young Clergyman* he expressed himself somewhat forcibly. Talking of the ideal parson he says:

> Of a few in his parish he stands in doubt. Some never attend public worship; two or three are noted poachers, and supposed to be smugglers; one man he suspects to be a Jacobin; and there are a few Methodists who are too proud to be taught by him. Against all these he has borne his testimony in the pulpit, and is therefore guiltless of their doom.[3]

It was the withdrawal of the Methodists from their parish churches and their attempt to build up rival congregations that angered Venn. He doubtless had the example of both his father

[1] *Ibid.*, pp. 364–5.
[2] The Rev. G. F. Nott, Fellow of All Souls, a High Churchman of the Daubeny school. In his Bampton Lectures, *Religious Enthusiasm Considered*, he condemned the work of Wesley and Whitefield as that of the Satanic spirit.
[3] *Christian Observer*, 1806, p. 211.

at Huddersfield and of Edwards at King's Lynn in mind. In 1795 Venn wrote to Charles Elliott from Lynn:

> Mr. Edwards is going on very usefully there, and were it not for the number of Methodists and Dissenters who are jealous of his popularity and success, and who keep no terms of regard for him, there would be a large number of serious people under his care. . . . Before a serious minister came the Methodists came to church; when Edwards came they felt and expressed their great joy, for the party spirit had not yet time to operate. But now were they able I believe they would expel him from the town.[1]

Earlier he had warned Edwards against admitting Dr. Coke into his pulpit, saying that if he did he would offend his proper hearers:

> They would esteem you a Methodist preacher in your heart who was restrained only by the love of emolument in the Church from openly connecting yourself with them. And with respect to the Methodists you would gain very little, the separation between you must come at some time and from some circumstances unless you wholly join them, and depend upon it, the further you have gone with them before the separation takes place, the less value will they have for you. *Keep in your own line.* I never saw this rule transgressed without manifest injury not only to the individual but to the Church. I think that were I in your situation I should not pretend to understand the hints of the Methodists, unless they were very broad ones, and then I should tell them plainly that their line and mine were different: that I thought I was called to labour in a regular way, and that therefore I should keep to that line of conduct unless very urgent circumstances determined me otherwise, that I hoped Dr. Coke's end and mine were the same, to glorify God as much as possible, and that I therefore, in the pursuance of this end, wished him success and hoped he would do the same to me in mine.[2]

At Clapham John Venn evidently had to contend with both Methodists and Calvinists. In 1795 he called on Wilberforce and Thornton at Battersea Rise one Sunday evening to tell them that because he did not preach the Gospel there was a threat to erect a chapel for a "gospel preacher" in the neigh-

[1] J. Venn to C. Elliott, Oct. 20, 1795 (MS.).
[2] J. Venn to E. Edwards, Jan. 15, 1793 (MS.).

bourhood.[1] His friends encouraged him to take no notice of these threats; so did his father, who wrote: "I am not displeased with the opposition of the Huntingtonians to your preaching: their hatred is much to be preferred to their praise. . . . It gives me great pleasure to see you stand in the place your father did —pelted on one side by ranters clamouring for sinless perfection, and on the other by Antinomian abuses of grace."[2] The actual situation at the turn of the century is described by John Venn himself in less violent language.

> A chapel has lately been opened about a mile and a half from my church in a neighbouring parish at which a young man, I believe not twenty, of Lady Huntingdon's class officiates. I am told that his place is crowded and many of the lower orders of my parish attend him constantly. A dissenting minister is also lately come to Mr. Urwick's meeting at Clapham who is a truly excellent man and who preaches very evangelically. His meeting is also well filled yet my own congregations are, I think, equally large, so that I trust it is a more general spirit of attending religious worship. I attribute it also in part to the improved state of our singing which has been the means of keeping many from the meetings who were allured to go by the excellence of the music.

He then mentions the vast improvements made by the introduction of his own selection from the Psalter, and concludes: "I am persuaded that the singing has been a great instrument in the Dissenters' hands of drawing away persons from the church, and why should not we take that instrument out of their hands?"[3] It sounds rather like a more modern argument that asks "Why should the devil have all the best tunes?", but it does show Venn's preparedness to learn from those from whom he had come to disagree.

[1] When Frances Turton was about to move to Clapham he writes: "Perhaps it may be useful to apprize you that though the village is spoken of in the world as the very throne of Methodism, the high seat of Calvinism, etc.—in fact the generality of the religious world would scarcely admit it into the number of places where the gospel is truly preached. Indeed many have left this place, or have been prevented from coming to inhabit it by an idea that we do not go quite far enough in religion" (MS.).

[2] *Life of H. Venn*, pp. 530–1. The Huntingtonians were the followers of William Huntington, another Calvinist. It is probable that Henry Venn is confusing this body with the Huntingdonians at Clapham.

[3] J. Venn to E. Edwards, Jan. 27, 1802 (MS.).

The chief difference between John Venn and both the Huntingdonians and the Methodists was about Church Order.

In his book *Simeon and Church Order*[1] Charles Smyth has shown how Henry Venn taught Simeon that ecclesiastical irregularity with its disregard for parish boundaries was possibly a necessary evil in the early days of the Revival, but it had to be abandoned if the Evangelical movement was to remain within the Church of England. The lesson Henry Venn taught Simeon he taught no less successfully to his son, who, as his own son put it, "was scrupulously regular in his ministrations". Although John Venn did not adhere strictly to his parish boundaries at Dunham, there was only one occasion on which he could be accused of gross "irregularity"; this was in 1791 when he preached in a farmer's hall near Fakenham to "his large family and a good congregation of his neighbours".[2] The fact that Henry Venn had been for a considerable time "irregular" in his ministry and Calvinistic in his doctrine led sometimes to embarrassing situations for his family. John Venn writes to Edwards in 1804:

> Till your letter came I did not know of Barnes's edition of my father's *Duty of Man*. I immediately sent for the book. The life prefixed is a vile and inaccurate and distorted account of my father published in the *Evangelical Magazine* by Dr. Haweis soon after his death, the evident design of which was to represent him as a High Calvinist and a patron of that irregularity and disorder for which Dr. Haweis may wish perhaps to plead as many examples as he can for his own justification. It so hurt me that I shall write a life myself of the same length, and if I cannot prevail on Barnes to insert it in the room of the present in all remaining copies I will advertise Barnes's as a spurious life and get Hazard to prefix it to all his editions.[3]

In some of the notes John Venn left for the Memoir of his father and which are now included in the *Life of Henry Venn* he explains his father's change of view, and in so doing explains the rigidity of his own position:

[1] Especially chapter 6.

[2] J. Venn to H. Venn, June 23, 1791 (MS.).

[3] J. Venn to E. Edwards, Jan. 11, 1804 (MS.). H. Venn himself came to have no opinion of Haweis. See p. 77, n. 5.

> Were I to deliver a panegyric agreeable to my own views of that excellent man, in whom I every day saw something new to admire and honour, I should draw a veil over what I am going to relate. But the faithfulness of an historian compels me to do violence to the feelings of a son. His mind was naturally ardent, and he was of a temper to be carried out by zeal, rather than to listen to the cold calculations of prudence. An intimate friend of his living in that neighbourhood, Mr. Berridge, was irregular in his ministerial labours. He deeply felt for the condition of perishing sinners and could not refrain from preaching to them the word of life without confining himself to his own parish or to the walls of the church. Influenced by his example and the probability of doing good, my father, in certain instances, preached in unconsecrated places. But having acknowledged this, it becomes my pleasing duty to state, that he was no advocate for irregularity in others; that when he considered it in its distant bearings and connections, he lamented that he had given way to it, that he restrained several other persons from such acts of irregularity by the most cogent arguments and that he lived long enough to observe the evils of schism so strongly, that they far outweighed in his mind the present apparent good.[1]

Venn's attitude was also influenced by that of Walker of Truro, whom he greatly venerated. In an article in the *Christian Observer* he praised Walker's insistence "upon the due observance of order and discipline. . . . He opposed the proceedings of the leaders of a modern prevailing sect, at a period when scarcely any minister holding similar doctrinal sentiments foresaw the remote evils which such a schism from the Church might occasion."[2]

What can be said on positive grounds of Venn's churchmanship? He was brought up in the "Protestant underworld" of his day. He tells Frances Turton:

[1] *Life of H. Venn*, pp. 176–7. This passage, first published in 1834 by H. Venn of C.M.S. and with his full approval, was very distasteful to A. C. H. Seymour, the member of the Houses of Shirley and Hastings who wrote *The Life and Times of Selina, Countess of Huntingdon* which appeared in 1839–40. Seymour loses no opportunity of attacking the Venns' defence of Henry Venn of Huddersfield. Henry Venn of C.M.S. replied in the *Christian Observer*.

[2] "Anecdotes of the Reverend Mr. Walker of Truro", *Christian Observer*, October 1802. For a full account of the difference between Walker and the Wesleys see G. C. B. Davies, *The Early Cornish Evangelicals*, chapter 5.

> The world at large little knows the sub-divisions of the religious world. For my own part, having from a child been in it, and seen much of the various opinions and practices prevalent in it, I have not followed any party implicitly or called anyone master, but have endeavoured as well as I could to follow the Scriptures and the truly apostolical writings of the founders of our excellent church.[1]

Like F. D. Maurice a generation later, Venn, tired of his experience of division, had come to long for the unity of God made visible in His Church. Unlike Maurice he was impatient of those whom he considered responsible for schism. In his sermon "On Soundness of Mind in Religion" he writes:

> Would to God that this rule of sound reason had been more generally observed! We should not, then, have to lament those fierce contentions which have agitated the Christian Church. We should not have seen one party unreasonably extolling every rite established by long usage, and proclaiming "the temple of the Lord, the temple of the Lord, are these!" and another party with equal unreasonableness and narrowness of mind, attributing an excessive importance to ceremonies, as though the observance of them were idolatry, and preferring rather to break the peace and unity of the church, and to introduce a spirit of schism, than to conform even in things indifferent. When will men learn to reason soundly?[2]

The stress on reason is significant. It shows his roots in the Hanoverian Church; it also, together with the stress on treating ceremonies as things indifferent, links him with the Anglican Reformers he so much admired, and also with the defenders of the Elizabethan Settlement against the Puritans. Venn, as time went on, came to enjoy not only the writings of Hooker but seventeenth-century divines such as Archbishop Leighton and Jeremy Taylor, though he considered the latter "rather inclined to the Papists". Hugh Pearson goes as far as to say that he nearly resembled Hooker in many respects:[3] this may well be too complimentary but certainly Hooker's position with

[1] J. Venn to Miss F. Turton, undated (MS.).
[2] *Sermons*, Vol. 3, pp. 363–4.
[3] *Sermons*, preface, p. XXII.

regard to the comparative authority of Scripture, Tradition and Reason was his own. John Venn was an Evangelical by inheritance and conviction, but he was very much an Anglican Evangelical, who valued his Anglicanism at times even more than his Evangelicalism. Though he had little conception of the Church as a divine visible society and could speak of the Anglican Reformers as "the founders of our Church", his attitude to his own church and other churches was noble. In his review of Nott's Bampton Lectures he says:

> The spirit of our Reformers was truly liberal; they endeavoured (and we think successfully) to ascertain what form of Church government was the most agreeable to Scripture and the most conformable to primitive usage. But while we admire that constitution which was the happy result of their labours, we admire also that Christian candour which led them to allow a participation in Gospel privileges to other churches, who, though differing from themselves in the mode of outward discipline, adhered to all the fundamental doctrines of the Christian faith. It is undoubtedly incumbent on us, as Christians, to allow that liberty of judgement to others which we claim for ourselves: and even were our duty in this respect less obvious than it is, yet we are convinced that the cause of our excellent establishment is better promoted by dispassionate reasoning, and candid discussion, than by violence of invective or the intolerance of party zeal.[1]

In this chapter we have been brought back again and again to John Venn's inheritance from his father. In conclusion it may be fitting to consider the only published comparison of the two men from one who knew them both; Charles Jerram. Jerram was one of the Cambridge undergraduates who made frequent pilgrimages to Yelling to sit at the feet of the aged Henry Venn; as Cecil's curate he often met John Venn both in London and at Chobham. He writes:

> If I might draw a comparison between the two, I should say he (John) possessed his father's talents, but not in all their splendour; he partook of his piety, but not of its fervid character; he devoted himself to the service of his Lord and Master, but not

[1] *Christian Observer*, October 1805.

> with that burning zeal which his father so pre-eminently displayed. Like him, he felt the constraining influence of the love of Christ, but not its rapturous transports. He diffused around him the savour of divine truth, but he was not borne away with the same irresistible impulse to spread it abroad. He enjoyed much communion with God in meditating and prayer, but he did not rise to the ecstasy of scarcely knowing whether he was in the body or out of the body. He was a faithful soldier of our Lord Jesus Christ, but he did not, like his father, lead a victorious band of warriors to fresh triumphs. He died with "a hope full of immortality" but he had not, like his father, such a transport of joy, in the immediate prospect of it, as to keep the wheel of life in motion, when its powers had ceased to act.[1]

John Venn possessed some of his father's talents, but, as we have tried to show throughout this book, no one will understand John Venn who does not see him as essentially different from his father; different in character, different in temperament and disposition. Whereas Henry Venn was jovial and good company, his son was shy and had to be drawn out; whereas Henry Venn always gave the impression that his habitual faith, joy and serenity came easily, his son shows all the signs of inner conflict and wrestling with doubt; whereas both men were lucid in their thinking and gifted in their teaching, John Venn was far more of the philosopher and poet than his father. Henry Venn may have had mystical experiences but nothing he wrote or said compares with his son's unveiling in his sermons of the unseen world.

Both were successful parish priests: Henry Venn was the more remarkable as an evangelist, John Venn though not without his evangelistic triumphs was far more of the teacher of his flock in the deep things of God. In ecclesiastical statesmanship they both proved themselves men of vision and resourcefulness, but the difference of their opportunities prevents comparison. However, in the boldness of John Venn's parochial schemes and in the wisdom of his missionary designs lie qualities which his father nowhere surpassed. The two men were different, their characters were complementary. John Venn always willingly

[1] J. Jerram, *Memoir of C. Jerram* (1855), pp. 271–2.

acknowledged his debt to his father,[1] but he must stand four-square on his own feet. He must be judged as himself and not merely as his father's son.

[1] In the Eclectic Society discussions John Venn frequently quotes with approval the practice and views of his father.

APPENDIX A

Prayer for a Student educating for Holy Orders

O THOU Father of lights, from whom cometh every good and perfect gift; by whose goodness to me I am training up in knowledge and learning, that I may be thoroughly furnished in due time to be a preacher and a teacher in Thy church; to Thee I make my prayer for a blessing on my studies and undertaking, or all will be in vain. Sanctify and purify, I beseech Thee, my heart, that I may not study for reputation, and get the name of the learned and acute, but only to be an instrument in Thy hand of glory to Thy name, of good to the immortal souls of men. And as authors are infinite, as much reading is a weariness to the flesh, causing distraction, and tending only to unprofitable questions; for this reason, I beseech Thee, so to direct me, that I may know what books to choose and what to refuse, and constantly apply myself to that course of studies which will best prepare me for Thy holy service. Preserve me from the infection of false doctrine, naturally pleasing to the pride and corruption of nature, and, as the only way of being safe from falling into error, grant that I may give myself up entirely to be guided by Thy Spirit in daily and earnest prayer.

And as Thy written word is the only repository of Thy will, and of that wisdom which is far better than gold, O make me a diligent reader of the Scripture. May I exercise myself in it day and night. Let it richly dwell in me, and be as much more pleasant to my soul than all human writings, as Thou, O God, art wiser and better than men. Give me wisdom to associate with none but those by whose sobriety, gravity, and good example, I may receive benefit. Rather let me choose solitude, and be satisfied with reproach, than walk in the way of sinners, and for company's sake, destroy my soul or wound my conscience. Excite in me a constant apprehension of my amusements and recreations, knowing how difficult it is not to exceed the bounds of moderation, and how soon the affections are drawn off from better things and enslaved. Let my care therefore be to redeem my time, and to find my study and my God my exceeding joy. In all things do Thou order my conversation. Grant I may be temperate in meat and drink and sleep, grave in my deportment, respectful to my superiors, amiable to my equals, meek towards my inferiors, courteous and affable, without levity and folly, to all. Give me ability and aptness for scholastic exercises, which are to strengthen my faculties, to polish my mind, and to be the ornament of my future life; that so may I leave this place of education free from the vices too prevalent in it; sanctified and prepared as a vessel of honour fit for the Master's use. And may I take upon me the high office of a teacher of souls, not as one who prostitutes his conscience and lies unto the Holy Ghost for a morsel of bread, but as one who is really moved by a desire of saving perishing sinners. Hear me for Jesus Christ's sake. Amen.

H. Venn, "Offices of Devotion for the Use of Families and for Persons in Various Condition", which is an Appendix to *The Complete Duty of Man* (1779 Edition, pp. 495–6). It is possible that Henry Venn composed this prayer with his son in mind and probable that John Venn used it at Cambridge.

APPENDIX B

A Note on Clerical Societies, especially those of Elland, Hotham and Little Dunham

THE purpose of Walker's Clerical Club at Truro was for its members "to consult upon the business of their calling".[1] This remained the chief purpose of the other societies. At Truro the Director (as the Chairman was called) introduced the subject for discussion and the other members brought their contributions in writing.[2] Members took it in turns to be Director. The societies at Elland, Hotham and Dunham were also under a Director. Whereas at Truro it was always the host who was Director as the meeting moved round from house to house, at the other societies they always met at the same place and took it in turns to be Director. The Eclectic Society was guided by a Chairman; this office was also by rota. At the Eclectic "the next question to be proposed" was agreed at the beginning of each meeting.[3] At Elland, Hotham and Dunham, copies were made of the Rules and Regulations and these included a number of articles for discussion, which formed at least part of the business of the meeting. The title, content and wording of these rules are practically identical; there can be no doubt that Stillingfleet took his copy of the Elland Rules to his new society, they there discussed them and made some amendments. Exactly the same thing was done at Little Dunham with the Hotham Rules; in fact John Venn's copy which has been preserved is a manuscript copy of the Hotham Rules, with a certain amount of crossings out and with additions on the blank page opposite; most of the first meeting was occupied with this revision.

Some of the differences between thc three are significant: whereas the Elland Society refers to itself at the beginning of its Rules and

[1] G. C. B. Davies, *The Early Cornish Evangelicals*, pp. 75–6.

[2] *Ibid.*, p. 76.

[3] J. Newton. Summary of Rules established May 26, 1791 and published at the front of his *Eclectic Notes* (MS.). The manuscript is preserved in the Cowper Museum at Olney.

Regulations as "A Society of Ministers of the Gospel", Hotham adds "and Church of England", and Little Dunham follows Hotham. Further, they add the explicit Rule 7: "that none be admitted members of this society who are not ministers of the established Church or be occasionally present". (The Truro Clerical Club was likewise restricted but the Eclectic Society admitted both laymen and Dissenters from the beginning.) At Elland members were required to share the expenses of dinner, at Hotham and Dunham neither payment nor subscription is mentioned. The Elland Society held four meetings a year at first,[1] at Hotham they met "as often in the year as shall be agreed",[2] and at Dunham there were meetings each April and October. Other Societies met more frequently; Walker's Clerical Club met seven times a year and the Eclectic Society as often as "every second Monday".[3]

The original articles for discussion at all three Societies are almost identical, word for word, they are undoubtedly the articles that Henry Venn and his friends drew up at Huddersfield Vicarage in 1767. The seven subjects are: public preaching, religious societies, catechizing children and instruction of youth, "personal inspection and pastoral visiting the flock", visiting the sick, "ruling their own houses well", and "particular experience and personal conduct". At Little Dunham Truro's example was followed in so far as each member was required to bring with him in writing "a paper containing references to those particular subjects which he designs to mention to the Society in answer to any of the questions here proposed".

In 1777 the Elland Society assumed a dual role, and in so doing somewhat altered its nature and procedure, for at the meeting held on March 19 "a design was set on foot of raising a Fund for the purpose of educating poor pious men for the Ministry";[4] it thus became an Ordination Candidates Society as well as a Clerical Club. This meant that much of the time was now given up to the interviewing of candidates and the administration of the considerable fund soon placed at their disposal for their training.[5] To-day the

[1] In 1796 it was reduced to three and in 1837 to two, April and September, which is the custom to-day. From 1804 every member had to pay half a guinea into the Dinner Fund.

[2] In fact September was one of the times usually agreed upon, judging by John's attendance there on Sept. 21, 1789 and his wife's writing to him from Hull in 1792: "The meeting is at Hotham this week."

[3] Newton's *Eclectic Notes* (MS.).

[4] *Rules, Regulations and Forms of Prayer for the use of the Elland Society* (1914), p. 65.

[5] Contributors to the Elland Society from 1778–98 included: William Wilberforce £2,565, Henry Thornton £3,880, Charles Simeon £275, Earl of Dartmouth £241, Sir Richard Hill £175.

meeting comprises Prayer, a reading of the Greek Testament, examination of candidates, business and a discussion of one Article. This procedure may be very similar to what has been the practice since 1777. The original procedure was as follows:

"When a proper time" had been "spent in making inquiries and in conference about the whole or a part of the above-mentioned subject-matter for consideration", the Director himself, "followed by the members in their turn according to the order of sitting", might do one of several things; he might comment on some passage of Scripture which would be of profit to the rest "as private Christians or public preachers", or he might recommend a new book and read an extract, or he might read from one of his own sermons and invite comment, or draw attention to a new heresy, or give an account of the work of God either in his own parish or outside it, or he might take counsel with the other members on problems concerned with his ministry, or he might suggest some subject for "either present or future consideration".

These suggestions are all taken word for word from the Hotham edition of the Elland Rules, apart from the provision that the others may follow the Director. However, it seems that at Dunham this part of the proceedings was probably dealt with more briefly, for there "after these subjects have been gone through, two of the members shall read a dissertation or discourse prepared by them beforehand, upon some subject which has a reference to the due discharge of the Clerical office in general, or any particular branch of it. If any member whose turn it is (according to the alphabetical order of his name) to bring his dissertation should be prevented from coming, he shall bring it next time."[1]

From the accounts we have, this was the main business of each meeting. The rules conclude with "Instructions to members" on their attitude towards membership of the Society and towards one another. Each is reminded to "endeavour to keep himself and others from all evil divisions and animosities both in heart and voice, in temper and conduct that Christian love and unity may be kept up and promoted, and that where there shall be any profitable Conference there may not as a necessary consequence be any unprofitable disputations". He is also reminded that at home in private

[1] At Elland the same need was felt, and in 1781 it was "agreed that each member write on some subject by rotation, that the subject be fixed by the Director at the meeting and given to the member whose turn it is to write, that the paper shall at the next meeting be read by the writer, and no excuse admitted for neglect. Forfeit half a guinea to the fund for educating young men. The papers to be left in the hands of the Minister at Elland." Elland Journal (MS.).

before the meeting day and in the morning of that day in private devotion, he be very earnest in prayer to God for his direction in and blessing upon the Society, its nature and design and several members. He is also bidden to "remember the Society in evening devotions the first day in each month". Apart from this last sentence these instructions are in substance identical with those of the Elland Society.

APPENDIX C

Account of a Society for Missions to Africa and the East instituted by members of the Established Church

Of all the blessings which God has bestowed upon mankind, the Gospel of our Lord and Saviour Jesus Christ is thc greatest. It is the sovereign remedy for all the evils of life, and the source of the most substantial and durable benefits.

Under its benign influence, the understanding is illuminated by the light of truth, pure and holy principles are implanted in the heart, the passions, those fruitful causes of vice and misery, are regulated, the whole conduct is reformed, peace reigns in the breast, and a well-founded hope beyond the grave, soothes the sorrows of life. Fallen man becomes a new creature, happy in himself, fulfilling the will of his Maker, and living to His glory.

In social and civil life also, wherever the Gospel is cordially received, its benefits are equally experienced. The husband and wife, the father and son, the master and servant, at once learn from it their respective duties, and are disposed and enabled to fulfil them. Human intercourse is sweetened by the charity it inculcates. A mild and equitable spirit is infused by it into legislation and civil government. Rulers become the fathers of their people, and subjects cheerfully yield obedience. Civilization is promoted upon sure and permanent principles, and nations are taught by it to dwell in friendship with each other.

Such are the benefits which Christianity is calculated to diffuse in the world; but these are its least blessings. It not only meliorates the state of man in society, but it saves his soul. It cancels his guilt, reconciles him to God, raises him from death to life, makes him an heir of the kingdom of heaven, and crowns him with glory and immortality.

A just conviction of the value of these benefits has produced several societies for the more general diffusion of the Gospel; and lately, zealous Christians, of various denominations, have laudably united to send missionaries to enlighten even the far distant islands of the South Sea with the knowledge of the truth.

In the CHURCH OF ENGLAND, two venerable Societies have long been engaged in the excellent design of propagating Christianity abroad. That for PROMOTING CHRISTIAN KNOWLEDGE has undertaken, though not professedly the object of its institution, "the management of such charities as should be put into its hands, for the support and enlargement of the Protestant Mission formerly maintained by the King of Denmark at Tranquebar in the East Indies"; and it has since extended its care to several other settlements in that quarter of the world.

"In the year 1701, King William the Third was graciously pleased *to erect and settle a* CORPORATION, *with a perpetual succession, by the name of the Society* FOR THE PROPAGATION OF THE GOSPEL IN FOREIGN PARTS, *for the receiving, managing, and disposing of the contributions of such persons as would be induced to extend their charity towards the maintenance of a learned and orthodox Clergy, and the making of such other provision as might be necessary for the propagation of the Gospel in foreign parts, upon information that in many of our* PLANTATIONS, COLONIES, *and* FACTORIES, *beyond the seas, the provision for ministers was mean; and many other of our said Plantations, Colonies and Factories were wholly unprovided of a maintenance for ministers and the public worship of God, and that for lack of support and maintenance of such, many of his loving subjects wanted the administration of God's word and sacraments, and seemed to be abandoned to atheism and infidelity, and others of them to Popish superstition and idolatry.*"

In consequence of this incorporation, the Society proceeded to receive subscriptions: and by the liberal benefactions afforded them, they have been enabled to supply with ordained ministers and schoolmasters many of our factories abroad, which else would have been destitute of the public worship of God, the administration of the sacraments, and almost of the knowledge of the Gospel. To the British Plantations in North America they have principally extended their benevolent exertions. It is evident, however, that, although they have not been backward, wherever a proper opportunity has occurred, to instruct their missionaries to embrace it, by preaching amongst the neighbouring heathen; yet the primary and direct object of this society has been rather the religious benefit of the British colonists and those heathen immediately dependent upon them, than the conversion of the heathen in general.

Room, therefore, is still left for the institution of a society which shall consider the heathen as its principal care. The whole continent of AFRICA, and that of ASIA also (with the exception of a few places) are still open to the missionary labours of the Church of England. To these quarters of the globe, therefore, the promoters of the present design turn their chief attention; and from this extensive field their denomination, not however considering their name as binding them to exclude their attempts from any other unoccupied place which may present a prospect of success to their labours.

A difficulty has occurred in establishing missions according to the regular constitution of the Church of England, which it is necessary to state, in order to justify a part of the present institution which might else appear exceptionable. It is obvious that the Church of England can allow no persons to officiate in any respect as Ministers who have not been *episcopally ordained.* Episcopal ordination, bearing respect to the present improved state of society in this island, is justly conferred upon those only, whose education and learning qualify them for the rank the English clergy hold in society. It is evident, however, that a missionary, dwelling amongst savages rude and illiterate, does not require the same kind of talents, manners or learning, as are necessary in an officiating minister in England. But ordination admits not of distinctions correspondent to the degree of refinement in society. He who is once episcopally ordained, though with the sole view of acting as a missionary to the heathen, would possess the power of officiating, and holding any benefice to which he might be presented, in the English Church. This circumstance necessarily requires extreme caution in ordaining persons for the purposes of missions only. For what security can be afforded, that a person of inferior station, offering himself upon this ground for orders, is not influenced by the desire of a more elevated rank in society, or of a life of greater ease, rather than by a pure zeal for the salvation of the heathen?

To obviate this difficulty which lies in the way of sending missionaries episcopally ordained, the conductors of the present institution have recourse to the expedient of sending their missionaries in the capacity of *catechists* only, where persons already in holy orders do not offer themselves, or circumstances do not justify an application for regular ordination.

The office of catechist[1] in the primitive church was exercised by

[1] *Vide* Bingham's *Ecclesiastical Antiquities,* Book III, chap. 10, sects. 1, 2.

any of the inferior ecclesiastics.[1] It was his business "to address in continued discourses the Gentiles or unconverted Jews in behalf of the Christian doctrine, to expose the folly and absurdity of the pagan superstition, to remove prejudices, and to answer objections. He also instructed those who had embraced the Christian faith, but had not a sufficient knowledge thereof to qualify them for baptism, who were therefore only admitted catechumens, which was done, in process of time, with great solemnity by the imposition of hands; whereupon they were esteemed a sort of Christians, and were divided into several classes."[2]

Catechists were thus esteemed as candidates, under trial and probation for the greater orders; and the church took this method to train up fit persons for the ministry, first exercising them in the lower offices, that they might be the better disciplined and qualified for the duties of the superior functions.

The utility of employing catechists has indeed been experienced in all missions. The missionaries employed by the SOCIETY FOR PROMOTING CHRISTIAN KNOWLEDGE have selected some of their ablest converts, and employed them as catechists with singular benefit to the Christian cause. We tread therefore in a beaten path when we follow these examples. Catechists indeed appear to be in several respects the most suitable persons to plant the Gospel amongst the heathen; and when such have approved themselves as faithful labourers in the vineyard, when they have instructed the children of the heathen, when they have laid the foundations of a Christian church, there may be just ground for application to admit them, if necessary, into a higher order.

Other particulars, respecting the present institution, will be understood by the annexed rules.[3] It will be seen that scrupulous care has been taken to insure as much as possible a right choice of missionaries, for upon their fitness for the work depends, under God, the whole success. The Committee to whom the choice of them is entrusted, may indeed be deceived, but it will be their aim to recommend such only, as unite a fervent zeal with discretion and know-

[1] Clemens Romanus plainly distinguishes the catechist from the bishops, presbyters and deacons: for comparing the church to a ship, he says, the bishop resembles the *πρῳρεύς*, or pilot, the presbyters the *ναύται* or mariners, the deacons the *ναυτολόγοι* or chief rowers, and the catechists the *τοίχαρχοι*, or those whose office it was to admit passengers into the ship and contract with them for their passage.

[2] *Vide* Bishop on the Catechism.

[3] The rules are printed as an appendix in C. Hole, *Early History of the Church Missionary Society*.

ledge; such as have themselves experienced the benefits of the Gospel, and therefore earnestly desire to make known to their perishing fellow sinners the grace and power of a Redeemer, and the inestimable blessings of his salvation. It is scarcely necessary to add, that as members of the Church of England they consider its doctrinal articles as exhibiting the standard of that faith which it should be their endeavour to propagate.

It remains now only to solicit the assistance of all those, who have the glory of God and the good of their fellow-creatures at heart, for the furtherance of this useful design. Wide is the field which lies before this Society, great is the importance of their object. They require not indeed the pecuniary aid of those who already, to the extent of their power, contribute to the support of other similar institutions—of all such persons they regard it as the duty to continue undiminished the support they have hitherto given. What they ask of them is their counsel, their good wishes, their prayers. Let not this Society be considered as opposing any that are engaged in the same excellent purpose. The world is an extensive field, and in the Church of Christ there is no competition of interests. From the very constitution of the human mind slighter differences of opinion will prevail, and diversities in external forms; but in the grand design of promoting Christianity, all these should disappear. Let there be a cordial union amongst all Christians in promoting the common salvation of their Lord and Saviour.

With a firm reliance on the divine blessing, and confidence in the piety and liberality of Britons for the support of their undertaking; the conductors of the present institution embark in their work without fear though not without solicitude. They hope that since God has so signally defended this island with His mercy as with a shield, His gracious hand, to which, amidst the wreck of the nations, our safety has been owing, will by us be acknowledged and His goodness gratefully recorded even in distant lands. They pray that while every country under heaven brings the tribute of its stores to Great Britain, she may return to them treasures more valuable than silver and gold. They trust that the wrongs which Africa has so long sustained will at length be repaired by the offerings of spiritual peace and Christian freedom. They expect that the petitions daily offered up by the Church that "the kingdom of God may come", will in time be answered; and they hail the rising day when the glad tidings of salvation, being conveyed to the lands lying in darkness and the shadow of death, "the wilderness and the solitary place shall be glad for them, and the desert shall blossom as the rose".

GENEALOGICAL TABLE OF THE VENN FAMILY

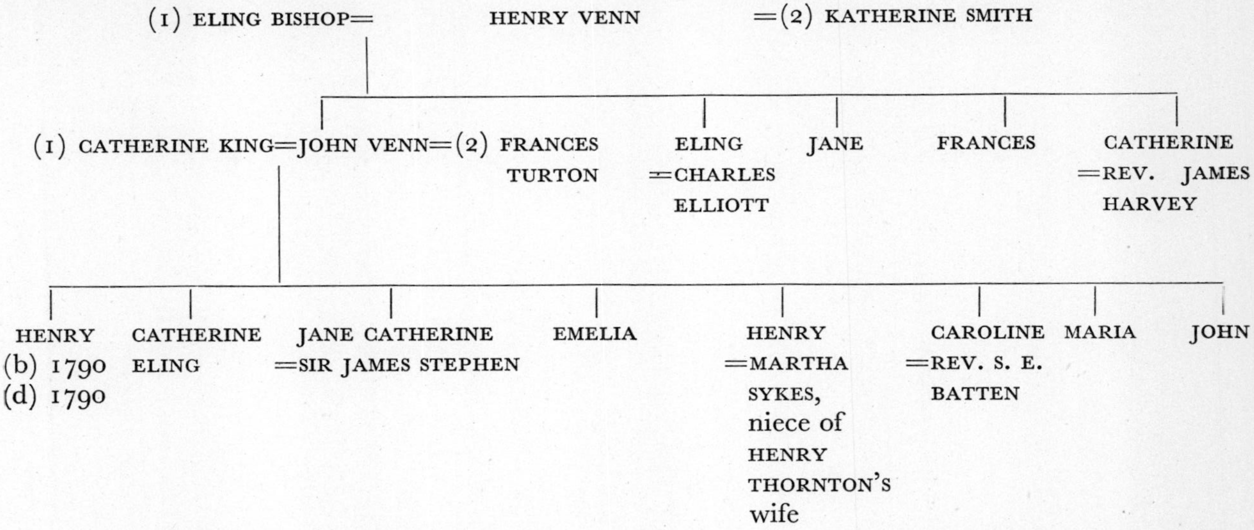

The intermarriage of the Venn family with members of other families of the Clapham Sect is well illustrated in two genealogical tables compiled by Mr. N. G. Annan in *Studies in Social History*, edited J. H. Plumb, 1955, pp. 275–6.

BIBLIOGRAPHY

The footnotes provide some contribution towards a general bibliography. A detailed guide as to the manuscript sources consulted and the published works of John Venn may be of interest and of use to others, and is therefore appended.

The Venn family papers contain the following manuscript material relevant to the life of John Venn of Clapham:

John Venn's Diaries for years 1806, 1808–13.

Parentalia (2 volumes).

Notebook of John Venn dated August, 1803.

Stock-Accounts. J. V. 1762–1815.

Rules and Regulations of the Little Dunham Clerical Society.

Extracts made by J. Venn from articles, pamphlets, sermons that he had written and copied out for his children.

Notes about last illness and death of Reverend John Venn of Clapham, by his daughter, E. V. (2 volumes).

Notebook of one of the daughters (probably Catherine), on the same subject, to which copies of some of J. Venn's letters are appended.

J. Venn: Letters, 3 volumes copied by his daughter, Emelia.

J. Venn: Letters, 1 volume copied by his daughter, Catherine.

J. Venn: Letters, 1 volume to his children and copied out by them.

By Henry Venn of C.M.S.:

Sketch of Life of John Venn of Clapham.

Sketch of the Character of the late John Venn of Clapham.

Notes on the Evangelical Revival.

Diary of a Visit to Yorkshire, 1824.

Letters received by the Venn family and preserved include letters from:

C. Simeon, W. Wilberforce, J., H. and S. Thornton, J. Newton, Z. Macaulay, Miss H. More, T. Scott, R. Cecil, L. Richmond, I. Milner, J. Stillingfleet, J. and H. Jowett and J. Pearson.

Henry Venn of Huddersfield: Sketch of Life of Eling Venn.
J. Riland: Eusebia, A Sketch of the Character of Eling Venn.

Other Manuscripts consulted include:

Clapham Vestry Minutes.
Clapham Vestry Committee Book.
Clapham Parish Register.
The Thornton Wigan Book. Contains a short autobiography of Henry Thornton and some of his letters copied for his daughter, Lucy Thornton. (Wigan Public Library.)

Journals of the Elland Society.
J. Newton's Eclectic Notes (1787–9) in possession of Miss C. M. Bull of Newport Pagnell and (1789–95) to be found in the John Newton Room of the Cowper Museum, Olney.

At Church Missionary House are to be found:

W. Goode's Notes on the meeting of the Eclectic Society held on April 1, 1789.
Josiah Pratt's Eclectic Notes in manuscript.
Official correspondence files of the Society to 1813.
Committee Minutes to 1813.
Brief manuscript biographies of C.M.S. founders and supporters including John Venn of Clapham, compiled by Charles Hole.

Ridley Hall, Cambridge, has inherited a number of papers from the family of Richard Cecil.

Many of the Wilberforce family papers are in the possession of a great-great-grandson, Mr. C. E. Wrangham of Castle Headingham.

Published Writings of John Venn

John Venn left his family a list of "every publication of mine which I can recollect". To this must be added the three volumes of his *Sermons* which were published posthumously.

The Nature of the Gospel as stated in the Writings of St. Paul. A Sermon preached at the visitation of the Archdeacon of Norwich held at Litcham, 10 May 1789. (1790.)

Reflections on this Season of Danger. Sermon preached at Clapham. (1798.)

Select Portions of Psalms extracted from various versions and adapted to Public Worship, with an appendix containing Hymns for the Principal Festivals of the Church of England, (*for the use of Clapham Church.*) (1800.)

The Easy Spelling Book—Part 1 containing words of one syllable. (1797.)

Published in "Cheap Repository Tracts":
Daniel in the Den of Lions.
Character of Onesimus.
Reflexions on Harvest. (All 1795.)

Account of a Society for Missions to Africa and the East instituted by members of the Established Church. (1800.)

Report of the Society for Bettering the Conditions of the Poor in Clapham. (1800.)

Articles and Reviews published in the *Christian Observer*, 1802–10.

INDEX